TAKING ON DIVERSITY

HOW WE CAN MOVE FROM ANXIETY TO RESPECT

A Diversity Doctor's Best Lessons from the Campus

RUPERT W. NACOSTE

Prometheus Books

59 John Glenn Drive
Amherst, New York 14228

Published 2015 by Prometheus Books

Cover design by Jacqueline Nasso Cooke

Cover image © Juanmonino / iStock Photo (middle row, second image); tixti / iStock Photo (top row, fourth image); MariaBobrova / iStock Photo (bottom row, second image); richellgen / iStock Photo (top row, second image); franckreporter / iStock Photo (remainder of images)

Prometheus Books recognizes the following registered trademarks mentioned within the text: Bojangles®, Facebook®, iPad®, iPhone®, PowerPoint®, TEDx®, Twitter®, YouTube®, Xbox Live®.

Inquiries should be addressed to
Prometheus Books
59 John Glenn Drive
Amherst, New York 14228
VOICE: 716–691–0133
FAX: 716–691–0137
WWW.PROMETHEUSBOOKS.COM

19 18 17 16 15   5 4 3 2 1

Library of Congress Cataloging-in-Publication Data Pending.

ISBN 978-1-63388-026-9 (pbk)
ISBN 978-1-63388-027-6 (ebook)

Printed in the United States of America

To the spirit of Curtis Mayfield
Whose words and music inspired many in the civil rights movement
When he told us,
"Keep on pushing"
"We're a winner"
And who called out to alert all Americans
When he wrote and The Impressions sang
"People Get Ready"

CONTENTS

PART 5: I HEAR THAT TRAIN A COMIN', SHE'S COMIN' ROUND THE CURVE

PART 6: LOOSENED ALL HER STEAM AND BRAKES, STRAINING EVERY NERVE

PART 7: THE FARE IS CHEAP AND ALL CAN GO, THE RICH AND POOR ARE THERE

PART 8: NO SECOND CLASS ABOARD THIS TRAIN, NO DIFFERENCE IN THE FARE

INTRODUCTION

"**I**'m at a party right now." That was the subject line of the e-mail that I guess on her end was sent as a text message. Maggie was the "her," and Maggie, a White female, was in the midst of a moment she wanted me to know about. Maggie texted:

> Dr. Nacoste, I'm at a party right now. . . . And a 21-year-old White male just said the word "nigger." I told him that I didn't think that any use of that word was acceptable in any situation. This started a conversation with everyone explaining to me it all mattered about the "inflection" and "connotation" it was used in. I was at a loss for words. What can I say if that happens again?

For today's generation of young people, there are no offensive words. It's all good, if you say it with the right inflection.

How have we gotten here? Here is a time in American history where the language of racial hate is OK to too many; a time when some Americans think it funny to call each other niggers.

In 2009 I was flabbergasted to read a letter to Amy Dickinson who writes the "Ask Amy" newspaper advice column (*Raleigh News & Observer*). Here is the letter:

> DEAR AMY: I have a few White friends who throw the "N word" around with an "a" at the end. It makes me uncomfortable when they use it, especially when they use it to describe me (I am White). I don't condone the use of that word in any form flippantly, as they are doing.
>
> They say having an "a" instead of an "er" at the end makes it acceptable, but I don't agree with them. How can I ask them to stop? I feel stuck between a rock and an awkward place.—Not the N Word.

Really? I thought. This is going on? Talking to my students, I came to know that, yes, this *is* going on. Later I learned about what was going on during episodes of the reality TV show *Big Brother*. I have never watched this show, but it came to my attention in the summer 2013. News items I saw on various websites reported that a number of *Big Brother* contestants were using racial slurs as well as antigay and lesbian slurs with casual ease. Unworried use of that language while knowing that most everything you are doing and saying is being shown to a national television audience is bold. The very public use of anti-group slurs, made without concern, means that the behavior was not new to the person. It's everyday. It's all good, I guess, if you say it with the right inflection or, you know, in a funny way.

One of my students wrote:

I recently had a group of friends over to my house to have some drinks and watch some movies on a Saturday night. Everyone was having a good time, hanging out, catching up, making jokes, etc. It was around 11:30 or so and everything was starting to wind down. We were all sitting and talking in the living room.

I was sitting and talking to my boyfriend and out of the corner of the room I hear the statement ". . . those Spics . . ." come from a "friend" sitting a couple feet from me on the couch. I am half Puerto Rican and half Black, my grandmother came from Puerto Rico with her mother and siblings when she was about seven. I am extremely connected to my mother's side of the family and every aspect of my grandmother's life is penetrated by her culture.

I responded with "What did you just say?" and without hesitation he repeated his statement, "I said those Spics." I explained to him that his statement was offensive, that I found derogatory terms toward any group inappropriate and they would not be said in my house. His response was that "it is okay to say, if you are saying it in the funny way, like nigger."

After his response I immediately told him to leave my house.

How did we get here? That's what I wondered. But I already had my answer. In my faculty office, I was talking with a young Black male college student. "It pisses me off," I said, "It pisses me off that there are African American students at this university who talk about our people still being enslaved. It really pisses me off that those students speak of themselves as being oppressed."

"Well, do you think it's all gone?" he asked.

"You see, that's what pisses me off. Did I say there were no racial problems or problems of injustice associated with race? Did I say that?"

"Well, no . . ."

"No . . . I did not. What pisses me off is to have college students who never experienced anything like slavery talk about being enslaved. I grew up in the Jim Crow South; I know what real racial oppression and hate look and feel like. I grew up when the signs said 'Colored' and 'White' and you had to follow those laws. They were laws, not customs. And that is not on this campus."

Looking into my eyes intently, feeling my intensity, this student of mine, this young Black man said to me, a sixty-two-year-old Black man, "Yeah, OK . . . but when we hear about that, it just sounds like a big joke."

I went breathless. Shock, sadness, and anguish took my breath away. Inside of myself I heard and felt the lament of the Hebrew prophet Jeremiah: "My eyes fail from weeping. I am in torment within. My heart is poured out on the ground because my people are destroyed. Because children and infants faint in the streets of the city" (Lamentations 2:11). "A big joke," I thought to myself. My eyes fail from weeping. . . .

"Well, that explains it," I said. "No wonder Black college students call each other niggers. No wonder Black kids let White kids call them and each other nigger. It's just a big joke."

Young people have no faith in what they hear in high school about the struggle for racial equality in America. Part of the problem is they only hear it. Hearsay learning is not enough. Too often in our middle and high schools, our children are only exposed to hearsay teaching about the modern civil rights movement. The fault is that of adults who do not want their children exposed to the harsh truth. Hearsay teaching, you see, is a sales pitch for America the Beautiful.

Hearsay teaching about the civil rights movement is so distant from the reality of what happened that it sounds like a joke; a loud, bad sales pitch on TV. But I am not talking about distance in history. Hearsay teaching about the civil rights movement is distant because it is empty of emotion. The impression given is that Martin Luther King Jr. gave a speech about his dream, and

White America said, "Oh . . . is that what this is about . . . then, OK, . . . I wish we had understood this before."

How false. How belittling of the mortal sacrifices made to force America to live up to its founding constitutional creed "that all men are created equal." But that's why hearsay teaching has no emotional impact on young people. Sparse descriptions of selected, tidy events of the civil rights movement are so unemotional and deceptive that it sounds like the teachers are making a joke. Hearsay teaching makes a joke of the legal work, marches, arsons, beatings, murders, boycotts, bombings, lynchings, and assassinations that moved our nation from Jim Crow, legally enforced racial segregation to equal rights under the law.

"When we hear about that," the young Black male said, "it just sounds like a big joke."

Something was happening to me. That very semester, fall 2012, I kept hearing my favorite song from growing up in the 1960s. Curtis Mayfield's "People Get Ready" kept coming into my hearing. As a teenage Black male growing up in the Jim Crow South, I loved that song because it declared that a train was coming down the line bringing change. I was taken with the grace the song promised when it proclaimed that no one would need a ticket to get onboard, that all anyone would need would be faith, belief in the inevitable change being brought by the train. I did, indeed, love that song. Yet now I was puzzled about why, in 2012, I was so often hearing the original on the car radio.

As if to put a fine point on that experience, toward the end of that fall semester, in December 2012, the song came to me in both my classrooms. It first came to me in my "Interpersonal Relationships and Race" course, where I introduce students to my concept of neo-diversity. Neo-diversity is this time in American life when each of us has unavoidable encounters and interactions with Americans from many different racial, ethnic, religious, mentally conditioned, socioeconomic, sexually oriented, bodily conditioned, and gender groups. For that class, a White male student started his final paper this way:

> I have been listening to the Alicia Keys version of the song "People Get Ready" from the movie *Glory Road*. I believe this song could be meant for us to hear in this day and time in this current neo-diverse world that we are

currently living in. Ms. Keys is telling us that there is a train coming and all we have to do is just believe and get onboard.

I believe this song is talking about neo-diversity, which if we really try to understand that world, some positive changes could be made. There have been small changes made in the United States today to make it a more welcoming and diverse country, but there is still work to do.

I was stunned.

One week later, I was teaching the final class of my other undergraduate social psychology course, "Introduction to Social Psychology," which is about what it takes to develop and maintain an interpersonal relationship. I use a lot of pop music in that class to illustrate relationship hopes, dilemmas, mistakes, and failures. That music, the songs I play, cuts across opera, country and western, rock, R&B, rap, and folk. Puzzled by that variety a student usually asks, "What's your *personal* favorite kind of music?" Ah, the naive rigidity of young people. Telling the truth, I give the Duke Ellington answer to that question: "Good music."

As our relationship of teacher, student, and classmate was coming to its formal end, I gave the two hundred students twenty minutes to "ask me anything." It is always an interesting twenty minutes. That day, the music question was different. The student asked, "What is your favorite song?" Without hesitation I said, "'People Get Ready' by Curtis Mayfield and The Impressions." I sang a few bars. I went on to say, "Funny that you should ask me that. For some reason that song is all around me over the last couple of months."

At home that evening I got an e-mail from my teaching assistant for that course. Jaime wrote,

Dr. Nacoste, when you mentioned "People Get Ready" is your favorite song, it reminded me of a YouTube my sister linked me to. It's Aaron Neville and the Five Blind Boys of Alabama together singing "People Get Ready." I think you'll enjoy the video.

I clicked on the link. Aaron Neville's soft, commanding falsetto voice is first, high in a hum. Then a big, husky voice of one of the Blind Boys of Alabama sings out . . .

"People get ready . . ."

Aaron Neville's falsetto retakes the air, now is the lead, high, sweet, wavy . . .

Electric guitar picks up that lead, keeps it, cries out . . .

Then all together the Five Blind Boys take over, lifting and pushing the lyrics, the meaning, the message . . .

"People get ready . . .

Suddenly a melody of voices . . . baritone leads, baritone harmonics, guitar, Aaron Neville's angelic cries, Blind Boy's deep bass . . . *"I believe . . . I believe . . ."* Confessing . . . *"I believe . . ."* asking, do you believe . . . do you know . . . it's time . . . *"People get ready . . ."*

Tears came into my eyes.

Aaron Neville's falsetto echoed over the guttural, emotional harmonic of the voices of the Five Blind Boys. Blind though they are, those old Black men seemed to be looking out onto a divine landscape as their voices moved the song through their audience and me, demanding that we all understand that now is the time to get ready. I heard the message loud, clear, and personally.

I knew one thing for sure. I was in the midst of a calling. More than once in my life, I have experienced a calling. When patterns repeat, when a theme emerges from different sources, when the repeating pattern and theme resonate in your being, that is a calling. I have learned this, and I have learned not to ignore a calling. You see, some very powerful force is calling, and it will not be quiet until you answer.

I started outlining this book because I know we are on the verge of losing the American Dream. Today, somehow, we have let young people feel that it's OK to speak about other Americans using the language of hate: niggers, bitches, spics, ragheads, retards. What's the big deal? It's all just a big joke anyway, right? Now I was being called to help our nation penetrate that thick fog of dangerous confusion.

All my life experience, all my scholarship, all my teaching; it all fit this calling. A still, small voice was going from a whisper to a shout in my consciousness: Time for you to call out to America, to proclaim that the neo-diversity future is now coming up the line.

In the station, attention, please! Your attention please!

People . . . get ready. The Neo-Diversity train is pulling into the station.

In the station, your attention, please! Attention!

People . . . get ready . . .

PART 1

THE TRAIN'S A COMIN', I HEAR IT JUST AT HAND

CHAPTER 1

NOBODY TELLS US WHAT THAT MEANS

America just ain't what it used to be. We no longer live in a society where our racial contacts are controlled and restricted by law. We no longer live in an America where the law makes one racial group more powerful than another. Not only that, but nowadays, every day, each of us has some occasion to interact with a person from another racial, gender, ethnic, physically challenged, religious, mentally challenged, or sexually oriented group. Today our interpersonal encounters with members of other groups are not just in Black and White, not just diverse, but neo-diverse. We are living, working, and interacting in the same desegregated, unisex, neo-diverse spaces. So we no longer live in a society where people can just decide it's all right to use group hate words any old kind of way, anytime they feel like it.

America just ain't what it used to be. The night of Tuesday, November 6, 2012, America heard the loud whistle of the Neo-Diversity train coming down the line. It wasn't because President Barack Hussein Obama won reelection. We heard the whistle and roar of the twenty-first-century neo-diversity main-line train because of how Mr. Obama won. He won through a coalition of groups that are growing from minority to majority status: women, Hispanics, young people, Blacks, lesbians, Asians, single people, gays, and Latinos. President Obama won because he captured the neo-diversity that is America.

With that it became ever more important for Americans to learn to accept and respect our neo-diversity. Not tolerate, but respect and embrace America's neo-diversity. I am forever flummoxed that people still think the solution to intergroup matters is tolerance. We just have to learn to be more tolerant. Really?

Tolerance is an awful relationship goal. It is awful because to take a stance of tolerance is to assume oneself to be superior to those being tolerated. When someone says we have to be more tolerant, I wonder who the "we" is. Only the more well-established, only the more powerful have to be tolerant. Parents are tolerant of their children. And not all that long ago, men were told that they had to tolerate the silly whims and emotions of women.

Tolerance is based on the assumption of unequal status. In twenty-first-century America, tolerance is outdated, obsolete, and out of place. No matter what racial, bodily conditioned, ethnic, sexually oriented, religious, or gender group an American identifies with, together we are a country of citizens with equal status under the law. We will not secede from that great American truth. And we ain't going back.

When people talk about going back to the good old days, what days are they talking about? The days of Jim Crow, when dark-skinned people like me had no right to life, liberty, or the pursuit of happiness? Or maybe they mean back to the days when women couldn't vote and were told to stay in the kitchen and not "worry their pretty little heads" about important matters? No American should want this country to be what it used to be. That is why it is so important for people to learn not to tolerate but to respect and interact with Americans who are not like them. That is why it is important for Americans to accept and respect the neo-diversity leadership of those we elect to office. Right now instead of acceptance, too many in America are living in a state of anxiety and anger about the neo-diversity that is in all our everyday lives.

In 2005 I could see my North Carolina State University students struggling with their anxiety about the neo-diversity of our campus. Their struggle was made clear to me by an interaction I had with a student who was taking my "Introduction to Social Psychology" course. That spring semester I was teaching the section on race as an interpersonal phenomenon. I teach this topic late in the semester because I want students to have gotten to know me. Otherwise, having me, a broad-shouldered, six-foot-three-inch, 270-pound, dark-skinned Black man as the professor might dampen the discussion of racial dynamics. To a certain degree my strategy had worked in the past, but this time the class of two hundred mostly White students froze up. The tension in the room was palpable. Discussion was strained.

After class I returned to my office. I sat and waited for a student from that class to show up for a previously arranged appointment. When this young White female came into my office and took her seat, we exchanged our quick hellos, I said,

"Sorry, but before we get to your questions, I have a question."

She looked at me as if to say, "I knew he was going to do this."

By that point in the semester my students know me pretty well. Sometimes they think they know more than they actually do or could. But for sure they know that I notice things and will ask about what I think is going on.

"Did you feel that in the class today?"

Still looking at me in that way, she hesitated.

"Yes . . ." she finally said.

"What was that?" I asked.

She looked into my eyes then dropped her gaze to the floor. I waited. Again, she looked up, dropped her gaze briefly then looked back up at me.

"Everybody says we have to be more accepting," she said. "But nobody tells us what that means."

This was a profound statement about the state of neo-diversity on our campus and elsewhere in America. During orientation, some university administrator runs out in front of the crowd of four thousand new students at North Carolina State University and says something like, "Now that you are here, you have to accept all kinds of people." Looking out over the crowd of young people who are eager for guidance, that person in effect says, "Good luck with that!"

College and university students are told that they have to accept all kinds of people. But, as this young woman said, nobody tells students what that means. Students are left to their own devices.

My interaction with that young White woman would not leave me alone. It called to me. It started me down the path of creating a new academic course. I was disturbed, you see, to hear this young person say, "Everybody says we have to be more accepting, but nobody tells us what that means." I was disturbed because I know for sure America just ain't what it used to be.

Born in 1951, I grew up in deep-South Louisiana—the Jim Crow South, that time of legal racial segregation in America. I was not allowed to, and so did not, go to school with White kids because it was against the law. For me, "a colored person," it was against the law to be in school with White kids. Yet today we live in an America where neither law nor anything else controls our racial encounters and interactions. Today we live in a time and circumstance in which contact with people who do not look like us is unavoidable.

Called by that young woman's profound insight, in 2006 I created a new undergraduate social psychology course, "Interpersonal Relationships and Race." I did so because I also knew that in America we have been traveling on a fast-moving train but on the wrong line. Hear the poet Sterling Brown:

> This is the wrong line we been riding
> This route to get us where we got to go.
> Got to get transferred to a new direction
> We can stand so much, and then don't stand no mo'.

Not willing to stand any mo', I left the comfort of my office. Now I stood at the train station and waited. When the old Wrong-Line train pulled in, I called all of the students off who would come. For a while those young people stood on the station platform confused, looking at me and at the same time trying to read outdated schedules of the train lines. But I pulled those from their hands. I gave them the schedule for the Neo-Diversity line.

Good kids: female, Black, Muslim, White, homosexual, Christian, Arab, heterosexual, Northern, male, Jewish, Southern, Brown. They're good kids and having had one class with me already, they recognized and trusted me as I called them off the Wrong-Line train. So they got off and followed me inside the station. I directed them to the benches and they sat. I started giving them some idea of what I was going to teach. I gave them enough information so that they knew I was going to teach them concepts that would show them how to live in the social world of twenty-first-century neo-diverse America.

I was compelled to do this because I knew that we had been putting our children on that Wrong-Line train and then telling them that when they reach the wrong destination, they'll be all right. "You just have to be more accepting," the adults say. Almost cruelly, we send them on their way unprepared. We put them in situations where they are left to wonder: How should

I interact? Should I say something? What should I say? How should I say it? Damn it, what are the rules?

As a college professor, I know this. Even so, seeing the evidence of that confusion in a real person's life is painful to me. I understand that there are times when we as individuals are confused. Sometimes that confusion is just the way of things. But there are times when our confusion hurts us, or when because of our confusion we hurt others. Then it is not so easy to pass it off, because at those times, in those instances, it matters. That is a confusion that matters.

Here's the thing: After teaching these young people for a while, in my students' writings I see their confusion about neo-diversity in their interpersonal lives. Every semester, one or more of my students writes, "For me, coming to North Carolina State University was a culture shock." Reflecting on their own social experiences, students who take my course tell a personal story that shows why and how so many young people struggle with the demands of interacting with someone from a different physically capable, gender, racial, mentally capable, ethnic, religious, or sexually oriented group. A story like this:

> My freshman semester at NC State I was enrolled in tennis PE. The second week of classes the professor selected partners for each one, and I was assigned to be the tennis partner for a Black male. It was one of my first interactions with an African American and his first interaction with Guatemalan Hispanic.
>
> Our first interaction was nothing but awkward and weird. Not only because it was interracial, but also because it was the first week of class when no one knows anybody. Before we started to play, we approached each other slowly and shook hands as we introduced ourselves.
>
> I said, "Hi, my name is Carlos."
>
> He responded, "Hi, my name is D, it is nice to meet you."
>
> Although our greeting was polite you could tell that there was some tension between us. I remember standing a little too far, and having a non-receiving body posture. I had no prior experience with interactions with a Black male, I was guided by stereotypes and was afraid to say the wrong thing or appear to act unwelcoming even though I was already doing it without noticing.

When students enroll in my "Interpersonal Relationships and Race" class, I get them off the Wrong-Line train. As they sit in the station, I begin to give them an orientation, an outline of the lessons they need to learn to be ready for the Neo-Diversity train that is coming down the line.

And a funny thing happens every semester. As the train I called these students off of sits for a little while, other people begin to get off Wrong-Line as well. Intrigued by seeing those young people get off and come into the station, some adults get off the Wrong-Line train and they, too, come into the train station. Some of those adults start to listen to the outline of the lessons. Having heard something that caught their attention, some decide to stay, to let the Wrong-Line train move on without them.

So all of a sudden I am being asked to teach about neo-diversity to people from adult communities: elderly (mostly White) women from One-By-One, the race relations improvement group from Sanford, North Carolina, the Wednesday evening congregational learning community of Raleigh's (White) First Baptist Church, and the nursing staff from UNC-Hospitals.

Just my outline of the meaning of neo-diversity catches people's attention. Everyone had been sensing that something new was happening, but they couldn't identify it; they couldn't name it.

Sensing something is not enough. "Feels like rain," we say, but we don't know for sure and are often wrong. Standing in that train station, talking to the students I had pulled off the Wrong-Line, I was in more demand than I anticipated because I was not only talking about what people were sensing; I was naming it, describing it, and explaining it. Something new was, in fact, happening. America, you see, just won't be what it used to be, many long years ago.

People—students and nonstudents, young and old, male and female, Muslim, Christian, Jewish, Hindu, atheist, homosexual, and heterosexual—had been sensing the Neo-Diversity train coming down the line. All kinds of people were sensing that truth. Some of those people wanted to get ready. Me, I started my teaching about neo-diversity with college students.

To get them ready, I know that my students need more than hearsay teaching. They need me to activate in them a new mindset that will give them the strength to lift off their backs the heavy baggage that hearsay teaching has put there. If I am to help, I have to teach in a way that enables these young travelers to develop the faith they need to see through the fog of their neo-diversity anxieties to see the truth.

On the first day of class, I let the students know we have real work to do. I exhort them:

"We've got some difficult days ahead," I declare. "That's what he said," I go on.

On that fateful night, when it seemed he knew he would be dead the next day, the late Reverend Dr. Martin Luther King Jr. said, we've got some difficult days ahead. On that fateful night, after so many battles had been won he said, we've got some difficult days ahead.

Understand, if you don't already know, Dr. King always chose his words carefully. That's why I am convinced that on that night in Memphis, Tennessee, it was no accident that he said, we've got some difficult days ahead. But what, what was he thinking of? What was he alerting us to? What did he know? It was clear he knew, somehow, he already knew.

And what I believe Dr. King knew was that change is difficult. And I believe he knew, too, that the most difficult change of all still awaited America. Change in the interpersonal environment.

He was telling us to get ready, get ready! For what? For neo-diversity. He was alerting us to the coming Neo-Diversity train. Dr. King could already see that with the elimination of the laws of racial oppression and segregation, all Americans would have to learn how to interact with, travel with each other no matter the groups we come from. He could already see that with elimination of the laws of racial oppression and segregation, America's diversity would grow. He could see that it would mean that all Americans would struggle with the question "Who are the 'we,' and who are among the 'they'?" He was telling us to get ready for the difficult days of learning how to interact with each other with respect.

All of you here who have gotten off the Wrong-Line train have gotten off with some unnecessary baggage that you are going to have to leave behind. Understand that the lessons I will impart are not lessons for any one group. That idea is a piece of unnecessary baggage.

These lessons are not and will not be about fixing White people. These lessons are necessary because all of you have been too long on the Wrong-Line train on which you were given some obsolete baggage to carry. That includes some bad lessons about interacting with people who are not members of your particular group. That unnecessary baggage does not depend on which group you are from.

There are no innocent.

In our social interactions, none of us is innocent.

That's why we've got some difficult days ahead.

So get ready, I say, . . . get ready.

Then I give them a reading assignment. Tim Tyson's *Blood Done Sign My Name* is a historical memoir by a White man who, as a ten-year-old boy, was witness to racial events in Oxford, North Carolina, in 1970. Tyson is now a PhD-trained scholar of African America history. The book jacket of his historical memoir reads:

On May 11, 1970, Henry Marrow, a twenty-three-year-old black veteran, walked into a crossroads store owned by Robert Teel and came out running. Teel and two of his sons chased and beat Marrow, then killed him in public as he pleaded for his life.

Like many small Southern towns, the civil rights movement had barely touched Oxford. But in the wake of the killing, young African Americans took to the streets. While lawyers battled in the courthouse, the Klan raged in the shadows and black Vietnam veterans torched the town's tobacco warehouses. Tyson's father, the pastor of Oxford's all-white Methodist church, urged the town to come to terms with its bloody racial history. In the end, however, the Tyson family was forced to move away.

Tim Tyson's riveting narrative of that fiery summer brings gritty blues truth, soaring gospel vision, and down-home humor to a shocking episode of our history. Like *To Kill a Mockingbird*, *Blood Done Sign My Name* is a classic portrait of an unforgettable time and place.

My students are assigned to read the book in thirds. After reading each section, students write a reaction to that part of the reading. Not an analytic reaction but a personal "What hit me" reaction. Breathless come those reactions.

"I almost don't know where to start."

"It hit me like a pile of bricks."

"This is not what I learned in history class."

"I cannot imagine."

"It baffles me."

"It made me cringe."

"I was astounded."

"I cannot believe that this is actually based on a true story."

"I find it shocking that such racial discrimination was happening in my state."

"I reacted right away with shock and sorrow."

"It breaks my heart, and frankly, it pisses me off."

"With every turn of the page, I feel my blood boiling. . . ."

"The stories and ideas made me gag."

"It brings over a sadness in me that is uncomfortable, painful even."

"The amount of violence is absolutely crazy."

"I was shocked by all the violence."

"Why were people so cruel? Why?"

"This book is appalling, intriguing, heartbreaking, and inspiring."

"My eyes have been opened."

"I never realized how damaged this nation really was."

"I was shocked."

"It left me with my jaw dropped open."

"I knew things were different back then than they are now, but wow!"

"Many emotions, sadness and pure anger."

"Wow, just wow!"

"As a young White woman I have been severely lied to about past events in NC."

"I was surprised by how much I really didn't know."

"Wait a minute, this is the story of a little White boy living in the segregated South. Oops."

"It was absolutely astonishing to me that my hometown was mentioned in this book."

"So eye-opening."

"Shocking to read."

"I was really caught off guard."

"I do not like this book."

"Where to start, there are so many things to talk about."

"I still cannot wrap my head around it. It is hard to comprehend. Shock and awe."

"Blew my mind. I was speechless, dumbfounded. Absolutely mind-blowing."

"A powerful book. Heartbreaking; tears were in my eyes."

"I put the book down and thought about it."

Such are these young travelers' reactions to the first third of Tyson's witnessed, documented, true telling of America's racial history. Here is a more extended version of those reactions from a White female. She wrote:

> I was truly amazed that I had never heard of Henry Marrow. I was surprised that the schools never mentioned the horrific murder of this young man. As I read these chapters it became clear that Henry Marrow's death sparked a revolution among the Black townsfolk. Why is something so important, someone so important, forgotten throughout the years? The book portrayed a movie in my head as I read these chapters. I saw with my own eyes Henry Marrow running for his life, I saw the Teels shoot Ben Chavis in the face at close range, and I saw the blows the Teels dealt Marrow as he lay dying in the street.

Why so much shock and awe? Well, how would you react if you found out that all you were led to believe about something turned out to be a sales pitch?

CHAPTER 2

A SALES PITCH?

O beautiful for spacious skies,
For amber waves of grain,
For purple mountain majesties
Above the fruited plain!
America! America!
God shed his grace on thee
And crown thy good with brotherhood
From sea to shining sea!

—Katharine Lee Bates,
"America the Beautiful," 1913

"America the Beautiful": that is a praise song. It is a song designed to make us, and keep us, proud of America, proud to be Americans. And pride in our nation is important, but not if it's based on a commercial; not if it's based on a sales pitch.

I was talking with Dr. Doug Gillan, one of my colleagues in the Psychology Department. I was telling him about how shocked and angry my students become while they do their assigned reading of Tim Tyson's book, *Blood Done Sign My Name*. I told Doug that my students ask, "Why did I have to get to college to learn the real, ugly truth about the civil rights movement in America?" They become even angrier because they had to wait to get to college even to learn about North Carolina's racial history. One of the young travelers wrote:

It angers me that we were taught the "fluffy" version of what happened, but not even that. We were lied to about the events that took place and how it all happened. I think people do this because they don't want to remember. They don't want to acknowledge that that was the mindset not all that long ago; for some it's how THEY thought. I think people think that by not acknowledging it and "sweeping it under the rug," so to speak, that they're just hoping it will go away. I think that's the opposite of what needs to happen. I think we need to embrace the fact that this was an issue, and work through the gruesome details to ensure that something like this doesn't happen in the future.

Another student wrote:

I am shocked that I never learned about this in any of the schools that I attended. It bothers me that our country is so ashamed of admitting that it was wrong that history rewrites itself to make events in the past not seem so terrible, especially slavery and the entire civil rights movement. Growing up learning about these events, the history books almost made it seem like a cakewalk to achieve equality. I think that it is important for people to learn about these tragic, brutal events that occurred during history in order for people to understand the significance of the civil rights movement and how far we have come since. It really bothers me that these things are not learned, almost as if Americans cannot own up to the past and admit its mistakes. This has been my main reaction to the reading. Those who believe that we should not focus on the past do not understand that we must recognize and accept our past in order to move forward as a whole.

And yet another wrote:

The more I read this book, the more I am astonished by our nation's history. Every new detail I hear makes it more uncomfortable to think about all the events that transpired in a time not so long ago.

Most of the time we think about racism in our country to be a long-ago event, yet we are constantly surrounded by people who have had first-hand accounts of this terrible time. When I take that into consideration, it reminds me that this wasn't so long ago; it's still a fresh wound in our nation's history, yet we act as if it was hundreds of years ago. We are a country that takes pride in our right to excel, having a diverse population, and encouraging the growth of all individuals. Yet we are hypocrites; we say all these things and look down on other countries that persecute their own people, but we have committed these same acts. I am ashamed of all those that participated in this horrible time.

But I am even angrier with those that let this behavior of hatred continue. It should not have taken all that it did to bring this to a stop. All of the leaders in our government as well as law enforcement, even if they did not participate in this type of behavior, still condoned it by not bringing it to an end at the first opportunity they had.

My students' anger came up in our conversation because Doug and I were talking about what good teaching is supposed to do. We were agreeing that good teaching is about giving the learner true, factual information in a way that transforms the learner's understanding of the world. It was in that context that I was talking about my students' anger about not learning in high school the real history of race in America. When I said this, Doug commented: "Well, we all know that what is taught in middle and high school about American history isn't the history. It's a sales pitch."

That hit me.

"What's it going to take to get you into this America," the salesperson says. Then that salesperson gives our children a sales pitch. "Trust me, have I got a deal for you." The salesperson offers a deal, all right: a false identity—no car facts.

It's a sales pitch.

To tell you the truth, I had not thought of it that way. Maybe that is why I was so struck by Doug's comment.

> O beautiful for spacious skies,
> For amber waves of grain,
> For purple mountain majesties
> Above the fruited plain!
> America! America!

It's a sales pitch. Well, I'll be . . .

No wonder so many Americans get so upset about learning real truths about American history. Some Americans act as if showing patterns of past racial, gender, religious, and ethnic injustice is just too much.

"You're just being critical. America . . . love it or leave it."

If you have bought the sales pitch, you don't want to have to rethink the purchase you have already made. My students pick up on that as well. One White male wrote:

> It's hard to believe that this racial murder and all the other racial stuff was taking place just forty years ago. About this time in our history we are taught about everything BUT the intense racial war. They'll teach about hippies, Vietnam, Kennedy, a few protests, legislation passed, and even Bill Russell's eleven NBA championships with the Celtics throughout the '60s and '70s, but not this stuff. They show people images of Blacks like Bill Russell to desensitize us about the hardships Blacks faced during that time. It really blows my mind that while Henry Marrow was beaten to death and his killers acquitted in Oxford, we have Bill Russell over here winning championships in Boston. How does that work out? It hurts me to admit it, but I believe that our country's attempts to change history will ultimately work. So many people are not taught this stuff that the "sales pitch" is what will endure over time.

I understand this young man's anger and his puzzlement about the duality of America. Still, I disagree with his conclusion that the sales pitch will win out. I am not alone. One of his classmates, a young White woman, wrote:

> In order for us to ultimately "conquer" our past we must address it from a true perspective, not all the hogwash that we are informed as children and teenagers with the animated films in history class of Martin Luther King. Race relations are still a touchy subject in America; nobody ever wants to offend anyone, or we are scared that if we say the wrong thing people will think we are racist. This is the problem—we have not confronted the issue as a generation of proactive young adults that want equality for anyone whether you are Black, White, gay, lesbian, Muslim, or Christian. Until we all are confronted with the truth and taught how to overcome and deal with our history, it's always going to be an underlying tension in the back of our minds when faced with the diversity that constantly fills our lives.

She calls the middle school and high school American history she was taught "hogwash," and she mentions "animated films" about the civil rights struggle. Really? Come on, don't we have actual film footage of what went on during the marches and sit-ins? Don't we? Yes, of course we do. So there is no need to use animated films when the films of the actual events can be seen on PBS and the History Channel and elsewhere. It can probably be found in the Library of Congress. Why wouldn't teachers attempt to find and use this footage?

Hearsay teaching is killing our democracy. Hearsay teaching is us giving our children invisible but heavy baggage to carry on their backs. After reading all of *Blood Done Sign My Name*, one of my students wrote:

> Reading this book, I have found myself to look at the world around me much differently. I cannot help but wonder how our ancestors could have lived lives filled with such hate against fellow Americans who in reality only differ in color from themselves. It's heart-wrenching to think about the devastation that the race-provoked violence left on American history.
>
> We are a nation that supports and encourages the freedom of all people around the world, yet our nation's history is composed mostly of us taking and/or limiting the freedom of our own citizens within the US. I am ashamed of the shared past that a majority of Americans have of our ancestors. Reading this book has opened my eyes to a history that I had always envisioned of another place and time, and had never really brought it home and connected with.

Without that connection to our identity as Americans, our racial history is heavy baggage we carry around without knowing why we feel so tired and anxious. That is the legacy of hearsay teaching.

Let me be clear. To teach in a way that is not hearsay teaching does not mean you have to have been there to witness the events. Having been a Black boy growing up under the oppression of legal racial segregation gives me a powerful perspective, but that is not the basis of the passion I bring to my teaching about intergroup matters. To teach with a passion that is in the moment requires that you study the events and connect what happened to your personal values. If part of your personal American value system is a real belief and commitment to the American Dream; if the words "All men are created equal" are more than just words to you, then reading, studying, and seeing the pictures and film clips of events during the civil rights movement should fuel your teaching with outrage and personal indignation.

I am not gay. But when it was reported on the local Raleigh news that antigay graffiti had been written in bold on the front of the North Carolina State University Gay, Lesbian, Bisexual, and Transgender Center (GLBT), I was outraged. When I read about that event in our student newspaper, I was infuriated. When I saw the picture of the hateful graffiti with the words "FAG . . . Burn . . . Die," I was enraged. I was outraged, infuriated, and enraged because that act violated my personal values for myself and for the campus on which I am a citizen.

When that happened, as a professor I had a number of teaching outlets available to me. Since the election of President Barack Hussein Obama, we have had a number of racial-graffiti incidences that caused uproars on the NCSU campus. During the first of these in 2008, I wrote a guest column for both campus newspapers: the *Nubian Message* and the *Technician*. My full column, "In Racial Transition," appeared in the *Nubian Message*:

> Much ado has been made about the racial graffiti and threat to President-elect Obama that was found in the NCSU Free Expression Tunnel. Yes; the words written by those four students were reprehensible. And NCSU has responded appropriately, vigorously, to the full extent of the law. We all know it is impossible for an educational institution to guarantee that there will be no students enrolled who harbor racial, religious, or gender, biases. No employer can make such a guarantee either. What the institution must do is when biases come out in behavior, strike hard and fast at the perpetrators. Yet that must be within the limits of the law. Civil-rights are not African-American or Caucasian-American rights, but rights that protect US citizens equally. We become Nazis when we want people persecuted in ways that go beyond what is lawful. If the state and federal laws are a problem, protest those laws. NCSU does not make the laws; the State of NC and Congress do that.
>
> We live on a new racial frontier. In deep-South Louisiana, I grew up when Jim Crow still lived. All of my early education through high school (1957–1969) was racially segregated from Whites. So in my lifetime, we have gone from segregation-by-law, to desegregation-by-law, to having an

African-American President-elect. Yet, as dramatic as the election of Mr. Obama is, even saying that President-elect Obama is African-American isn't quite enough. Mr. Obama is bi-racial. So, we have also gone from segregation and race in Black and White, to race as multicultural.

No wonder that leading up to election-day, there was interpersonal electricity. People couldn't stop talking. When the election results flashed and thundered, people cried, laughed, threw up their arms, danced, collapsed, shook hands, and hugged each other, held their mouths; all in belief, shock, disbelief, joy, fear that this was happening in America.

On campus the next morning, I ran into Dr. Tom Stafford, who is NCSU's Vice Chancellor for Student Affairs. He told me about the racial graffiti that threatened the person of President-elect Obama. Dr. Stafford was shaken but went on with handling that business. My thoughts turned to what I would do in my "Interpersonal Relationships and Race" class. Instead of the scheduled lecture, I had already decided to have my students talk about the conversations they were now having given the interracial event of Senator Barack Obama being elected President. Now I knew I would also lead a discussion about the racial slur and threat in the Free Expression Tunnel. All semester, you see, I have been introducing my racially mixed class to social psychological concepts that helped them to understand the forces acting on interracial interactions. Part of that has been helping those students understand how things were, and how much things have changed in America.

It's a new racial frontier. That is why in interracial interactions, people feel uncertain. We wonder, what is the right way to interact? But that anxiety does not make a person a bigot. After all Whites *and* Blacks are experiencing this anxiety. That anxiety indicates that as a nation we are living in a transition-time of interracial uncertainty, tension and change. In interracial interactions, that is why people feel confused and jumpy. That is why hours after the election of our nation's first African American President we learned of threatening racial graffiti being aimed at that person. Both the positive and negative are in the interracial mix that is our nation today. Stalked by our uncertainty, events like the election of Senator Barack Obama and the simultaneous appearance of a racial slur and threat against him make Americans feel even more confused and jumpy.

Even so, there are a few certainties. Despite what people may say, the Civil Rights Movement was not about changing the hearts and minds of White America. It was about obtaining "equal protection under the law" for

Black Americans. So in the case of the racial graffiti, the issue is not that at NCSU there are Whites who dislike Blacks. There will always be ignorant people. The question; what is the response of the institution?

Since becoming a member of the NCSU faculty in 1988, among other things I served as the university's first Vice Provost for Diversity and African American Affairs (2000–2002). So when it comes to diversity issues, I watch what the administration does with a careful eye.

By my judgment, the university's response to the discovery of the racial threat was swift, dramatic and unambiguous. A strong statement from the Chancellor denouncing the behavior; an immediate investigation in cooperation with the Secret Service came quickly. Also coming quickly was a strong editorial from the *Technician* and a racially mixed student sponsored protest rally. Racism is not an individual problem. Racism is always institutional; does the institution support and encourage bigotry? Clearly our institution does not.

Editors of the *Technician* were a bit more skittish and published only a short version of my essay as a letter. Yet, after that, the staff of that paper invited me to write a guest column whenever I had something I wanted the campus to think about seriously. I have used that open invitation since 2008 to try to give students an understanding of neo-diversity matters writ large. After the incident of the antigay graffiti, I was quick to write an essay for the *Technician*. Published on October 19, 2011, two days after the occurrence, to the whole campus I said:

> On our campus, it appears that some believe our gay and lesbian peers and colleagues have no right to life. The graffiti on the front of our GLBT Center tells them to "die." Yet, the first words of the preamble of the Declaration of Independence are:
>
> "We hold these truths to be self-evident, that all men are created equal. That they are endowed by their creator with certain inalienable rights; among these are life, liberty and the pursuit of happiness."
>
> Self-evident. Meaning it's so obvious that there's no need for a discussion or explanation.
>
> Yet, for a long time, the whole country said that these words did not apply to someone with my dark skin color. Slavery and then racial segrega-

tion was all evidence of no right to liberty; to choose where to live or go to school; no right to vote until 1965. No right to choose who to marry, and no right to the pursuit of happiness until 1967.

Racial segregation did something very important. It made it clear who was part of "we" and who was part of "they."

With those immoral laws gone, we now live in a time when interacting with someone who does not look like us is unavoidable. Now we struggle with neo-diversity anxiety that is causing some to want to keep other American citizens in the category of "they" and "them."

Regarding the preamble, General Colin Powell said, "This beautiful statement was not the reality of 1776, but it set forth the dream that we would strive to make a reality. . . . Governments belong to the people and exist to secure the rights endowed to every citizen."

Diversity is the first American promise. That makes diversity the American value. As citizens, we are all required to accept and work for that American value.

Whenever we have fought diversity in the past, we have held ourselves back. In fact, that seems always to be the point in fighting against diversity—to have America stay the same, to stagnate. But when we have come to accept diversity, we have moved forward. We have grown as a nation because we have begun to use all the talents available to us, making our nation stronger.

I served in the US Navy from 1972 to 1976. I served with men of honor. Some of those men were gay. On board ship, 5,000 men on aircraft carriers, did we know that? Yes, we did. Yet, all that mattered was that everyone did their job.

About finally eliminating Don't Ask, Don't Tell, the outgoing chairman of the Joint Chiefs of Staff, Admiral Mullen said, ". . . we have been asking American citizens to lie about who they are in order to serve our nation. That is not who we are; we are better than that."

Yet, some of us still want to condemn gay and lesbian American citizens, some of whom are willing to risk their lives to serve and protect American freedoms. Some of us want to tell gays and lesbians they have no right to marry or to the pursuit of happiness. And some say they have no right to life; die.

Will we on this campus stand for that?

Right away, in my more traditional teaching mode, I began to use the antigay graffiti event as an example of neo-diversity anxiety gone unchecked. In my lectures, in my presentations to audiences on and off campus, I objected to the hatred of gays and lesbians that that event demonstrated existed on our campus. But I also objected to how that event dehumanizes all of us by demeaning our relationship to each other as campus citizens, as citizens of America, and as human beings.

In the context of getting my students to understand the social psychology of slurs, I point out that there are no innocent anti-group slurs. Slurs have divisive social psychological effects on us all.

Anti-group slurs rest on what we social psychologists call the minimal group effect (Gilovich, Keltner, Chen, Nisbett). We humans have a tendency to quick-think of people either as members of our group or not. Slurs motivate people to think of everything as being us versus them. That can then lead to a tendency for us to want competition between the groups. That minimal group effect makes it easy for each of us to treat others in demeaning ways; it makes discrimination easy. Making that analytic point, I also express my personal objection to the particular event at our GLBT Center by saying, "This happened on *my* campus, *my* campus. I will not let this pass; I will not!"

I teach this example, this way, not because I am gay. I teach it this way because, as with any anti-group slur, it violates my personal values, my American values.

In the midst of the emotional mind-bending experience of reading the Tyson book, my students are coherent about what hit them and how it begins to trouble them. A Mexican American female student wrote:

> From reading the first third of *Blood Done Sign My Name*, I was shocked to read about many of the struggles that African Americans and at times even some Whites went through in order to be able to get where we are today—a racially integrated society. I cannot even imagine having to go through some of the things they were faced with. Not being able to sit down and eat a

meal at a restaurant, not getting the same education, treatment, or justice because the color of my skin was looked down upon—I do not know how or if I would have been able to cope with everything that they went through.

A White female wrote:

Denying the events of the past does us no good, nor does it heal the wounds that are a result of racial warfare. I've mentioned earlier how surprised I've been when reading the history of North Carolina as told by Tim Tyson; it's amazing how many things have been left out conveniently from textbooks.

I grew up in Topsail Beach, North Carolina, 26 miles outside of Wilmington. Because there was not much as far as commerce goes in my town, it's not a stretch to say that I grew up in Wilmington. I had heard a little bit about the Wilmington 10, but I did not know too much about it until they were pardoned last year by the governor. How can an event so catastrophic, so large that it caught the interest of international headlines, not be mentioned in a single history class that I was sitting in 26 miles outside of where it happened?

Then there's the Wilmington Race Riot of 1898. As Tim Tyson said, "The Wilmington race riot was probably the most important political event in the history of the state. Its omission from North Carolina history may have been the biggest of the lies that marked my boy-hood." I could not have said it better myself and I sincerely hope that the history books are changed to make sure that important events are not overlooked and left out. To make matters more interesting, my great-grandparents as well as grand-parents were living in Wilmington at the time. Unless they lived under a rock, they obviously witnessed these race wars, but not a word about it was ever mentioned, not even in casual conversation. It's probably not a surprise to you, Dr. Nacoste, that because I know very little about what happened in 1971 in Wilmington, I had never heard about what happened in 1898 until I read this book. While Conservatives took over the political life of the city, exiled their opponents, and Blacks fled the city, a new order was created, and it did not include Black citizens. To this day it is unclear what the death toll was of African Americans during this overthrow.

Although I have been shocked about things that happened in what I consider my home-town, I am pleased that I am now aware of the past events. In the future, I hope that I can be a proactive member of society that contributes to acknowledging our past and help our communities move forward.

Although the shock continues as they read, these young travelers begin to wonder why. They begin to ask, "What was really going on?" They begin to develop hypotheses. A White female student put her thinking this way:

> The apocalypse is here. The world is officially coming to an end. That is what I could not help but think while reading the second part of *Blood Done Sign My Name*. The amount of violence, tragedy, and injustice that existed just forty years ago was enough to make me wonder, "What in the world was wrong with people?" Did White people really think that what was going on in their communities was morally right?
>
> Robert Teel and his sons brutally beat a man and then murdered him while he was pleading for his life, based on the poor assumption that he had "flirted with a White woman." Yet none of them were found guilty for anything. Witnesses on both the prosecution's side and the defense's side stated evidence that incriminated these men and yet none of them were found guilty. It is no wonder why Blacks chose to retaliate against them, burning down buildings and bringing fear deep into the souls of the White people living around them. Honestly, what choice did they have?
>
> I have never been a big fan of violence. The idea that some people immediately jump to punching someone in the face because they do something wrong is not something I condone. But, Black people were driven to it. I am not trying to start a "White People Suck" campaign, but I find the injustice that I have been reading in these pages too sickening to think anything else. Part of me wishes I had been an adult during that time. Maybe then I would understand where this backward way of thinking was coming from.
>
> Maybe White people reacted so negatively towards integration and the fair treatment of Black people because they were afraid of change. They were afraid of losing this so-called "power and control" they had in the world. But, I still think this is all a copout. No one is entitled to power and control over other people, no matter their race, ethnicity, gender, sex, etc.

Entitled or not, the power and control hypothesis is one that comes to many of my students. One wrote:

My immediate reaction is: "I just don't get it." How can people believe that their actions are justifiable? At what point do they allow themselves to be brainwashed, thinking that what's going on around them is okay? Granted, at this point, the people only knew what they grew up with, but it still surprises me that so few people came to the realization that what was going on during this time was extremely inhumane and unjust. Color? Really? Color to separate humans.

And then it all becomes clear. Power. It comes down to power and fear. At one point White people created a power over Blacks. From then on, anything was formulated; ideas, stereotypes, false facts, to separate Whites from Blacks. To create an illusion that Blacks were a different species, and that species was lower than Whites. Really?? My reaction is frustration. Frustration and a lack of hope in human beings. I understand how this situation got to where it did, and I understand why so many people went along with it. What was created was huge, and nobody wanted to be on the wrong side.

We've already got ourselves stuck in the position, it's what we know, so we continue to live this way because we are afraid of the unknown and not threatened with the comfortable current state. But things began to change. The Blacks began to stick up for themselves, bringing fear to the people and the necessity to make a change.

Maybe it's because I was a witness. Maybe that is why I am so surprised that so many of today's young travelers believe that the civil rights movement was about changing the hearts and minds of White Americans. No, it wasn't. Yet some young people actually try to argue with me that it was.

That is an element making up the thick fog of fatigue that has been stopping these young travelers from seeing the reality around them, and the real destination ahead. Anyone who believes that the civil rights movement was about changing the hearts and minds of White people is lost in an ahistorical fog. Reacting to *Blood*, a White male student wrote:

Has there been progress over the past few generations? Obviously. Great strides have been made. As I look at my town, and those running it, however, not much has changed in its operation from decades ago. I can count on one hand the number of African-American businessmen or professionals that are prominent in my town. I also know that despite Blacks and Whites seemingly getting along and even catching up with old friends or coworkers in passing, things change once the conversation stops.

Any given day that I'm home, I guarantee I will hear the word nigger or other forms of bigotry from friends, family, or other Whites in town including those in political offices. My ex-girlfriend's grandfather is a former North Carolina State House of Representatives member. I've heard the man say some of the most bigoted shit out of anyone in my life, and he's been in the state government for decades. Times have changed for sure, but it still makes me wonder how far people themselves have progressed in my small town and those like Oxford.

Even though that is enough to make the point about a change in hearts and minds, I want to be clear. This is not just a small-town Southern problem. One of my former students is from Long Island. After taking my course and returning to Long Island, I got this e-mail from her. She wrote:

Dear Dr. Nacoste,

How have you been? I hope your classes are going great. I forgot to mention in my last email when I moved back to New York I noticed a lot that had to do with language communities once again and was afraid of slipping into my old habits. It's definitely a lot different to be in different states and be surrounded back home with everyone who makes constant racial judgments. It's kind of sad to see it all play out in front of me again because I can see that it's very easy to slip into old habits. I wish I had a chance to catch up with you in North Carolina, I hope all is well. I would love to read your new book! My home address is . . . South Bay Shore NY 11706. I look forward to reading your book and hearing back from you.

If the language of racial stereotypes and racial hate is still so prevalent, then I say again, the civil rights movement didn't just fail; it was an epic fail. But that is not true. The truth is that the civil rights movement was a magnificent success. The success came through the focus being put on attacking racism; attacking unjust laws.

Understand, to believe that the goal of the movement was to change White people's feelings about Black people is to confuse prejudice with bigotry and bigotry with racism. Right now that confusion is all over America because we have tried to downplay and ignore our history.

Prejudice is a prejudgment. We all have prejudices. I grew up in the bayou country of Louisiana, not New Orleans; there is nothing city about me. I am a bayou-born, Louisiana Black Creole from Opelousas, Louisiana, in the heart of what is called Cajun Country, Acadiana. We Creoles, along with the Cajuns, have a reputation: we eat just about anything. And it's true that our orientation is that all you got to do is "put a little sauce-piquant on that and you got yourself something." Right now, one of our newer delicacies for the dinner table is nutria rat. Put a little sauce-piquant on that skinned and gutted nutria rat and you got yourself something.

If you squirmed at that statement, and you have never eaten nutria (or any other rat), that is a prejudgment; a prejudice. Now, more seriously, when it comes to racial, mentally challenged, gender, physically challenged, ethnic, sexually oriented, or religious groups, prejudice is an unfair, negative judgment of any whole group of people. It is a prejudgment because no one can know (or interact with and experience) a whole group of people.

Answer me this: does a person who has such a prejudice have to show it in the presence of a member of the group? Answering for you, I say no. Turns out, the well-socialized person can be quite cordial and (apparently) open to a person from a group for which he or she holds a prejudice. As my student (above) wrote: "I also know that despite Blacks and Whites seemingly getting along and even catching up with old friends or coworkers in passing, things change once that conversation stops." What he is saying is that when the interaction is over, when those people go back into their racially segregated groups, the negative racial language comes out.

In the presence of someone from a group you prejudge, you do not have to show that prejudice in your behavior. When, however, a prejudice is shown in external behavior, that is bigotry. Bigotry is the behavioral expression of a group prejudice.

On the matter of racism we are, in fact, deeply confused. We show our confusion about these matters especially in our glee to call someone else a "racist." It turns out that racism is never in a person (Vander Zanden). Racism is institutional and organizational (Simpson and Yinger).

I admit that nowadays it is perplexing to see pictures of events from the civil rights movement and look upon the hateful behavior of Whites screaming out their hate, spitting on, hitting with bats, throwing bricks, all at Black people simply because of their skin color. Modern Americans see that and say, "What racists!" But the real question is why were those Whites so comfortable showing their bigotry in public? Why? Because their behavior was authorized and supported by the law. Unless a White person actually murdered a Black person right in front of the police in broad daylight, nothing was going to be done to Whites for screaming out their hate, spitting on, hitting with bats, or throwing bricks at Black people. And the case of the murder of Henry Marrow in 1970 showed that the police and the whole criminal justice system might overlook even the murder of a Black man.

Racism is never in a person. Racism is always institutional and organizational. That is one of the lessons I teach and one of the truths my students learn from Tyson's book.

What the civil rights movement was about was killing the social structure of law that supported and encouraged prejudice and bigotry. Killing that social structure, obtaining equal protection under the law for African Americans was necessary to reduce and stop the free occurrence of bigotry from Whites. That took real strategies and work. Sometimes a horrendous event was part of the energy. The racial murder of Henry Marrow in Oxford, North Carolina, was one such event for that town. That's why the conclusion from one of our young travelers about the effect in Oxford is so important to comprehend. She wrote:

> The Blacks began to stick up for themselves, bringing fear to the people and the necessity to make a change.

We have been giving our children hogwash as history lessons; hogwash that makes them more than ignorant. We make them insensitive to the struggle of a people. "It's all just a big joke." That ignorance and insensitivity is the baggage these young travelers are being weighed down by. Carrying such a heavy weight, they become tired, especially because they don't know they have this baggage on their backs. It's carrying on your back an invisible, full, and heavy backpack. Tired out by this weight, hunched forward under that weight, they give up in the face of intolerance. They are so blinded by the fog of fatigue they cannot identify bigotry. These young travelers are so close to exhaustion, so weary, they get so punchy that when someone uses the word nigger, that's funny. Anything said about race is funny.

Real information, real car facts, knowledge lets them reach around, grip that backpack, and take it off. With that weight gone, their vision clears; they have sudden sight. With that abrupt sight they are startled to see that they have been carrying on their backs filthy baggage that is filled with useless pieces of iron deadweight. Relieved of that burden, even the way they hear will change. Intolerant language that they once laughed at will have the true sound of its growling bigotry.

Yet I acknowledge and admit that receiving the truth they get through my course is not an easy process for my students. No, it is not easy. It is not a pleasant experience. That is another reason I tell them up front, "We've got some difficult days ahead."

PART 2

I HEAR THE WHEELS A RUMBLING, AND ROLLING THROUGH THE LAND

CHAPTER 3

WE'VE GOT SOME DIFFICULT DAYS AHEAD

On the first day of my "Interpersonal Relationships and Race" course, I exhort to the fifty to seventy students, "We've got some difficult days ahead." Forewarned, they are, by my introduction. Even so, I still know that the reading and the lecture lessons of the course will be a jolting, painful experience for those who have been misled by hearsay teaching up to that point in their lives. So I am not saying that students or anyone else will like the lessons. Oh, god, no. Real learning can be psychologically painful. A Chinese American male student wrote:

> I was utterly disgusted toward the results of the Henry Marrow case. It is obvious that Roger and the Teels were responsible and should be guilty of murder. The fact that the jury acquitted the defendants is an absolute disgrace to the US judicial system. Personally, I feel like if the defendants are still alive right now, which I believe they are, they should be retried to make sure that justice is served. Nonetheless it might be too little too late.

Some are even more overtaken with disgust. In a two-page, single-spaced reaction, a White female student wrote, in part:

> I don't like this book.
>   I avoid confrontation at all costs. I mentally prepare myself for altercations to make sure I can be calm. I don't hate people I don't know. If I don't like someone it is because they have done something wrong to me. But the people in this book, they just hate. They hate people they don't know, and they hate people they do know. You commit one "nigga loving" act and you are exiled off the island. Everything is focused on everyone's race. You have to follow the rules in order to stay in the "club."

Just this whole book for me is "Ugh!" and "What?" and then "Why?" and then "What?" and then a lot of bad words go through my head. Then I want to throw something at someone.

Hit hard by reading *Blood Done Sign My Name* and reeling, a Black female student wrote:

The book is done, but I seem to have even more questions now that I can sit back and reflect. I realize that because I did not live through this, I will never understand it fully, but it scares me that I still do not understand how we got to this point. The reason why this unknown scares me is because if we do not know how we got to this point we do not really know how to stop a situation from getting to that point again.

People know that African Americans were a group that was discriminated against, so people know that that race will not be targeted again, but in this neo-diverse world, there are always new minority groups that could easily take their place in the future if we were to go back into that behavior. And we have already begun to target groups such as Arabs and Hispanics as they are becoming larger and larger in our population, and some of the same mindsets in the book about Black people are the ways that people are thinking about these groups. People look at them as if they are coming into America and taking over when really they are just trying to live the same American Dream as all the other citizens in this country, much like African Americans were trying to do in this time of *Blood Done Sign My Name*.

We are being haunted by an unacknowledged history. There are things in our history that linger around us, a fog influencing how we see, what we see. That fog gets thicker because we are hiding a smoldering, brutal history. A White female student wrote:

After reading the middle third of *Blood* I have come to a very dark and serious conclusion. Although it is not official, this time in our nation's history commenced a second civil war. History books state that the conclusion of the Civil War, the North versus the South, was in 1865. If you ask the average person, they might tell you that this was the last war to take place on US soil. I wholeheartedly disagree.

It may not be deemed a formal war in textbooks and in society, but *BDSMN* shows that this disturbing era in our history has war written all over it: Weapons, violence, murders, riots, major traumatization, and mayhem. It was not North versus South, but it was Blacks versus Whites, equality versus inequality, justice versus injustice; a war so paradoxically conspicuous, so up close and personal, that no one at the time even realized it. Just like the wars before and after, Civil War II, as I call it, was no isolated incident. There were battles taking place nationwide and headquartered in the Jim Crow South.

Reeling with this discovery of the truth, something important starts to happen to my students. One White male wrote:

There is a line on page 242 of *Blood* that reads, "After they shot him down, and while he was laying there, flat on his back, unable to get up . . . they kicked him and stomped him and hit him in the head with a shotgun butt over and over again. They beat him while he begged for his life, beat him until he was probably unconscious. And then they shot him in the head like you or I would kill a snake."

This sort of murder is a type that I have heard of before on crime documentaries, but now that I've been primed to consider racial aspects, I realize the significance of this. The men weren't killing Henry Marrow simply because they misinterpreted his words; it was because they viewed him as inferior and worthy of death to even consider touching one of their women; inferior only because society taught them that Black people were in fact inferior to Whites. This kind of murder is not calculated, it is not technical; it is primal and heinous, and those committing it should be locked away immediately. No sort of hate would merit that; self-defense is even pushing it, and the fact that it was his race that justified it in those men's minds makes me sick, to say the very least.

I don't even know what to say about the verdict of the case. I honestly have never felt so disheartened about racial incidences in the past, mostly because our school systems dress it up as a pretty package that has led to equality nowadays, which we know is not even true. The fact that a man's life was taken when beaten senseless like an animal would go under the radar of being reported to modern youth in the very same state as it occurred, even when a key court case was held, is a testament to how uninformed we are about what happened in the past.

It's a disgusting reality, but a reality nonetheless, and to have always been taught about the successes of the movement and given bare-bones explanations of the murders of some leaders means that it needs to be taught differently. So much happened that it is not worthy of being confined to old textbooks but should serve as an example of the horrors that can unfold when we demean the existence of other people based on any physical factors and allow them to face hell by other people around them.

I'm actually offended that, in retrospect, I never learned about these sorts of murders; the closest mention being a quick aside such as, "The KKK practiced the murder of Blacks." This is why I am so glad to have come to this class. . . .

Something important starts to happen to my students. Almost always, after reading the first section of *Blood* and hearing my "It Was a Hell of Time" lectures, one or more of the students struggle with the idea that some Blacks didn't choose the Martin Luther King Jr. nonviolent strategy. Further on with the reading and lectures, something else important begins to emerge from that psychological struggle. One White male wrote:

While reading this second section of *Blood Done Sign My Name*, I was immediately taken aback by the viciousness of Dickie [Henry] Marrow's murder, and its description in such detail. I wasn't . . . shocked, exactly . . . I guess the closest thing I could describe was . . . disappointment? Just complete and utter disappointment in the three men who committed such a heinous crime.

They didn't just kill Dickie. They completely and utterly destroyed who he was—his mind and his body—before putting a bullet in his head. His brain was spilling out into the street, he was beaten beyond recognition, and he didn't even have the good fortune (though terrible) to simply die and be alleviated of his terrible suffering. I guess that may sound callous, but I mean it in the kindest way possible. One of the men broke his gun stock on Dickie's face—that's how hard he was hit. I just can't even comprehend such anger and violence, simply due to one comment that might not even have been made to Larry's wife.

I can totally understand the backlash that followed, if not completely support it. Black people were, to put it lightly, pissed. And deservedly so. While I don't agree with the methods many of them used (firebombs, etc.), I do like some of those who used more peaceful strategies that nevertheless showed the Black refusal to accept that murder as what Dickie deserved. I really liked how Ben Chavis led the school to the courthouse on the day of the preliminary hearing. That to me showed their discontent with the situation, their support for consequences brought against the murderers, but it was done in a nonviolent way. To me, the nonviolent way, while rarely the easiest, is usually the best way to resolve a situation like that. Violence only fuels the interracial (or intergroup, in another case) fire, sometimes literally, as it were. . . .

We see how complex the struggle becomes: "I can totally understand the backlash that followed, if not completely support it." And that struggle is good. Without struggle we look back on the past and blame individuals. We would say they knew better; the Black people who threw firebombs knew better. It's all their fault. It's not so easy when you see the fullness of what was really going on. A Black female wrote:

I knew from the first section of the book that this book was going to be anything but a breeze to get through. The more I keep reading, the more uncomfortable I get because I just cannot understand this time. I mean I do not know if I would have been strong enough to make it through this time period without my spirit being broken. I think that the biggest thought in my mind would be the color of my skin and how it is holding me in a place that will not have allowed me to be great and do what I really wanted to do. I do not think that I would have been able to fight all of the people and obstacles to become something more than what society allowed me to become, and this thought makes me rethink about myself as a person and about the people that went through that time. I never realized how strong they had to be and exactly how bad it was for EVERYONE and not just the people we read about in history books.

All of my students are thrust into a struggle. Not just a struggle to understand but a struggle with how to feel; simpleminded judgment and blame, they come to see, lacks respect. And so now, something important is happening to these young travelers. One White male wrote:

> It is very easy, especially for me as a White male having grown up in the culture that I did where family is very influential, to associate "Black Power" with Jesse Owens, Black Panthers, Malcolm X, and violence. "Black Power" is so often directly associated with violence, conflict, and insubordination, and although there were events by radical men who encourage this stereo-type, I can't give a firm answer as to why this is. Maybe it is the result of a shift in power that threatens, or seems to threaten, the classical White social structure. It could also be that demands as passionate as those involved with the civil rights movement were fighting for were usually accompanied by force and pressure. One thing is for sure though: the Black Power movement was not one centered around violence as a means of achieving ends. Had they used force, fear, and pressure as the primary motivators for change, I do not believe it would have happened in the way it did. I also believe they had a great understanding of this.
>
> How Tyson reflects a different light on the whole movement has allowed me to empathize with that cause on a more rational level; it seemed more normal and typical of other movements—somehow, the stigma was lifted. I cannot exactly explain why (or how, for that matter) I feel as though I can empathize or better understand the oppression faced, but through reading this book, I am developing a much better internal grasp of the nature of the discrimination and oppression faced by African Americans.
>
> I do not feel guilty. That is not my place to feel so. I was not there, and they were not my actions. It is difficult to describe my emotions, because honestly, I feel more empowered in my now deeper understanding than guilty on behalf of my race.

Guilt has no point. Those pseudo-psychologists, some of them White, who want young White people to feel guilty about America's racial past, have no idea of the psychology of guilt. Guilt is unnecessary baggage. Guilt is so heavy it slows the person's travel to our neo-diversity destination. Guilt holds a person in place. Guilt does not motivate new action; it motivates hiding and denial. In the case of racial matters for young Whites, it also activates anger at being blamed for the actions taken by others before they were even born.

I am against White privilege. I am against the use of the gut feeling of White privilege in discussions of racial matters in America. I am against White privilege because it is used to make Whites feel guilty.

"White privilege" is not an analytic concept. "White privilege" is a catch-phrase that comes out of one person's sudden gut feeling that she could operate in the world in ways that other people could not. White privilege comes out of one person's "aha" moment of realization that she has privileges that other people don't have and that some of those privileges are race-based. Naive to that reality until some event provoked self-examination, this person now is, for whatever reason, for the first time looking clear-eyed at some of the social realities of life in America.

"Some people have more opportunities than others," and "Some people have to deal with less crap than others." I guess because it is a catchy label, too many have latched on to that person's quaint self-revelation and tried to turn that catchphrase into a diversity discussion tool. By doing so, diversity facilitators have overgeneralized and overused "White privilege." To the detri-ment of productive interracial discussions of the neo-diversity of America, too many have reified one person's anecdotal observations of her own life into the "reality of race in America." But there are all kinds of privilege in America. Yet one person's self-revelation, one person's recognition of the privileges in her life, has been put on a pedestal. So shiny and compelling from way up there, it is widely used as a "gotcha." That is why it doesn't work. That is why it is counterproductive to meaningful discussions of racial matters, of neo-diversity matters in America. Captivating for diversity discussion facilitators or not, relying on "gotcha" ideas does not move us through the new thinking and discussions we need to have in America. Using the catchphrase "White privilege" pushes people to think and interact with each other at the group level of us versus them. Diversity discussion facilitators should know better.

When it comes to wanting to talk about White privilege, I have been sur-prised by the vehemence of the pseudo-psychological thinking among people who facilitate diversity discussions. I critique the idea. I say that it is only a catchphrase that is used to make Whites feel guilty, and the replies come:

"I think they ought to feel guilty."

"I think they ought to be ashamed."

Both those comments came at me from Whites. With intentions that pave the way to hell, good-intentioned people say those things to me.

Shame and guilt is what you should feel when you realize your own behavior has been bad. Shame and guilt are not what should be thrust upon you for the actions of someone who shares similar skin color with you. Do none of these people see the irony? African Americans, Black people have always had to fight the automatic associations that people make when one Black person does something reprehensible and now all non-Black eyes fall on all Black people.

Worse yet, shame and guilt freeze the person in place so as to eliminate thoughtful action. Almost all psychotherapy is aimed at getting the person to disconnect from feelings of shame and guilt so that the person can grow. Any psychologist, even I, a research psychologist, knows that.

Yes, my teaching about issues of American neo-diversity does require that people, all of us, admit to the details of our American racial history, but not to make Whites feel shame and guilt or Blacks to feel anger and envy. We must admit to the details of our individual and collective American racial history in order to know and acknowledge what we have to work on.

It is important for White Americans to acknowledge the details and feel disappointed in their ancestors, and to then pledge no more, never again. "No more will I let stereotypes drive my behavior because I now see how that dehumanizes other people."

It is important for Black Americans to acknowledge the details and feel the pride of strength beyond just survival and pledge never to stereotype others, to dehumanize others. Never. "No, I will never dehumanize other groups of people the way we African Americans have been dehumanized. I will respect the human dignity of others."

Remorse is important but applies only to things you yourself have done, not what "your people" have done in the past. You cannot have rational remorse for the actions of others. All you can feel by association is guilt, shame, and disappointment. And these would be to the detriment of your goal if you spend your time trying to get Whites to feel shame and guilt about their ancestors and those Whites' current lives; you activate a relationship-damaging dynamic. Black and White students have told me about the negative racial feelings they experience in discussions of White privilege. One of my students, a Black male, said that discussions of "White privilege" always left him with the feeling that "White people are guilty and it sucks to be Black."

And I have seen this come to life. When I observed a "White privilege" exercise, here's what I saw happen:

Students started out as one large group in the middle of a big classroom. Then the leaders told them that a list of benefits and material goods would be read out. If you have "x" benefit or good, step forward, if not, step backward. Pretty soon it was Whites forward, Blacks backward. That was not a pure racial effect, it was also a class effect, but it looked pretty racial.

One young White male was no doubt from an affluent family. Toward the end of the exercise he was flinging himself against the front classroom wall, laughing as he did so. I walked over to him, and he said, "I'm used to this, it always happens to me." That was one side of the racial relationship dynamic.

At the same time, there was a young Black female at the other end, all by herself. Every time some benefit or material good was called out, she moved backward. I walked over to her. She looked at me, distraught. She said, "I hate this exercise. . . . I always end up back here by myself." I wondered if I saw tears in her eyes.

The young White male was resigned and tried to eradicate any feelings of guilt by making fun of the material situation of his family, flinging himself against the wall and laughing each time he had to do so. The young Black female was resigned to the less-well-off material situation of her family. She was almost in tears.

White people are guilty and it sucks to be Black.

Is that the point of the "White privilege" exercise? As used, the ungrounded notion of White privilege is a two-headed spear of attack. Lack of real substance means that using the notion of White privilege in diversity discussions activates the minimal group effect: "us" versus "them" with a tendency to compete. As used, the catchphrase "White privilege" activates guilt, and that activates anger and envy. As used, it pushes a racial social comparison that is counterproductive to any open discussions of racial issues in America because it puts everyone on the defensive. Whites feel guilty and it sucks to be Black. It reinforces a racial divide.

If there is some reason to talk about the causes of socioeconomic, educational differences by race, I do so in the context of legacies of racism. That's easy enough. But I have talked to enough diversity facilitators to be convinced that at least some want to attack.

One of my students told me this story: An African American male, he was at his off-campus job. A customer asked him if he was a student. When he answered, "Yes, at NC State," the customer perked up. The customer, an African American female, asked my student if he knew "Dr. Nacoste." When this young man said, "Yes, he's my mentor," the customer launched into her awareness and admiration of my work on campus. But then in her comments, in my student's opinion, she veered off-track.

A diversity discussion facilitator on campus, this customer veered off the track when she said to my student, "Dr. Nacoste spoke to a group of students about neo-diversity. After he spoke, I was trying to get my group of students to talk about their 'White privilege,' but they didn't want to give it up." My student told me that when she said what she said, "That's when I realized she really didn't know anything about how you teach about neo-diversity. So I found a way to change the subject."

It was this young Black male who characterized his feelings about discussions of "White privilege" as "White people are guilty and it sucks to be Black." "White privilege" is used as a spear of attack. Too many use that spear without realizing the attack is relational and so hits both groups in a negative way. That is counterproductive to real conversations about neo-diversity matters in America. So never in my class or in any presentation do I use the phrase "White privilege." Never.

When asked about "White privilege" by an audience member, I am quick to reframe the question as being about "legacies of racism." I am quite ready to talk about racial inequalities that persist and that are the result of past, overt, legalized racial discrimination; income inequalities, educational inequalities, housing inequalities. I am quite ready and willing to talk about those and other legacies of racism, but I am ready to do so without calling up "White privilege." Why? I teach about the social psychology of modern diversity issues. I am not locked into the 1950s. I center my course on the theory-grounded concept of neo-diversity anxiety. Although I can point it out in real life, I derived that social psychological concept through an integration of interdependence theory (Kelley and Thibaut) and the well-researched social psychological concept of intergroup anxiety (Stephan and Stephan).

There are no innocent. With that stated and consistent approach, I conduct frank discussions of neo-diversity dynamics in America. When I lead these frank discussions about situations in our neo-diverse nation, young White people don't have to feel guilty, and young Black people don't have to feel that it sucks to be Black. Everyone has to be shown that in this age of neo-diversity, in his or her everyday social interactions, there are no innocent.

Over and over I say to my students, when it comes to racial matters in America today, there are no innocent. Rightly so, we eliminated the legal racial segregation and organizational discrimination parts of American apartheid. Yes, there are still legacies of that apartheid in institutions and organizations that have to be rooted out. But for individuals, racial matters are matters of interpersonal interaction. And when it comes to interpersonal mistakes being made when two people from different groups are trying to interact with each other, reliance on stereotypes, use of intolerant language when it comes to those things in social interaction, there are no innocent.

Hearing and feeling that, a worry is lifted from all my students. A White female wrote:

> When I started taking this course, I was excited and very nervous. Coming from a semi-bigoted family already made me feel guilty for being the race I am, so I was concerned that my guilt would just be confirmed. This course has actually freed me from that guilt. Just knowing that "there are no innocent" is comforting to me, and it helped me understand that feeling guilty for something we cannot control does no one any justice.

With the burden of guilt gone, my students look with a clear eye on their own experiences. A White female wrote:

> My reaction to the last part of the book was that I started looking back at my experiences of living in a small town. Although obviously racism is not

as prevalent today as it was during the 60s and 70s, I definitely witnessed bigotry in my small, basically all-White private school. I had not really thought about these experiences very much until reading this book, which made me realize how often I witnessed bigotry throughout my childhood.

Not guilt, but a clear eye on and openness to the truth is what it will take for us to live a new way in America. A White female student put it this way:

> Black people getting freedom was more violent than Americans wanted to remember. Why? Because they want to take the easy way out.
>
> Americans still face issues with race because of its history in this country. To erase the past would mean that we, Americans, wouldn't have to deal with the backlash, anger, consequences of discriminating against an entire group of people. This is impossible.
>
> Would stereotypes eventually fade away if Americans decided to ignore the past? First of all, in order for stereotypes among Blacks and Whites to completely fade away, the past would actually need to be erased. This is impossible. But if they were ignored, I think the stereotypes would get worse. They would get worse because people would grow up learning these stereotypes, *not knowing where they came from.*
>
> So, we are faced with taking the long route. We cannot erase the past, and memories will always exist. We have to know where, why, and how our people, Americans, ostracized the entire Black community. We have to know the origins of all the impeding stereotypes that exist today, and change the way we have learned to act and think. We have to face our consequences.

Consequences. That is why the reading of *Blood* is an important part of my class. The book is important to give my students a solid, truthful history of race in America. Race, you see, is the prototype for intergroup matters in America. To understand any intergroup matter in the twenty-first-century American context, one must have a clear understanding of where we have been and come from as a racial nation. But reading *Blood* is not the whole class. That would be a history course.

My course "Interpersonal Relationships and Race" is taught through the Psychology Department based in the discipline of social psychology. So at the same time the students are reading *Blood* in the evenings, during the day

I am teaching these young travelers the social psychology of interpersonal-intergroup dynamics. I am teaching them what activates intergroup tensions today when the two people interacting are from different group backgrounds. Making that connection, one student wrote:

> Reading the second portion of the memoir *Blood Done Sign My Name*, I literally put down my book at one point, stopped and thought—"What did that just say?" When the mayor and city manager of Oxford were planning to try and stop the Black citizens from marching to Raleigh, they announced that six new basketball goals would be built on city property. As the author said, "They thought that Black people might stop complaining if the town simply built enough basketball courts."
>
> At first, I honestly laughed at the ridiculousness of the statement they made. I couldn't help but think how ignorant the government of the town was for letting their actions be guided by a stereotype that Black individuals could be persuaded to give up their fight if there were more basketball courts in the town. Now, it could have been pure coincidence that they released this news on the same day as the march; however, after what I have learned in this class, I know that people make cognitive shortcuts to avoid conflicts (the problems the march would cause) and that avoidance leads to the use of stereotypes (all Black people like basketball).

CHAPTER 4

DJANGO UNCHAINED

*D*jango Unchained. I had to see that movie. Not because I am a Quentin Tarantino fan. Even though I enjoyed *Pulp Fiction*, it was a disturbed enjoyment. I had to see *Django Unchained* because the controversy about the movie connected directly to my teaching about racial slurs.

Probably the most intense lecture I give in my "Interpersonal Relationships and Race" course is the one on anti-group slurs. A central lesson of the lecture is that the point of using any anti-group slur is for the person using the slur to show the interpersonal power relationship (Thibaut and Kelley) between the two people who are interacting with each other. Slurs are designed to establish quick, who-is-superior-and-who-is-inferior-in-this-moment of social interaction. No matter the instance, no matter, so to say, the skin color or the gender of the person who speaks the slur toward the other person, the effect is to put the hearer in their place. "Remember, you're just a _____." Nothing the hearer does can change that intent of the utterance. That's the interpersonal power of the slur. That established, I end the lecture saying,

> Again, my point today is that all of the issues we have to deal with around neo-diversity and intergroup dynamics are relationship issues. Three semesters ago, during class a White student said in frustration, "I just want to know what to call them." At the interpersonal level, the question should never be, What can I call "all of y'all" or "all of them"? That means you still want to interact with the group, not with the person standing in front of you.
>
> It would be easier, you see, if White people were all the same: honkeys, peckerwoods, rednecks, and crackers.
>
> It would be easier if all males were the same: man-whores, wankers, dicks, mama's boys, and dogs.

It would be easier if all people with disabilities were all the same: crips and retards.

It would be easier if all Mexicans were the same: wetbacks and spicks.

It would be easier if all gays and lesbians were the same: faggots and dykes.

It would be easier if all people of Middle Eastern descent were the same: ragheads and sand monkeys.

It would be easier if all women were the same: bitches, sluts, and whores.

It would be easier if all Black people were the same: niggers, jungle bunnies, spear chuckers.

It would be easier if all Vietnamese, Chinese, Korean, and Japanese people were the same: slant-eyes and chinks.

It would be easier, but real life is not so.

We have to deal with real, individual people. We live in the age of neo-diversity. We live in a society and country filled with people from many different groups: neo-diversity. So, welcome to the twenty-first century. What are you prepared to do? That's the question because calling people names just won't do.

With that as a major lecture in the course, I assumed that the *Django Unchained* controversy would be brought up in class. How many times the slur "nigger" is used in the movie is the controversy. A story set in the Deep South, in the time of slavery, with a slave owner who calls his Black slaves niggers whenever he speaks of those slaves. "Too many times," some said. "The word is used too much. Something is wrong with Quentin Tarantino."

Really?

The late Mr. August Nacoste, a dark-skinned Black man, my father, a grass-roots politician in his day, was born in Louisiana in 1918. As my father grew up and became a man, were White people reluctant to say the word, to call my father a nigger to his face, over and over again? No. Not at all. He told me so.

People said that Daddy was one of the best cooks in Opelousas, Louisiana. That was saying something since food is such a big thing with us Creoles and with the Cajuns. You don't just put anything in front of people to eat. Whatever you feed people, it has to be right; it has to have some flavors and some heat. Being spicy isn't enough. Burning people's tongues is the wrong idea; the food has to have something for them to think about. It has to have some surprises in it.

That's what people said Daddy did better than anybody. Working with tomatoes, cayenne pepper, black pepper, filé (fee-lay), bell (green) pepper, onions, celery, and garlic, Daddy would cook some garfish, mudfish, crawfish, chicken, or whatever in a way that would bring a mist of ecstasy into your eyes.

I remember the time Daddy made crawfish bisque. That morning we had gone out to crawfish at Uncle Alton's. Uncle Alton and Aunt Helen lived between Opelousas and Port Barre (Port Bear-ree) on land that used to be a rice field. Rice fields hold water; they have to because to grow rice you need plenty of water. Where Uncle Alton and Aunt Helen had their little four-room white house, the land was dry because it had been built up. Behind their house, though, the land was a rice field with no rice growing. It was a wetland; green marsh, a shallow swamp, and the crawfish were a plentiful and hungry crowd back there.

Along with Uncle Alton and Aunt Helen's sons, Peter and Edward Carriere, me and my two brothers, Phillip and Brother (August Jr.), waded in and set our nets. It was an exceptional day. We caught two sacks full of crawfish. So my brothers and I had a whole sack of mudbugs—Louisiana lobsters—to take home. We had so many crawfish Daddy decided to do something special: make a crawfish bisque.

Outside over a fire, in a cast-iron kettle, Daddy boiled the live crawfish in seasoned water. When the boiling had just cooked them, Daddy broke off the tails, peeled and chopped the meat, and put that meat into a mixture of already cooking onions, bell pepper, celery, garlic, some cayenne pepper, a roux, and water. He let that simmer.

All that was blending and binding over the low heat while Daddy cleaned out the crawfish heads. Crawfish mixture right, he took everything but the liquid and poured it in a pot of rice. He then poured just enough of the liquid in that pot to dampen the rice and mixed all that together, then he stuffed that mixture into the cleaned-out heads of the crawfish.

We were no longer breathing air. Somehow we had been taken to a different planet with an alien atmosphere. On that planet, the atmosphere you pulled into your mouth and nose was thick and pungent. Carried on the steam of the boiling water was a slightly burned yet sweet odor: the mix of the smells of bay leaves, cayenne pepper, chopped onion tops, garlic, and the honey-tinged smell of whole crawfish.

That smell, that pungent atmosphere, was everywhere by the time Daddy said it was ready. When he served it, he wouldn't let anybody help, not even our mother. We each got ten to twelve of those stuffed crawfish heads, with some of the rice on the side and some bread.

"Talk-about-good, man."

Even when he was a young man with a young family, my daddy, Mr. Nacoste, could cook. Even then he had a reputation, and he would get hired to cook. He told me and my two brothers this story:

> I used to get hired to cook at that camp right there on the levee. One time I was out there to cook, and it was lots of big shots out there at that camp. I was cooking, and when I was done cooking I started serving. I think it was garfish sauce piquant I made. I made plenty 'cause there so many out there. They was all White men and they was drinking and eating. And they was talking.
>
> Some of that talk was politics, and I could hear them planning who they wanted in office and how they was going ta' make that happen. I wasn't saying nothing, just doing my job, making sure everybody had the food they wanted and the drinks too. That talk took a turn 'bout putting politicians in office who would keep colored people under control. I was standing right there.
>
> One of the men said, "Y'all need to be quiet when that boy is in here with us and we talking our business."
>
> That's when the man whose camp it was called me over. With me standing there he told the other men, he said, "Don't worry about what y'all say. This is my nigger and he knows better than to listen in on White man's business." Then he told me to go on and do my job. And that's what I did.
>
> Now you boys need to understand that what that man said made me mad. But I held myself. I held myself and my pride so that I could keep listening that night and other nights. I was learning a lot; so I swallowed my pride to learn all I could. Then when the time was right I let it be known what I knew and what I could do with it. That's why I can get them White politicians to do things around here and that's why they don't mess with me.

Daddy told me that to teach me about the racial world he grew up in and in which he fought his way to his own dignity. He told me that to teach me to find my own way to fight for my dignity in the segregated-by-law racial world of Jim Crow that I was growing up in.

So to act as if the word "nigger" is used too much in *Django Unchained* is to be ahistorical; it is to wish it had never happened. With the support of law and custom, Whites could and did call Black people niggers to their faces, over and over again. That was the point, to demonstrate both superiority and power.

And so countrymen, in my judgment it is clear that TV personality Paula Deen has been backstabbed by America. With angry fervor, the corporate assembly has surrounded Ms. Deen and then watched with glee as each Brutus has stepped forward to backstab her. Ms. Deen has made the willful, unforgivable mistake of telling a truth about the racial history of America. In being deposed for a 2013 civil case, Ms. Deen was asked if she ever used the "n-word." She said, "Yes, but it's been a long time." That is willful disobedience of the norms, nowadays, because we do all we can to not let the truth be known. One way we try to erase history is to say "n-word" rather than pronounce the word "nigger." That is a strategy designed to help the speaker feel safe, righteous, and disconnected from American history. But the major way we avoid our American racial history is not to speak the truth about what really happened.

If the outcry against Ms. Deen is all about the fact that sometime in her sixty-six-year life history she called a Black person a nigger, America has lost its historical way. For the sake of argument, let's ask, from 1940 (when Mr. Nacoste, my father, was twenty-two) to 1990, how many White Americans did not once used the word "nigger" to refer to a Black person or Black people? That bigotry happened because it was authorized and supported by law well into the 1970s. But now some want to demonize Paula Deen for the time and circumstance in which she was reared and grew up. The question should not be about whether Ms. Deen ever used the word; the question should be about whether she has done so while running her businesses. Whether she is a bigot and has created a climate of racial intimidation and discrimination at work. Instead we want to wash our hands of our collective history. We want to act as if our history didn't happen. We proclaim that anyone who admits to that history is a racial traitor.

That is why the corporate assembly has reacted with such vehemence to Ms. Deen's confession that she did in her life ever use the word "nigger." Riddle me this: if someone asked you if you EVER used a group slur of the nigger-type, how would you answer?

"Punk."

"Faggot."

"Dyke."

"That's so gay."

If you are asked about ever using such a slur referring to gays and lesbians, what would be your truthful answer? Then ask, does that mean I am forever a bigot? Can I not change, stop that behavior, and redeem myself? Can you? Did you? Will you?

Or are you an African American who believes you can use the word "nigger" in a way that is not "like that." Some Blacks say that now the word can be used without offense because we have changed the meaning so that it is now a term of endearment, affection. If so, you should have had no problem with NFL player Riley Cooper, a White man, yelling out from the stage at a Kenny Chesney concert, "I will climb this fence and fight every nigger here. . . ." (Schwartz).

If you thought that it was OK for Riley Cooper to use the word "nigger," then you should have been outraged that Cooper was suspended for his use of the word. In fact, you should have gone to Cooper's defense since the word is one of affection. OK, well, one of his NFL teammates did speak in Cooper's defense. The claim was that Cooper didn't mean it "like that." At the same time, though, another NFL player, one of Cooper's teammates, said he was upset because he didn't think Cooper would use the word, "like that," with the word's historical negative meanings.

But it turns out the racial slur "nigger" can only be used "like that." Cooper's use of the word was the classic use of the word to put down and demean a Black person. But some, a few, were willing to argue that in this case none of that applied, so Riley Cooper's screaming out the word "nigger" was OK. It was all good, right? But it's not all good because all the talk of using the word "like that" means the word still carries and will always carry the point that whomever the word is aimed at is inferior. You are fooling yourself to think otherwise.

Are you an African American who believes you can somehow call another Black person a nigger—not "like that"—with no racial malice, only with affection? Again, you are fooling yourself. In her last reflection paper for my course, an African American female student wrote:

> It was not until our lecture in class on racial slurs that I realized that the word is about power still until this day. I've heard all of the arguments for "taking back the word," but now I realize how stupid that is. I think all of this has to do with power. I realize that the only times I have ever used the word "nigger," I have used it to describe someone who I think is not acting the way they should. I have never used that word to uplift someone, no matter how jokingly I thought I was using it.
>
> As soon as I say someone is acting like a "nigger" I know exactly what I mean, and to delude myself into thinking otherwise makes me ashamed of myself. I know that using nigger and other words is just a way to express power over another group. If I think someone is a nigger I'm not expecting them to do anything worthwhile with their lives. In my head I've already decided who they are and what they are by labeling them as one of "those people," and I'm Black. The sad thing is that I have probably been called a nigger so many times it could make my head spin and I would be upset, but I have the gall to say it about someone else and think it is okay.

Or are you a non-Black person who believes that you can use the word as long as you pronounce it the "right" way? Remember Maggie's text:

> Dr. Nacoste, I'm at a party right now. . . . And a 21 year old White male just said the word "nigger." I told him that I didn't think that any use of that word was acceptable in any situation. This started a conversation with everyone explaining to me it all mattered about the "inflection" and "connotation" it was used in. I was at a loss for words. What can I say if that happens again?

Jabari Asim in his book *The N Word* writes:

The word "nigger" serves primarily—even in its contemporary "friendlier" usage—as a linguistic extension of White supremacy, the most potent part of a language of oppression that has changed over time from overt to covert. While "jigaboo," "coon," "pickaninny," and "buck," have been largely replaced by such ostensibly innocuous terms as "inner-city," "urban," and "culturally disadvantaged," "nigger" endures, helping to perpetuate and reinforce the durable, insidious taint of presumed African-American inferiority. (Asim.)

Even in the time of Jim Crow legal segregation, there were Whites who felt too genteel to say the word in its raw form: nigger. So those aristocratic Whites said "nig-rah" as in "Those poor nig-rahs just can't help being so filthy." Pronunciation didn't change the meaning back then and doesn't change it now. Spelling it as "nigga" doesn't change that either. You are still referring to a whole set of people as inferior and not human.

"Like that" is the only way to use the word "nigger." Today, long after the passage of the 1964 Civil Rights Act, Americans in private, and sometimes in public, are using the word "like that." But we are upset with Paula Deen because we do not want to have the mythology of racial change that we have created be not only challenged but shown to be false. And it is false.

Writing for the *New York Times*, standing in the shadow of the popular but false racial history of America, columnist Frank Bruni judged and backstabbed Ms. Deen for hinting at the truth of our collective racial history. Bruni wrote:

Others have urged clemency, noting that she's 66 years old and has lived her life far south of the Mason-Dixon line.

Please. All of her adult years postdate the Civil Rights Act of 1964. . . ." (Bruni.)

The glib Mr. Bruni writes as if everything changed the day the Civil Rights Act of 1964 was passed. That's ridiculous.

Write what you know, is what all writers are told. In my teaching and writing I follow that advice. Born of Black parents in 1951, I grew up in the Jim Crow South. Passage of the Civil Rights Act was an oasis along the continuing march of racial transition that America is on. No instantaneous change happened with the passage of that act by Congress. Martin Luther King Jr. was in Memphis, Tennessee, leading a racial protest march when he was assassinated in 1968. I graduated from a still racially segregated Catholic school in 1969. During the time I served in the navy (1972–76) there were some 350 major racial incidents on our bases and ships (Sherwood). That includes the January 1973 three-day race riot on the aircraft carrier USS *Intrepid*, onboard which I was serving at the time. A three-day riot onboard a ship carrying weapons of mass destruction that was set off because even into the 1970s too many White sailors felt free to call Black sailors niggers. Ten years after the passage of the Civil Rights Act, in 1974, in my golden-brown Ford Pinto, I drove into Johnston County, North Carolina, and looked up at a billboard showing a hooded man on a white horse with the words "Welcome to Klan Country." Yes, that was in 1974.

Nothing changed fast after the passage of the Civil Rights Act, not institutions, social norms for language, or individuals' use of racial slurs. Nothing changed that fast. That is why today we live in difficult days. We are still in a difficult transition. We continue to struggle with a history that is attached to words that are still used for the same old reasons.

A White female student wrote about the twenty-first-century confusion caused by the everyday use of group slurs. She wrote:

> The ambidextrous nature of these words fosters a constant vague interdependence with the use of the words. If someone walked up to me and said, "What's up, bitch?" I would respond, "What did you just say?!" Because I am not familiar with the context they are using it in. My interpersonal anxiety would activate, and I am sure it would be an awkward interaction. In general after this class I believe, as suggested, that we should not be using these words ever. We should not try to resolve a confused context of a word through the use of it. I understand now that people learn things in different places, under different contexts, and with different experiences, and if there was not enough confusion in interactions already, why add more by using those words?

Why indeed? As my student asks, if there was not already enough confusion about race in America, why use the word "nigger" anyway? It is a good question. If so much has changed, if we got past our racial history the minute the Civil Rights Act of 1964 was passed, why do people still insist on using the word "nigger"? What is the attraction that so compels young Whites to call each other "my nigga"? Is it just that they are so disconnected from America's racial history by hearsay teaching that it's all just a big joke anyway? No, this is still a superiority move. In an e-mail, one of my students asked me about the issue this way:

> The last class lecture we had really blew my mind. In high school and even now I know Caucasians who use the n-word amongst themselves, and I never understood why. I thought they were just trying to be cool or fit in with Black people. I was wrong! I didn't think of it as a power move or that it was about the Whites staying on top in their mind; I was just really confused. When you explained why during class, a lightbulb went off in my head. Duh! How could I not have seen this?! After thinking about this more after class I have a few questions. I've heard other groups of people use the n-word amongst themselves, like Hispanics and also Asians. I would think the power move applies here too, but I'm not sure of the source or train of thought when they use it. Do they feel like they have the right to say it because they feel higher up in status than Blacks regardless of how Caucasians view them? I almost feel they might think, "Well, I know I'm not White, and White people may not like my race that much either, but at least I'm not Black." I also thought maybe they may be trying to impress people, Caucasians specifically. Are they trying to get on their (Whites') good side so they will be seen as equals? I'm not sure what to make of it all, and I would love to hear your thoughts on this when you get a chance!

After giving it some thought, about a week later I responded:

> B. T., yours is a very good analysis. Turns out, the history of race in America is such that it is better to be anything but Black. And so, even non-Whites take the opportunity they have to say "I'm not Black . . . I'm not a n****."
>
> You also wrote: I also thought maybe they may be trying to impress people, Caucasians specifically. Are they trying to get on their (Whites') good side so they will be seen as equals?
>
> B. T., ah, once again, a very good analysis. In this case non-Whites are

trying to work the Us vs. Them tendency, by putting themselves in the Us with Whites. As you say, they are trying to be seen as the equals of Whites, and they are doing so by distancing themselves from Blacks. These are ways in which the history of race continues to do harm in our society.

Yet we shun and backstab Paula Deen, a sixty-six-year-old White woman who grew up in the Deep South, and who now admits that sometime in her sixty-six-year history she used the word "nigger." What a racist!

Why do Americans relish calling other people racists? If I were a Freudian, I would conclude that those who have had the most intense reactions to Paula Deen's truth telling are those who need a defense mechanism for self-protection. A Freudian analysis would tell me that these are people who in private let their friends and neighbors speak about "them" in ugly ways from the shadow of our American history. I would call these people consensual bigots: people who through their silence in the face of intolerant language agree with one or another anti-group slander. And now when the race stuff goes public these consensual but hidden bigots are outraged in self-defense. But Freudian analysis is only speculation, and it's not necessary to understand what is going on in the backstabbing of Paula Deen.

Turns out, we are a nation of Pontius Pilates. We wash our hands of the whole racial thing. We are distancing ourselves not just from the personal relevance (I'm not a racist) but also from the interpersonal relevance (I don't know or interact with racists) (Sommers and Norton). I am not responsible for any of it, not for what happened, not for what's going on now, not for thinking about any of it, not for taking any action. I wash my hands of the matter.

To me it's funny how Americans don't realize how much work we are doing to distance ourselves from America's racial history and ongoing racial struggles. It's funny that we don't realize how much work we are doing to distance ourselves from our present-day neo-diverse America.

You see, we no longer live in a society where our racial contacts are controlled and restricted by law. We live in a time and circumstance where, for each of us, encounters and interactions with people from different (racial, ethnic, religious, bodily conditioned, gender, and sexually oriented) groups are unavoidable. So, today our interpersonal encounters with the intergroup are not Black and White but neo-diverse. Neo-diversity, you see, is our twenty-first-century "race problem."

And can you say social media? Facebook, Twitter, YouTube? Now, for the first time, it is nearly true that every American has a chance to raise their voice in song and protest. This means that groups that have experienced injustice cannot be silenced. Today, we live in those difficult days when no one will stay in the kitchen. Not only do we live in an age of neo-diversity; we live in an age when no one is hiding. No one is ashamed of who they are. No one wants to be melted.

Now we as a nation are being pushed to crown our good with brotherhood, from sea to shining sea. With the elimination of legal segregation and the increase of diversity in our nation, too many of us want to avoid talking about our racial past. So we are engaged in all kinds of avoidance tactics. Classic, nowadays, is people saying, "Oh . . . I don't see color." That is said to avoid any conversation about race relations in our lives. For too many, you see, the equal treatment demands of neo-diversity turns into an anxiety about "who are the 'we' and who are among the 'they.'" That anxiety is living large in our everyday social interactions.

One way to try to avoid that anxiety is to deny history; to claim that if anything bad happened, it was only for a little while and everything changed fast. But Paula Deen has stepped out of the shadow and into the light to show us how much pretending we are doing. No wonder so many have been so quick and so eager to be Brutus. That is why, friends and countrymen,

I come to praise Paula Deen, not to bury her.

I speak not to disprove what Paula spoke

But here I am to speak what I do know.

You all, America, did love her once, not without cause;

O judgment, thou art fled to brutish beasts,

And America had lost all its reason. Bear with me;

My heart is in the coffin there with Paula

And I must pause till it come back to me.

We have got to stop reinforcing and defending a racial mythology. We need to stop the hypocrisy. A White female student wrote:

I'm glad Dr. Tyson ended the book that way. I didn't feel the need to throw it at him. I agreed with just about every word he said. The first time I heard about this book was when you assigned it. My friend Caroline, who is in this class, told me her background knowledge of the book and how her father knows the author. I thought that was really cool and had a respect for Tim Tyson before I even opened the book. The third time I heard about this book was when I left it on my kitchen table, my roommate walked by and asked me if I was reading it.

I said, "Yes, for a psychology class."

She replied, "Oh, I grew up right near there. I know some of the people in it. It's not all true, you know. Some of it is . . . you know . . . overdramatic."

I didn't reply to her as she walked out the door, but I did stare at the door for a while. We had already been in class for a month, and you, Dr. Nacoste, had introduced the book. You told us that we were going to realize that we had been lied to in the past about all of it. Her tone made me believe that she assumes that all Black people are overdramatic. This is kind of ironic since everyday she complains that "today is the worst day ever," and she does not know any Black people on a personal level, so I don't know how she could know one Black person was overdramatic, let alone all Black people.

You learn a lot about someone from living with them. My roommate is sweet and kindhearted and happily engaged to her boyfriend of eight years. She is probably one of the most overdramatic people I know, so I got scared that if she said this was overdramatic, that this book was all a lie and that it was going to be a waste of my time. I'm glad to say it wasn't. I've come to realize that there's no way this book could have been published as a true story if it wasn't. With how many names are in this book, someone would come after Tim with a shotgun.

My roommate is a sweet girl, but she has lived a sheltered, conservative life that her parents happily set up for her. She's been through some tough times like anyone, but I think she just doesn't realize that not everyone else lives in a perfect little bubble. Her parents could easily tell her this book was false, and she would have no trouble believing it.

We have got to stop doing this to ourselves, to our children. I do what I can through my teaching. I am a day breaker.

Stop worrying. Trust me. Young people are not so fragile that they cannot process the truth. Female, Black, male, lesbian, Muslim, gay, White, and Christian students who take my "Interpersonal Relationships and Race" course at NCSU almost always have the same reaction to reading Tim Tyson's historical memoir. My students become angry because they want to know "Why did I have to get to college to learn the real, ugly truth about the civil rights movement in America and even North Carolina's racial history?" But beyond anger, by reading Tyson's memoir students are brought from racial ignorance and naïveté to a more realistic view of the history of American race relations.

Reading a true story of race in America leads to reappraisal and appreciation. My students find themselves processing a full reevaluation of, and growing respect for, the hard work and different tactics it took to begin the difficult change of the racial environment of America.

"Yeah," some will say *"but what does that do to our children's pride in our nation, in our national identity?"* Look, I know that pride in our nation is important, but not if it's false pride based on a commercial, based on a sales pitch.

I am proud to be an American. I gave four years of my life to serve, protect, and defend America. But during the same time that I was in the navy, I also worked hard to help the navy, to help America, correct its racial mistakes.

Remember, I served during a very difficult time for race relations in the military. Imagine this: race riots aboard ships carrying weapons of mass destruction. I don't have to imagine that horror. In January 1973, onboard the aircraft carrier USS *Intrepid* at sea in the Mediterranean, it was three days of on-again off-again random attacks on White sailors and Black sailors. I was there and could not say for sure what got the riot started. But navy investigative documents uncovered by naval historian John Darrell Sherwood found simmering racial tensions brought to a boil by the use of racial derogatory language directed by White sailors and petty officers toward Black sailors, not to mention perceptions of racial discrimination (Sherwood, chap. 10).

The navy needed to correct the way Black sailors were being treated by White sailors in that time of racial transition. So an intervention was created that required all sailors, officers, and enlisted men to participate in racial sensitivity training that lasted two and a half days. I was trained to be one of the facilitators of those group sessions whether on land or at sea.

In those two-and-a-half-day sessions, sailors, officers, and enlisted personnel learned that they had to set aside their stereotypes and intolerant language in order to cooperate with the real people in their work group. Yes, I am damn proud to be an American. But the only America I can be proud of is the America that works to admit and correct its mistakes. As a nation, America has certainly made many mistakes. Still, I know that the real beauty of America is that its people can fight to correct their mistakes. That is not the case in every nation of the world, but in America we can and we do fight through our mistakes in the hope of changing for the better.

On January 1, 2013, America celebrated the 150th year anniversary of the Emancipation Proclamation, which started the process of making slavery in America illegal. That proclamation was America's attempt to correct itself. There are many other examples:

August 18, 1920: the Nineteenth Amendment to the US Constitution granted American women the right to vote.

July 2, 1964: the Civil Rights Act was passed, outlawing major forms of discrimination against racial, ethnic, national, and religious minorities, and women.

July 26, 1990: the Americans with Disabilities Act was enacted to prohibit discrimination based on disability.

September 20, 2011: The "Don't Ask, Don't Tell" law was repealed, thereby allowing gays, lesbians, and bisexuals to serve in the United States Armed Forces without having to hide their sexuality. It was about time.

We correct our mistakes.

March 18, 2014: "24 MINORITY VETERANS RECEIVE LONG OVERDUE MEDAL OF HONOR" (Carter and Abdullah). The CNN report reads this way:

> If not for the hue of their skin or their ethnicity, 24 soldiers who faced death in service to their nation would have received the most prestigious medals for their valor long ago.
>
> But they were born and fought in a time when such deeds were not always fairly acknowledged. On Tuesday, the US government corrected the oversight.

President Barack Obama honored twenty-four army veterans with the Medal of Honor—the country's highest military award, given to American soldiers who display "gallantry above and beyond the call of duty"—for their combat actions in Vietnam, Korea, and World War II. (CNN.com.)

In that same CNN report, President Obama was quoted as saying: "No nation is perfect, but here . . . we confront our imperfections and face a sometimes painful past, including the truth that some of these soldiers fought and died for a country that did not always see them as equal."

I say again, in America we correct our mistakes.

Even after reading *Blood Done Sign My Name*, my students still believe in America; they just want us as a nation to do better than we have in the past. They want the truth to be told, to be widely known. A White female student wrote:

> Another reaction I had was to the part in chapter 11 when Tyson discusses the Wilmington Race Riot 1898, which he believes was "the most important political event in our state." He discusses how many schools do not teach about this historical event. I am shocked that I never learned about this in any of the schools that I attended.
>
> It bothers me that my country is so ashamed of admitting that it was wrong that history rewrites itself to make events in the past not seem so terrible, especially slavery and the entire civil rights movement. Growing up learning about these events, the history books almost made it seem like a cakewalk to achieve equality. I think that it is important for people to learn about these tragic, brutal events that occurred during history in order for people to understand the significance of the civil rights movement and how far we have come since.
>
> It really bothers me that these things are not learned, almost as if Americans cannot own up to the past and admit its mistakes. This has been my main reaction through reading the entire book, especially the last few chapters. Those who believe that we should not focus on the past do not

understand that we must recognize and accept our past in order to move forward as a whole.

As blunt in her writing as she was in our class discussions, another White female wrote:

> We are a nation that needs to lay down our pride. We need to open our closets and let the skeletons tumble out. We need to lift up those rugs we swept filth under for decades. We need to admit that this was not just "racial tension": this was war. Irrational, crazy, stupid war, but war nonetheless. People's lives were taken, and normal and abnormal people alike did hateful and hurtful things. As Dr. Nacoste always says, "There are no innocent." So let's at least be a little more frank about admitting our guilt. Let's teach these stories in school.

Why is this so hard? Is it that we, the so-called adults, can't handle the truth? Are we using the claim of protecting our children as an excuse, when the real issue is that we want to protect ourselves from self-examination? Here is why I ask that: a White female was so motivated by the history, the story told in Tyson's book, she went home to have a conversation with her mother about what she had learned. My student told me that story of this encounter in one of her reaction papers:

> When I finished reading *Blood Done Sign My Name*, I stopped and reflected on how much I had enjoyed it. I did not enjoy it like one would enjoy *The Hunger Games* or one of the Lord of the Rings books because it was not that kind of story. By the end I felt enlightened. I had become more knowledgeable of that historic time period and was appreciative of the fact that Tim Tyson had held nothing back. As you constantly say in class, there are no innocent. I respect Tyson for going in and digging up the dirt of that time period that both Whites and Blacks had buried so deeply into the ground. It was a story that needed to be told.
>
> Herman Bennett's story was probably the most emotional experience I had while reading this book. "They killed my sister," he said. His family was racially mixed and because they moved into "the wrong neighborhood," someone who disapproved of his parent's union threw a firebomb in the

window and killed his infant sister, which is why Herman's family left the country. We all have our own stories. This is the story I told my mom after she finished telling me about her experience. She cried a little. She has never handled hearing about such tragedies very well, but then again, who does?

"I will never understand why such hatred existed during that time or why Whites felt so superior to Blacks. To this day it still makes me sick to think about," my mother said.

Then she got up and went inside.

It is for people like my mom that I think Tyson wrote this book. It is for those who wish they could understand the horror of that time, but just need some guidance to get there. I also think he wrote this book for people like me, who would have otherwise gone their entire lives living in a world of naiveté, with the past buried so deeply beneath their feet and no one willing to dig it up. This is why I enjoyed this book.

Every semester my students surprise me somehow. One semester a student got in her car and drove to Oxford, North Carolina, to visit the grave of Henry Marrow. The student whose reaction you just read went home and talked to her mother about the stories told in *Blood*. Her mother's reaction was powerful, but her mother was also shut down. But that is not what happened to that mother's child. That young woman finished the reading saying: "*I respect Tyson for going in and digging up the dirt of that time period that both Whites and Blacks had buried so deeply into the ground. It was a story that needed to be told.*"

We underestimate young people. But at the same time we leave them to their own devices. With no guidance, with hearsay teaching as their foundation, with a false racial mythology in their minds and hearts, we tell them, "You just have to be more accepting."

We should all worry about the state of our nation the way my students begin to worry. My students do not lose their pride in being Americans, but they do become scared about whether we will ever be a truly humane nation.

A Mexican American male student wrote:

My last point conflicts with my feeling of excitement for finishing the book and gaining knowledge on North Carolina's past because I now wonder, how many other stories like these are out there? Can we find them all? What can we even do to begin digging into the dirty past that has been hidden from us?

What makes America strong for me is that we correct our mistakes. But in order to do that, we have to acknowledge and face these errors. After reading *Blood* my students wonder if we will ever be able to do that. With real information about the history of race in America, my young students do not fall apart or lose pride in our nation. But these young travelers do ask, "What about now? What mistakes are we making that we can stop making, right now?"

An Argentinian American female in my class wrote:

This historical-memoir has brought understanding and empathy for what people, especially in The South, were going through during this era. Although I will never truly be able to grasp the hatred expressed and felt on both sides of the conflict, *Blood Done Sign My Name* has shown me a seemingly holistic view of the gravity of the situation. Now I wonder what are we missing, hating, and/or lacking to love that will make us seem like hateful people in 60 years?

PART 3

GET ON BOARD, LITTLE CHILDREN, GET ON BOARD

CHAPTER 5

PREACHING TO THE CHOIR?

"Well, the people who take your course aren't the ones we need to reach. You're preaching to the choir."

No, I am not. Let me say that another way. When it comes to neo-diversity matters in America, there are no innocent.

On the second day of class, I used to ask my students, "Why did you sign up for this course?" Hands would go up, and the only statement in the room was "To take another class with you." After two semesters of getting that answer I stopped asking that question. The answer, you see, made me uncomfortable because that was not the question I was asking. So, I changed the question to "What do you hope to talk about, what questions do you hope we get to address in this course?" In answer to that my students say:

To understand how to navigate racial differences in a workplace.

To understand why there are stereotypes about music regarding race (White people like Soul too!).

How does one successfully live with a member of another race?

To understand the development and progression of reverse racism—"I'm just voting for Obama because he is Black."

Why do racial groups mostly stay divided into cliques?

What purpose did racism originally serve?

How does a multiracial person develop their self-identity?

Why do only Muslims get stereotyped as terrorists?

To develop an understanding of romantic interracial relationships.

How about racial ignorance in general?—People assume I am this, but I am actually Cambodian.

I want to be able to take something and put it into action outside of the classroom.

83

What different races are associated with what cultures?

How do stereotypes form?

Why are people so nervous to talk about race?

What about within-group interactions?—"Why are you talking White?"

How about race in the courtroom?

How/Why do people internalize their stereotypes?

What is the difference between crime and a hate crime?

Why do people choose to conform to stereotypes?

How do groups who hate based on stereotypes get past it?

How to interact with different people.

How to quell roommates' fear of being robbed because they are the "only White girls on the street."

Why is it awkward to challenge your own stereotypes?

What kind of environments create "racism" or help to abolish those views?

Why are there pick-your-race/ethnicity forms?

What steps can we take as individuals to not stereotype?

What about stereotypes in the Greek community?

Is there an age where it gets hard to change thought patterns?

How about the language we use to enforce stereotypes?

How to control feelings of resentment from stereotypes/prejudice/bigotry.

"Isn't it bad that there are dating websites for "Blacks only," etc.?

Psychology behind prejudice—how does it gets so personal?

Do you feel Obama's election encouraged "racism?"

Diagnosis is what I have done. Allowing my students to express their interests and concerns lets me in on the neo-diversity tensions they carry around and have brought with them into my classroom. No, all of these topics and questions cannot be covered in one course, not even a university-level course. I let my students know that. I let them know, too, that we will confine ourselves to topics and questions that have to do with what goes on in an interpersonal interaction. Interpersonal psychology is the foundation for the course.

Different from general psychology, interpersonal psychology comes out of the broad interpersonal science of interdependence theory (Kelley and Thibaut). As I define it, "interpersonal psychology" is the area of study in which social psychologists develop theoretical and practical knowledge of how interpersonal relationships work (Kelley). Interpersonal psychology is based on the idea that all relationships are relationships of interdependence; that is, relationships in which each person depends on the other person to obtain interpersonal satisfaction (Rusbult and Van Lange). That is the theoretical guide for my two undergraduate courses. From the interdependence theory frame, I set up the relationship principles that students must keep in mind throughout the course. The most basic of these principles are the following seven:

1. "The essence of any interpersonal relationship is interaction" (Thibaut and Kelley, 10). You are not in a relationship if there is no series of face-to-face interactions that come close in time.

2. All relationships evolve through social interaction experiences. Real relationships are never, and cannot be, immediately deep. If it is a relationship with depth, it got there through evolution that went from surface contact to stages of deeper and deeper behaviors (and eventual feelings) of mutuality (minor, moderate, and major).

3. Self-disclosures are the engine of relationship evolution because "any failure to communicate adequately and fully in the initial stages of the relationship will affect the representativeness of the outcomes sampled." (Thibaut and Kelley, 72). Outcomes are experiences, and it is interaction experiences that influence whether one or both persons are willing to continue the interaction or relationship. That is one reason that self-disclosures must come over a number of interactions, and why self-disclosures must be asked for over time, not all at once and not suddenly.

4. A relationship cannot evolve without encountering and managing person-to-person incompatibility of preferences that come with honest self-disclosures. Turns out the social interaction experiences that help a relationship evolve must include self-disclosures that lead to the discovery of conflicts in preferences (e.g., Why would you want to go there? You eat that stuff?) and the management of that conflict (so-called response interference).

5. At some point in each of our interpersonal lives, we will have to adapt to a situation in which the rules for the interaction in that situation are vague. These situations of vague interdependence will cause interpersonal anxiety in us that will have the potential to cause us to behave badly.

6. Neo-diversity has created a social environment in which people experience lots of situations of vague-interdependence because nowadays no one can avoid having social encounters and interactions with people from different sexually oriented, bodily conditioned, racial, gender, ethnic, religious, mentally conditioned, or socioeconomic groups. Being vague, being without clear rules, those intergroup interactions can cause a person to feel interpersonal anxiety.

7. Push hypothesis: In social interaction, the simple awareness of an intergroup difference can push the two people to try to interact at a level of intimacy that the interaction or relationship is not ready for because there have not been enough social experiences between the two people for the relationship to have evolved that far.

For those in my "Interpersonal Relationships and Race" course, the focus is on what can influence the interdependence and interaction between two people when, by some group designation, the two people are different from each other and one or both is aware of that social fact. With the social diagnosis of my students done at the very beginning of the course, I am aware of some of the neo-diversity anxieties they experience in interpersonal-intergroup situations. And those anxieties make it clear that these young travelers are not the innocent Kumbaya choir.

Part of the mix in the classroom is because students do follow me around. From the first day of the first course many take with me, "Introduction to Social Psychology," students know that I am not kidding around. They know that I am not at the lectern worried about hurting their feelings. They know I am not worried about what they might say to their parents. I don't care.

From the first day of "Introduction to Social Psychology," students know I come to do business. They know because on that first day I make it clear that the room is mine and that there are certain rules that are not to be violated. I say:

I'm sure each of you has seen one or more of the Godfather films. And, while there is much to be concerned about when it comes to the lifestyle portrayed in those films, there is a philosophy that comes through that I like. That philosophy is:

Some things are personal.

Some things are business.

Never get the two confused.

So understand this: When I come in the classroom I am here because we have work to do; I come to do business. My style maybe different from what you expect from a professor, but that's because I haven't always been one. Before I became an academic, I served in the navy. For four years I was a sailor, an enlisted man in the US Navy, serving aboard aircraft carriers.

I served with men of honor.

But I also served during a time that brought out the worst in some of us.

Imagine this: race riots aboard ships carrying weapons of mass destruction. Well, I don't have to imagine it because I was onboard the aircraft carrier USS *Intrepid* during a race riot; five thousand men at sea, some of them trying to hurt each other on the basis of race. I served at the height of racial turmoil in the navy.

Understand that this class will be fun, but whatever skills you think you have in being able to not pay attention and do what you like . . . you've got nothing. I served onboard aircraft carriers; thousands of men living in close quarters, at sea, six months at a time, on a ship of war. I've seen things you haven't even thought about, ways of behaving you don't even know exist. So, don't cross me. Don't even consider it.

Some things are personal, some things are business. I never get the two confused. When we come to this class, we come to do business; we've got work to do. You need to keep that straight, because I always do.

I continue:

Navy pilots have a language. I was not a Navy pilot, but I served in air antisubmarine squadrons, so I got to know pilots. When they are in the air, bearing down on a target at high speed, they say to each other, "I'm coming in hot."

Every day I will come in and put this music stand where you can see it.

Then I will leave the room for a few minutes. The stand is your signal to get ready. Get your papers out, your pens; get ready to take notes because when I come back in, I'm coming in hot.

Make note of what I am telling you. I will close the doors, come to the spot where I have put the stand, wish you a good afternoon, and start lecturing. Every time . . . not sometimes, but every time . . . that's what will happen. Every time . . . I'm coming in hot . . . every time.

And . . . about those doors. Be on time! When I close the doors, they stay closed. If you are late, go to the third floor and, quietly, come in the doors at the back and top of this auditorium. If these front doors are closed that means I'm lecturing . . . and if anybody comes in the doors behind me, you will disturb me. You do not want to do that. Hear me loud and clear . . . once these front doors are closed, do not come in through them. If you do, I will embarrass your ass. Trust me on this.

Rules are also specified in the syllabus. A very important one that I go over on the first day is the safe space rule. Knowing the way I operate, having seen me in action, students follow me around. Advantage me, in teaching a "race" course at a predominantly White university. Many students do take the "Interpersonal Relationships and Race" course just because I am teaching it—partly due to my oratorical teaching style: lectures with recitations of poetry, a big voice, with big movements as I walk around the room. Students also follow me around because they know they will be safe to express themselves in my classroom.

Many of these students, you see, have watched me create, and have themselves experienced in the classroom, a safe space, from the first course they have with me. As part of the structure of my undergraduate social psychology courses I have a safe space discussion policy in the syllabus. For my general "Introduction to Social Psychology" course, that policy reads:

> Safe Space: Relationships have rules. And that applies to our interactions in Psych 311. There will be class periods where I will ask you, the class, to give me an answer to a question. During such a time, the rule is that when I call on one of your classmates, that person gets to say what's on her or his mind. This classroom will be our *safe space* for exploring what is going on in the social world. No one gets to judge, and try to shut down, another person's statement; no one. If anyone tries to shout down in judgment another classmate, that person will have to deal with my wrath. None of you wants that.
>
> We are at a university and that means we expect to hear points of view that conflict with our own. We don't all operate in the social world in the same ways. So understand that your opinions of "how things work" are yours and not the god-given truth. That means you have no standing to tell someone else they are wrong. Hearing your classmates' different ways of operating in the social world will be a big part of our class throughout the semester. Sometimes what you hear will make you feel challenged. When that happens, sit with that and learn.
>
> This is our *safe space*.

Especially early in the semester, an opportunity always presents itself for me to show that I mean what I say. For one discussion in that course, I ask the class to talk with me about one of the new social dynamics of dating: who pays? Who pays on the first date? That discussion is always fun and enlightening for my students because they learn from listening to their classmates that there is no longer one answer to that question. One spring semester, in the middle section of that two-hundred-person auditorium, a young woman put up her hand. I called on her and she said, "Well, it's really interesting when it's two women on a date."

Students started to "ooh," snicker, and lean forward or turn around in their seats to see who said that. I roared into navy-boot-camp-company-commander mode.

"Hey! Hey!" I boomed. "I will not have that in this classroom. You will respect your classmates or you will leave this auditorium now. And I mean right now!"

Total silence.

I waited. Head and body turning slight and slow, I let my eyes scan the auditorium.

Total silence.

"OK," I said. Then I again pointed to the center of the auditorium where the question had come from.

"Young lady, you were saying."

Everyone waited, silent.

"Well, what I was saying was that it's really tough if it's two women on a date."

"What makes it tough?" I asked. In the hushed auditorium, I kept my body posture to her, head inclined up in her direction, eyes focused on her, only her.

"I guess . . . it's that there are no cues, no roles to fall back on like with a boy-girl date."

"Indeed" I said, "that makes the 'who pays?' question even more difficult to negotiate without an upfront conversation."

"Who pays?" I said, continuing the discussion as I did after each idea from a student.

I ended that discussion by saying, "This is a new and widely discussed question in dating circles, online dating advice columns, all over the place. I say it's new because in my day, no such question was asked or even an issue. On a date, as a man, I knew I would be reaching in my pocket for my wallet to pay. I say it's new also because something has changed in the social world of relationships." Then I am off and running with a lecture on the American societal shift from a marriage-dating system to the modern relationship-dating system (Whitehead).

At the end of that class period, a young White man waited his turn to ask me a question. When his turn in the line came I faced him, we shook hands firmly, looking each other in the eyes.

"I just wanted to introduce myself," he said.

"Nice to meet you, young man. I appreciate you introducing yourself."

"I also wanted to thank you."

"Thank me?"

"I appreciate the way you control the class, Dr. Nacoste. Like what you did today to stop people from laughing at that girl's question. I had another class in this auditorium where the professor had no control. That was awful. So thank you."

"You're welcome, young man."

He turned and left the auditorium.

After that class period, after I took questions and self-introductions from students, I picked up my lecture notes, lifted my music stand, and walked out and down the hall. I took the elevator up to the seventh floor. I went into my office. There I sat down at my desk and composed and sent this e-mail to the 210 students in that course. I wrote:

Hello All,

Last class period, when I asked for your opinions about ". . . who pays," some of you forgot that we have a safe space rule. When I ask for an opinion, I am not asking for foolishness or for opinions everyone will agree with. The point is for you to hear and learn that there are a lot of different ways people inhabit the social world.

When your classmate brought up the very interesting issue of two women dating and ". . . who pays," some of you made noises like little children. I will not have any of you pass judgment on another student's experience or way of living in the social world. Not in my classroom. In my classroom, we have a safe space rule. Here is part of that rule from the syllabus. [I restated the relevant part of the rule.]

Some of you need to pull out your syllabus and remind yourself of my full statement of the safe space rule, which I went over on the first day of class. If you are uncomfortable with the rule, your only option is to drop the class because we will live by the safe space rule in my classroom. That is the interdependent situation of Psych 311.

Dr. Nacoste.

Nobody dropped.

Oddest thing about my class that spring semester was that only male students talked to me about the "I will not have that in my classroom" moment. A week later, a young Black male student came to see me. He came to talk because he said he wanted to figure out how to be the way I am in the classroom, on campus and in life. We were talking about how I operate when he brought it up.

"That was impressive what you did in the class last week."

"What was that?" I asked.

"When we were talking about who pays on a date, and that girl started to ask about two women on a date. The way you made it clear that you wouldn't put up with us judging her situation. And then the next day you sent an e-mail to the whole class making it real clear that you meant what you said. That was impressive."

"Humph," I grunted. "So why did that catch your attention?"

"I liked that you control the class. And I was thinking how that could really help somebody in the class express their opinion. Without doing what you did, somebody who's really shy or just a little unsure of him or herself might not ever talk in that big room. But what you did might make it easier for them."

Even at the end of that semester the "I will not have that in my classroom" moment was still on the mind of at least one student. With the last class meeting done, semester ending, I got this e-mail from a male student. He wrote:

Dr. Nacoste, I'll keep this brief, but I felt like writing you to let you know that your class was very enlightening. I really feel as if I learned a lot and I only hope that I can apply it well.

I would also like to thank you for your "safe space" policy.

In the beginning of the semester when a couple of people were sniggering at comments about lesbianism you let them know it was inappropriate. Many other teachers would have changed the subject or simply dismissed them, but you didn't, and I greatly appreciate that.

Quite telling that as part of thanking me for my course, even at the end he chose to highlight that early classroom moment; that moment where, for a young lesbian woman, I enforced the safe space classroom rule. Students do, indeed, follow me around, and the safe space policy and the way I enforce it is one of the reasons.

Following me around from course to course, then, is a mix of students. So mixed is this group that I know there are students who take my "Interpersonal Relationships and Race" course who are not all members of the Kumbaya choir, always ready to accept and respect everyone they interact with. None are innocent; none are without stereotypes; none are without anxieties about how to interact with people who come from different sexually oriented, ethnic, religious, racial, bodily-conditioned groups.

On the third day of class, I do even more social diagnosis by asking the class, "Why are first-time interracial encounters difficult to manage?" The responses always flow:

> Because you don't know how the other person sees race.
> Because people assume a boundary.
> People expect different behaviors, actions, and thoughts.
> It's a new experience.
> History of the races involved and their relation with each other.
> External forces—other people's reactions.
> Fear of offending.
> Trying not to appear "racist."
> Media portrayals of certain races.

Fear of being judged because of stereotypes (of your group).

People from different groups have different experiences.

Situation specific stereotypes.

Being in unfamiliar territory.

Uncertainty about what it's OK to even talk about (conversation topics).

Fear of judging (from hearsay or stereotypes).

Having biases.

Trying not to embarrass yourself (or others).

Worry about the person's (good or bad) experience with your race.

Overcompensation to avoid awkwardness.

Seeing or feeling a person's guard go up.

Trying to live up to the social norm of being accepting of all kinds of people.

Social pressure (to be accepting) from the situation.

Responses flow because on the first day of class I have gone over the safe space policy in the syllabus for the "Interpersonal Relationships and Race" class. My syllabus also includes a Class Discussion Policy, which reads:

Class Discussion Policy: We will have open and honest discussions of race, racial interactions, racial misunderstandings and confusions. To make our discussions authentic, we will not attack each other. And we will pledge not to take any person's name outside of this classroom. Leave here and talk about what was said, so that you can understand it better. But leave here (the classroom) with no person's name (except mine) on your lips. In other words, who says what in here, stays in here.

If this is the second course a student has had with me, they know for sure what this means. Even so, for this class I go over the policy on the first day. After the students have read the syllabus, I hit hard on this safe space policy. "Look," I say, "we all know that in America we live in an environment where no one wants to talk about racial matters. Bring up race, and people start looking for the exits. But for this class to work, we have to get past that and talk to each other, without judging or arguing with each other. That is how we will operate in here. For the next fifteen weeks; this classroom is our safe space."

I push the idea that the only way for the course to come alive and be educational about real life—not just theoretical life—is for us to have frank discussions during which we will not argue with or try to rebut each other. We will listen to each other's experiences and perspectives, but not argue.

Also, I say, we will not talk about who said what in here. I tell them:

> If you want to talk to your friends about the topics we cover, fine, but do not talk about particular people. If you want to talk about somebody, you have my permission to talk about me. You can tell your friends that I am a low-down, no-good, never was nothing, never gonna be nothing . . . mucky-muck. I don't care what you say about me. I facilitated racial-sensitivity discussion groups in the navy, with grown men, sailors who didn't want to be in the room. Those conversations were not polite. So whatever you want to say about me after you leave this classroom, go ahead. You got nothing. But you better not talk about your classmates because trust me, word will filter back to me. And you don't want me to come in here and deal with that.

From that first day on, whenever I open the class up for a general discussion, I remind them, "This is our safe space." I state that reminder every time because on the Wrong-Line train these young travelers have learned to avoid frank discussion of racial matters by acting as if it's all just a big joke. So I have to reinforce for everyone in the class that this is a different situation.

Honesty in my students' self-disclosures is the result. Confessional are their comments in class. Confessional are their papers. Confessional . . .

That is why I know that these young travelers do not all come from the Kumbaya choir cabin on the Wrong-Line train. Truth tellers they become in my class, and that is why I know the young travelers who come off the Wrong-Line train to me are young people who have been struggling. Their honest, truth-telling writing is how I come to know the struggles they have had during their short time traveling through life.

I am talking about confessional writing in which the students admit to their negative intergroup attitude, their neo-diversity anxiety. One White male wrote:

> I was lucky enough to grow up in a home where my mother and father were full of love and taught me to be the same. However, I have more family than

my parents, and many of them grew up with a different attitude towards race. As an impressionable child, this rubbed off on me and I developed my own personal prejudices that, at times, bled into my actions. I hesitate greatly to say that my prejudices are gone, because they are not. No matter how hard I try to convince myself that I do not harbor prejudice, I will be wrong.

A Black female wrote:

Times have changed a lot since the 1960s and 1970s. I know it's not them versus us, because everybody is a part of this conflict. The conflict in the past was worse than the present. I just find myself in a moment of why did he or she do that? Is it because I'm Black? These moments cause me to think about why people can't change. Am I wrong to think like that? I feel bad about certain thoughts I have about things people do. I do not want to think they are racist, but how should I feel when a White man opens the door for his White female friend and lets the door close in my face. I mean I was standing beside him thinking he was also holding the door for another female. How should I feel about this situation? I do believe things have changed. I wish people could change and also myself.

I am also talking about the confessional stories of struggle that they write and hand in to me. These are stories where the student has been surprised by the sudden introduction of race, gender, ethnicity, bodily condition, religion, sexual orientation as relevant to the interaction. Surprised is the key; they are blindsided and left to wonder, "Really . . . is that what this is about?"

A White female wrote:

I have always had Black friends, but most of my friends dressed in what most people would refer to as a more "White style." We were never treated any differently than anyone else, so I never really understood that some of the racial stereotyping still existed. That is until I started to hang out with my friend Byron. Byron is a nineteen-year-old male with dark skin standing about 5´11˝. He dresses in a style that is typical of people his age; he wears the big oversized shirts that go past his knees, the huge pants, baseball hats, and "bling." I never really thought anything different about him; he was just a kid that I worked with who I had become good friends with.

One day when we went out to lunch I really started to notice a difference in the way he was being treated. We went to a restaurant that I had gone to a million other times, every other time I had been given great service and the waiters seemed happy to serve me. However, this time it was a little different. When the waitress came to the table she didn't really look either of us in the eye, wasn't being friendly and outgoing, and she didn't really seem enthused that she had to take care of us.

There was never anything said about the reason behind the lack of service, but I had a feeling that I knew what it was. I have worked in restaurants for years, and there's a stereotyping that Black people don't tip. Due to that prejudice, you will frequently see Black patrons get worse service than White patrons.

I receive confessionals in which the story's truth teller is surprised and embarrassed by her own mistake, which is based on her own stereotypes. A Black female wrote:

Here's how it happened. I was about 17 years old. It was my senior year of high school, so of course I was under the impression that my friends and I were the baddest group of people walking the planet. It was springtime and the faint smell of graduation was in the air. Even the teachers were feeling it, which meant we often had pretty laid-back assignments and classwork to do, giving us ample time to fool around and gossip.

On this particular day, my friends and I had just made our way back to campus from "open lunch" at a chicken place. I had 6th-period art class with my favorite teacher. He was only a little older than we were—maybe his midtwenties, if that. He was so cool. We laughed and joked around in his class all the time. Today was the day we were supposed to be putting the finishing touches on our art projects to turn in. As long as you were done though, you pretty much had free run of the classroom.

As expected, about fifteen minutes into the class period, everyone's chatting. Since the teacher was so relaxed, we often had people from other classes, or early-release students come in and hang with their friends who were students in his class. He never minded, so when a couple boys walked through the door, no one really took notice. Except that after about thirty seconds, the eyes of every girl in the room made a beeline to the left, where stood the most amazing piece of Asian male I think any of us had ever seen.

Now, let me just clarify. I was raised in New Jersey, home to one of the most segregated cities in the US. I lived just outside of Newark for a while and still visit family there now. It's not that I didn't ever see anyone of a different race nor have friends from other cultures. But this was the first time in my life that I was physically attracted (I mean REALLY physically attracted) to someone of another race that was a feasible prospective for me to date. Of course I thought Channing Tatum was hot. But he wasn't standing ten feet away from me. This guy was.

Being (in my own mind) God's gift to those in my high school, I had to meet him. So I walk over with two friends behind me. He's leaning against one of the tables, bike helmet in hand, looking like the epitome of cool. Some guys are striking up conversation with him, and it becomes obvious that they are all friends. I try to work my way into the conversation, making little remarks here and there. He tells me his name, Li. He has no accent, but I assumed his parents were first-generation immigrants. So, in an attempt at being coy, I ask him where he's from. He doesn't respond.

Now I told you how unbelievably superior I thought I was. I was not used to being ignored. So I ask again. Where are you from?

He says "California."

I say, "No, that's not what I meant. Where are you from? You know, like Korea, China, Japan?"

He just looks at me, and then says, "What about you? Nigeria, Kenya, Madagascar?"

Needless to say, I was floored. I could tell by the way his eyebrows raised and his brow furrowed, he was irritated. He threw me one last cold glance and continued the conversation with his buddies.

I've never been more embarrassed in my life. And he was so CUTE!!

That's how it happened.

I have also encountered student confessions in which the truth teller is a teenager and is caught off guard by how racially mean a person of his or her own group can be. A White male wrote:

My best friend growing up was a boy named Leon. He and I met in the first grade and were basically inseparable most of the way through high school. Leon was of Hispanic descent. His father was Colombian and his mother was

El Salvadorian. Leon has tanned skin and jet-black hair. He started growing facial hair when we were in middle school. In my opinion, if someone looked at Leon, they would know that he was of Hispanic descent. When I was at their house, they would make ethnic meals and speak in fluent Spanish around me. It was something that I was used to.

One weekend, there was a Hispanic festival in downtown Winston-Salem, and Leon's family invited me to go. I thought it would be fun to see what Leon's family was all about, so I went. When we got there, it was a shock to see all kinds of people from Spain to Mexico, Colombia to Argentina. The food was great, the music was blasting, and people were dancing everywhere.

After we had been there for about three hours, Leon needed to get something from the car. As we were walking to the parking deck, an older White man approached us asking for directions. We helped him as best we could, being twelve years old in the middle of all the sky-rises. As we were about to leave, the man made a comment.

"It's hard to find directions with all these damn Mexicans around here. None of them speak any English."

Both Leon and I were shocked. Leon's shock quickly turned to anger. I could see his expression changing with each passing second. As Leon began to say something, the man turned and left. This was the first time that I had really been faced with such a harsh racist comment.

There are also confessions about the goofy, anxiety-driven reactions people have, about the very awkward situations people create to interact with you, because you have a visible bodily condition. A young man wrote:

I was born with a different arm. I am missing my ulna in my left arm, resulting in muscle loss, a loss of 1/3 length compared to my right arm, a curved shape, and only three fingers in my left hand. I have seen people mess up many times. I can see anxiety about what to do and what to say and in result they take our interaction to an intimacy level before it is ready to be there.

They ask the most absurd questions, such as, "Are you left or right handed?" Also, some people tend to be very invasive for a first-time interaction with questions like, "Does having a different arm bother you?" People also just make gaudy exclamations such as, "Whoa, you don't have an arm!" or attempt to mirror, so their left arm matches mine, I assume, to understand how it physiologically functions.

I understand. I do. People are interested and fascinated, but they go about it in such a half-witted way, making them appear to be an ignoramus. The anxiety of the new interaction with someone with a perceived physical difference throws him or her off guard and he or she loses socially acceptable behavioral action.

It's tough out there. And when you have been traveling on the Wrong-Line train, it's even tougher. You see, as the Wrong-Line train rumbles along, there is no conductor to whom you can ask questions. No one will give you a concrete answer about how to interact with other people on the train, or what to do at the stops along the way. No conductor, no information car; you travel with a lot of unanswered questions. How should I interact? Should I say something? What should I say? How should I say it? Damn it, what are the rules? "You just have to be more accepting," is all the young travelers hear through the train's overhead speaker, from a disembodied voice.

CHAPTER 6

PISTOL SHOOTING?

Almost all of the students who take my courses have had some puz-zling interpersonal-intergroup interaction they have struggled to understand. So they have no trouble responding to the major assignment for the course.

Yes, there are regular, multiple-choice exams, but those are just to make sure students are retaining technical definitions and the basic theoretical ideas from the lectures and reading. To pull all that together, to make the course educational in the deepest sense, at the end students should be able to use all that they have learned to make sense of some interpersonal event in their own life. If they can do that, they will be seeing anew and clear how the world works. If they can do that, then they should have a new perspective on social interaction that means they behave in new, more productive ways. When they use that new perspective to guide their behavior later, they will have become a truly educated person.

Hence the first part of the major assignment:

As you are now well aware, we are using a "story" methodology to learn how to analyze interpersonal-intergroup interactions. As part of the learning experience, you will need to be able to analyze dyadic (two-person) interac-tions that you have been a part of at some point. So, here is your assignment.

Please type out your answer to the following question: *What is the most intense (odd, angry, happy, curious, threatening, challenging) interpersonal-inter-group (by race, gender, ethnicity, religion, sexual orientation) dyadic interaction you have experienced?*

Be sure to think through *what happened*, and be honest with yourself about what (behaviors) actually occurred. In other words, describe the interaction from beginning to end, *focusing on the behaviors* of both members of the dyad. Do that to answer the question:

What is the most intense (odd, angry, happy, curious, threatening, challenging) interpersonal-intergroup dyadic interaction you have experienced?

Write an honest description of the dyadic interaction. Tell the story, giving all the details of the situation and the encounter that you can. You might want to start with "Here's what happened:"

Do not try to analyze the interaction. At this point, your job is to *describe* the details of the situation (the time, the setting or place, the two people, the group of people, the conversation or other interaction features, the progression of the interaction, and the behaviors that brought the interaction to a close). Do this in *no more than* one (1) typewritten page (300 to 600 words).

Please *e-mail this to me.* I will give each of you feedback on whether you are on the right track. After I read them all, I will tell you what we will do with this exercise.

I make that assignment due right after the second exam. I take about five days to read the fifty to seventy stories. As I read I give each student feedback. I make suggestions only about one of two things: length and commentary. Obvious, length means too long, but usually that has to do with the writer making commentary about what happened in their story. Once I have reminded the writer that all I want is the "Here's what happened" story, the writer edits (sometimes with my help), and then I say, "Save your story; you will need it to complete a major assignment later in the semester." That is where the stories come from.

On the last day of the class I give out the assignment for the final exam. That assignment reads:

Earlier in the semester, you wrote up a story in response to the following:

What is the most intense (odd, angry, happy, curious, threatening) interracial, interethnic, intergroup dyadic interaction you have experienced?

For your final exam, you are to *analyze* the story of that intense interpersonal-intergroup interaction *using the relevant interpersonal concepts that have been covered in this class.*

Generally speaking, when you use a concept, be sure to *make it clear how* the concept relates to the behaviors that happened in the situation that made the interaction intense.

You are to write your analysis as an essay, using and *formally defining* the models and concepts.

Since 2007 this assignment has evolved just a bit—but it is an important bit. Always, neo-diversity has been the concept around which the course is built. I started out with a focus on interracial interactions because race in America is the prototype for intergroup relations. Even so, when asking me questions about their experiences, students started to ask "Is it only interpersonal-intergroup if it's Black, White?" I was focused on the interracial aspect at first, but I would still say, "Tell me what you have in mind?" Their answer was neo-diversity: interactions in which two people are from different groups—gender (male, female, transgender), sexually oriented (gay, lesbian, bisexual), religious (Christian, atheist, Muslim, Jewish), ethnic, and so on. Neo-diversity is what young people are experiencing in America today. My students helped me to broaden the way the final exam assignment is set up. I will be forever grateful for that because I began to see just how broad the intergroup dynamic is in their lives.

Nothing interpersonal-intergroup is easy, not in this age of neo-diversity. Even between females and males I have been struck by the extent to which modern-day interactions are filled with neo-diversity anxiety. But it's not just anxiety. Sometimes—in fact, too often—there is real hostility. I am deeply troubled by this, by what I have learned about twenty-first-century interactions between young women and young men. A young woman wrote:

One particular afternoon, about a month into my job at the Bookstore, my boss asked if I could dust and wipe down the glass fixtures in the store. I, of course, said I would. About ten minutes into cleaning, one of my male co-workers came over to me. He stood there for a second and looked at me with a smirk on his face. He then said, "Ahhh. You're doing exactly what you're supposed to be doing." I was shocked and I didn't even know how to respond to the words that just flew out of his mouth. I said nothing, but I am sure he could tell I was not happy with what he just said. He then proceeded to walk away without saying anything else after his rude remark.

I began to actually process what he said to me and became more and more frustrated. I could not believe that someone could still have those kinds of views about women. I barely even knew him at the time, which baffled me as to why he would say something like that.

Let's dispense, right away, with any attempts to downplay what happened in this interaction. Social interactions are sensitive. So, no, the young woman, the writer, is not being "too sensitive." Brief as it was, what happened in this interaction was a gender-identity put-down. "Oh, good, you know your place."

In that brief interpersonal moment, a negative judgment of women was displayed to a woman. In her analysis of this moment, she said:

> Neo-diversity played a role in this particular interaction. Neo-diversity is the new social uncertainty brought about by the rapid and substantive changes in the spheres of communication-technology, gender-relations, race and ethnicity, and international relations. This particular case is purely categorized under gender-relations. Today there is much conflict on what a women's role should be. Should women be home-makers, as that was the only job a woman could hold back in the day, or, as our society becomes more accepting, should women venture out into the workplace? There isn't one answer, and many individuals hold different opinions on this subject matter. There is social uncertainty.

She went on with her analysis to point out the possible role of a language community:

> A language community is a set of people who give specific words and phrases unique meaning in order to define the group, its mutual understanding and its distinctive way of interacting through verbal and sometimes nonverbal manners of speaking. Language communities may present problems for members of a dyad if the shared cultural knowledge does not match up.
>
> My co-worker, being a male, was from a different language community just by the fact of gender. Males may have a different set of phrases and words, also known as what males call "guy code." He may have spouted

out that particular remark by mistake because that is the type of phrase he would say with all his other male friends and would be considered acceptable. I could tell once he saw my facial expression and how I reacted to the situation, he realized he was in the wrong.

Carrying your language community norms around with you is unavoidable. That is why knowing that you cannot just use the rules of one language community in every interpersonal encounter is an important social skill. It is one of the fundamental lessons I teach early in the semester. I realized I had to teach this when one student tried to justify the offensive way people sometimes talk by saying, "Maybe that is just the way they talk to everybody."

I stood in the front of the classroom and took a breath, rubbed my bald head with my right hand. Then I used the relationship principles of the class to point out the errors in the claim. I said:

Remember that this course is grounded by a set of theories and related research about how interpersonal relationships work. One of the relationship guidelines that came out of that research is that nonfamily relationships evolve. All voluntary relationships evolve.

A new acquaintance is not the same kind of relationship as an old friend. To be specific, a new acquaintance is a surface-contact relationship; it's just a set of superficial interaction moments strung together between two people. If that surface-contact relationship is to become more than that, the two people must engage each other in honest self-disclosures. And from Altman and Taylor's social penetration theory we know that those honest self-disclosures should come slowly, as if peeling an onion. Just that should be enough to alert you to the social fact that no one should "talk to everybody the same way." Anyone who believes that it is OK to talk to everybody the same way will always be in situations where their attempts to communicate are inadequate and off-putting.

Acquaintances are not friends or not necessarily co-workers or, heaven forbid, bosses. To be successful in social life, which is all real life, no matter where you are, relationship awareness is a critical social skill.

In that context, let's consider a young man who interacts with a young woman this way: *He stood there for a second and looked at me with a smirk on his face. He then said, "Ahhh. You're doing exactly what you're supposed to be doing."* Clearly there was no relationship awareness here until it was too late: *I could tell once he saw my facial expression and how I reacted to the situation, he realized he was in the wrong.* And the language community he is used to, "guy code," was likely an influence but is no excuse for his being so socially inept. It's no excuse also because "guy code" can activate a group dynamic that is dangerous. Another young woman wrote:

> Two years ago I was dating a guy who was in the army. I hardly ever got to see him because he was home for short periods of time. Therefore, whenever he was home we often hung out in big groups of our friends, so everyone else would be able to visit with him also.
>
> One evening, my boyfriend asked me to come over because it was his last night home for a few months. When I got over to his house there was a big group of our friends, just happening to be all male. We all hung out for a while and were having a good time. Then it happened. My boyfriend turned to me and said, "Go do what a woman's supposed to do for her man and go cook me up something nice."
>
> He did this in front of all his male friends, not even realizing that what he said had made me upset. His friends laughed along with his joke and then proceeded to tell more "female" jokes and explained why men were "better" than women.
>
> Of course, everyone thought this was hilarious . . . except for me. I didn't want to be disrespected like that. I left the room soon after (not bringing the sandwich, I might add) and was shocked that my boyfriend would say those things, even in front of our friends. Needless to say, he and I didn't work out.

Say what! Go do what! What year is this? That's what I want to know.

Taking apart her own story, the young woman hit on a number of important analytic points. First, she addressed the nature of the relationship. About that she wrote:

> My ex-boyfriend, we will call him "G," was a very interesting and funny guy. Of course, this is what drew me to him in the first place. We had gone to high school together, but it wasn't until my sophomore year in college that we started hanging out and eventually started dating.

The Nacoste Interdependence-Integrative Relationship Development Model could be used to help examine this situation. This model demonstrates how a relationship will go from an exchange dimension (where everything is payment, repayment) to a communal dimension (when people do things just to please one another). It shows how a relationship can go from zero contact, to mutual awareness (with no interaction), to surface contact, and through the different levels of mutuality (minor, moderate, and major).

This model applies to my interaction because this was still a new (minor-mutuality) relationship to me and we had only been together for about a month and a half when my interaction occurred.

Yes, she was attracted to this young man. At that point in their series of interaction moments, there had been very little opportunity for the two to exchange honest self-disclosures about anything meaningful. No surprise, then, that she is surprised to learn that he held this kind of attitude toward women. People, young and old, make this social interaction mistake all the time. Attraction and desire are not information about the person you are interacting with. Attraction and desire are only in your head and in the heat of other parts of your body. Attraction and desire do not and cannot tell you anything about the other person's beliefs. All attraction and desire tell you about is what you want.

Second, our writer offered a deeper assessment of the group dynamic of the situation.

Another way to analyze this interaction, between G and I, is through the Nacoste-Nofziger Model of Intergroup-Interdependence. This model helps analyze situations that create interpersonal anxiety in a person. Social interactions, such as mine that included gender, can often result in intergroup anxiety stemming from contact with out-group members. According to the model, with me being the out-group member, G started to have anxiety because he was unsure how to act toward me with his guy friends present. Because of the group composition, myself being the only girl with many other males, I was uncomfortable because I was in the out-group. However, because G was in the in-group, this caused him to be more comfortable, possibly explaining why he made the statements he did.

All of a sudden my boyfriend says, "Go do what a woman's supposed to do for her man and go cook me up something nice," right in front of everyone. I was embarrassed, shocked, and angry. Although we had not been together that long, he had never said anything like that to me before, and here he was joking about women right in front of me and everyone else. I felt offended, and that is why I left the room.

Her analysis here is nicely done. And yes, I agree that the social psychology view is that the males in the room are a group. I am disturbed, though, by her report that *all* of these young "men" laughed. Not one of these males had a notion that their behavior toward this young woman would be viewed as offensive and scary—by their behavior, not one.

There are things I want to know here. I want to know who is rearing these males in this way that pushes them to demean women, to resist treating women as equals. One of these males said, "*Go do what a woman is supposed to do.*" So I want to know what these males think of their mothers.

My father, Mr. Nacoste, made a point of teaching his three sons to respect our mother. When I was about thirteen or fourteen, we boys were starting to develop real height and weight. August Jr. was already 6′1″ (on his way to being 6′6″), I was 5′11″ (on my way to 6′3″), and little brother Phillip at the age of ten was not far behind me (on his way to being 6′2″). One Saturday we were in the house doing nothing while our mother was in the living room on her hands and knees waxing the hardwood floor. Daddy walked in the front door.

When we heard the door we, the boys, came out of our room to meet him. When we got to where we could see him and he could see us, we watched him lean over and ask our mother to get up. "Oh, no, O-geese, I need to finish this." (My father's name, August, is pronounced "O-geese.") Daddy insisted and helped our mother up. He asked her to have a seat, and she did. Then he turned his eyes on us.

"Come over here," he said. His voice was calm but stern.

We stood before him.

"You three are going to wax and polish this floor for your mama."

We stood there, squirming a little. Then Daddy spoke on.

"Look, you three need to understand this. She is your mama, but don't you ever forget that she's my wife. And you will not treat my wife this way. Now get to work."

I want to know who is rearing males today in ways that keep them boys. I want to know, because, as we all know, boys will be ignorant.

What century are we rearing males to live in? For sure it's not the twenty-first. Indeed there was a time in America when women were forced to stay in the kitchen and not worry their pretty little heads about important matters. Let me say again what I have said before: those days are over, and we ain't going back. Although it might make inappropriate stops, even the Wrong-Line train can't go backward.

We have a clear and present danger. Too many young males are threatened by gender equality. We should not be cavalier about that form of neo-diversity anxiety. It is dangerous. Young women in my classes are too often reporting male attempts to devalue and undermine their thinking prowess as women, their goals and accomplishments.

One female student wrote of undermined goals:

It was a cool summer night on Lake Gaston the summer of 2010. I was surrounded by good friends and family outside on our deck, talking about this and that. I was about to start my senior year of high school, so naturally all I could talk about was where I wanted to apply to college. My cousin's friend asked me where I was thinking about applying, and I told him a few of the places that I had in mind. I told him that I would really like to go to the University of Georgia. He asked me why, and I told him that it seemed like a good fit for me. He quickly replied, "No, you just want to go to Georgia so you can marry a frat boy and have a lab." Our conversation quickly ended after that when I became very offended. The entire deck silenced after this comment, and I simply walked inside.

Another female student conveyed a story that speaks to undermining a person's thinking prowess:

I'd read Emily Brontë's *Wuthering Heights* one summer in a fit of boredom and had unexpectedly fallen in love with the story line. I was really looking forward to reading it again, only this time in a classroom setting.

One day over lunch, a friend brought up the subject of *Wuthering Heights*. His teacher had assigned a lengthy paper on the novel just before lunch period. I asked him whether or not he was enjoying the read so far, and he explained that the assignments put a damper on his ability to appreciate the plot.

Another male friend P chimed in, bemoaning the fact that they even had to read the book in the first place. I asked him why. "*Wuthering Heights* just doesn't compare to the other books we've read. The plot and writing is horrible. It's a joke. I don't understand why it's even considered a classic."

I piped up, telling him that I thoroughly enjoyed reading it through for a second time. "It's not for everybody, I guess, but I really liked it."

"It's a glorified romance novel. Of course you liked it!" P shot back. "You're a girl."

I sat there, stunned. I couldn't even form a reply. The lively conversation came screeching to a sudden halt, all because P had used my gender to explain away my love for the novel.

Looking back on it now, I wish I would have said something, anything to stick up for myself. Instead I kept quiet for the remainder of lunch and fought back tears. I was insulted by his sexist remark, but his "you're a girl" quip was part of a bigger issue. For me, the thing that struck home was the realization that he genuinely believed my appreciation for the novel stemmed from the sordid nature of the love affair and nothing more. Because if there's one thing girls thrive on, it's drama, right? Wrong, P. So wrong.

I didn't get the chance to explain my interpretation of the story's themes or Brontë's repetitive use of symbols. I'm a girl, and to P that meant my love for the novel was superficial-level at best.

Other women find themselves in situations that undermine their achievement:

It was my first day working as a waitress at Pappy's BBQ in my hometown. The staff was predominately male, but there were a few other female employees like myself. I had been training for several days beforehand with other members of the waitstaff, but this was my first night waiting tables on my own. After an extremely hectic night of running back and forth from the kitchen, taking orders, and filling drinks, I sat down at a table to calculate my tips to see how well I had done as a waitress. I was anxious to see what I had earned, and to my surprise I did well. I actually made more tips than some of the other, more experienced, waitstaff, so I felt very proud of myself.

However, my proud moment was cut short when one of the male waiters, Brad, asked me how much money I had made for the night. When I answered him, he replied: "You're a *waitress*; of course you made a lot of money. I bet you don't even know what hard work is like. Customers always give the waitresses more money." I knew he would never say something to the other male waiters, even if they made more money than him.

Here is an example of an interaction in which a woman's entertainment preference is being undermined at an early age:

At one point, a guy across the room from me said, "That was terrible! You're playing like a girl!" I turned, disheartened that the gendered insults had already started.

The boy's name was Matt, and he was a year ahead of me. We had a math class together in middle school, but we had not really interacted. All I really knew about him was that he struggled in school. I walked over, noticed that they were playing "Guitar Hero II," and asked if I could play next.

His first reaction was to laugh, but then he gauged the look on my face as serious. "It won't be much of a game, but whatever," he said, nudging his companion and laughing again. I did not say anything but waited patiently until they were finished. Matt beat the other boy soundly and addressed me with a smirk. "Are you sure? I wouldn't want to hurt your feelings." I nodded, controlling my growing anger, and took the guitar from the other player. "If I couldn't beat him, I don't know why a girl thinks she can," he said, just loud enough for me to hear.

"We can play this easy one." Matt said, choosing "Surrender" on Medium Mode. Nervous and anxious to prove myself, I missed the first few notes. I won, but Matt was hardly impressed.

"I was just being nice." he said indifferently, moving down the list of songs we could choose from. "But I won't let you win this one." My heart fell when I realized he had chosen "Hangar 18" by Megadeth on Hard. Thankfully, Haleigh had ceased whatever game she was involved in and had come over to encourage me. "You'll beat him, Bristol! He's got nothing on you."

He certainly thinks he does, I thought as I struggled through the song. It reached the riff that was the most challenging, and I thought that I had lost whatever lead I had. The end came, and somehow I had managed to win. I smiled, but I tried not to rub it in Matt's face. Rather than force him to apologize, I waited to see what he would say. No one had ever told me I was incapable based on the fact that I was a girl, and I was elated that I had proven this person wrong.

Matt glared at me. "It doesn't make any difference." he said. "Girls can't play real video games." Knowing that I could not change his mind, I left the club and went home.

Some of this may seem trivial, but it's not in the immediate psychological experience of the young woman. It's also not trivial, because the neo-diversity anxiety sometimes introduces raw gender hostility to an otherwise casual social interaction between two people who happen to be different on the intergroup factor of gender. Giving her story the title "No Barbies in Basketball," a young woman wrote:

Let me start my story by stating two facts about myself. First, I love basketball. Both NBA and college basketball games are what I have grown up watching, so I tend to be more knowledgeable about them than the average female, especially when the games involve my favorite teams, the Miami Heat and, of course, NCSU. Second, I am not the "girliest" girl in the world. I like to wear a dress on occasion, but for the most part, sports and debating with my dad about which teams are the best is my thing. I am telling you these things so you will understand why this particular situation was, for lack of a better term, unpleasant for me.

So, here's what happened. I was sitting in my living room at home with my dad, brother, and one of my brother's guy friends. We were watching a basketball game with the Heat and some other team. My brother and his friend started debating about which team was better, the Heat or the Boston Celtics. Feeling that I was knowledgeable enough on the subject to contribute my own opinion, I moved over to the couch with them and started debating as well. I had never met this particular friend, but I am not a very shy person, so being loud and confident in what I was saying did not really bother me. I noticed him giving me odd looks anytime I would speak, but I ignored them and continued saying what I believed to be true, that Miami was better because of Lebron James, Dwyane Wade, etc.

My brother and I were playfully going back and forth on the issue, with this guy friend giving his opinion every so often. Apparently we were really entertaining because my dad kept laughing at us. But, eventually this guy stops talking altogether and just stares at me, frowning. It was really odd and very noticeable to everyone in the room, so I asked him what was wrong. He looked me straight in the eye and said, "Nothing is wrong. I just think you don't know what you are talking about and should just go upstairs and play with your dolls . . . Barbie. Leave this conversation to the boys."

I just gaped at him. I was infuriated, but what could I say? Everyone was staring at the two of us, probably wondering what was about to happen, but I just got up and left the room. It was either that or punch the guy in the face. The nerve of some people.

He stares at her. Frowns. That is hostility, all because "a girl" knows NBA basketball. Unable to handle equality, the young male comes close to bullying with his gender put-down. That is not an innocent moment and not a moment to be ignored. So I do wish the father had spoken up at this point to defend his daughter, in her presence, because something sinister was going on. In this case, there seemed to be no long-term effect on the young woman. That may attest to how this NBA-knowledgeable young woman has been reared to think about herself as a person, to believe in her own personhood.

A number of young women wrote stories that showed that they, too, had been reared, by their fathers, to explore the world fully. Disturbing in those stories, however, is how other males have had such powerful neo-diversity anxiety responses to young women so reared.

One young woman wrote: "Over the summer while I was home in NY, I really got into pistol shooting with my dad." Every time I read that sentence I have to read it again, because I misread it the first time. I misread it to mean she is telling me that she and her father get into arguments: pistol-shooting contests. My gender stereotypes are showing. Indeed, there are no innocent. I have learned to catch mine and set them aside as soon as I do. That takes time; it takes work because we start to learn stereotypes before we are able to speak. Anyway, what she wrote was:

> Over the summer while I was home in NY, I really got into pistol shooting with my dad. It was a lot of fun, despite having to wake up really early in the morning to go.
>
> I'd been asking and asking and asking my dad to take me shotgun shooting at the gun club, as they do it every Sunday and Thursday. Something would always get in the way: bad weather, business appointment, etc. So finally, while I was home on spring break, the last Sunday I was home we went. It was a perfect day, sun shining, cool, but not cold.
>
> I was nervous as we pulled up but tried to hide it. It's a big difference shooting at a small, still metal target than it is trying to hit an even smaller, moving clay pigeon. So, we walk up, and it's all old men, probably somewhere in their 70s. There were about eight to ten of them around. They were all really encouraging and thought it was cool that my dad was teaching me to shoot. First round my dad shadowed me to make sure I was doing OK. Then he went. I decided I wanted to go again, so this time I was on my own. While I was at the bench, a few of the guys came over to give me pointers and help with what I was doing wrong. It felt really nice to be so welcomed.
>
> The second round I was in though, the old man to the left of me kept looking at me and had been silent since we got there. Now this was my first time ever doing this, so naturally I wasn't as fast as everyone else, but they all seemed to be patient and understanding, except for this guy.
>
> He never said anything directly to me, but he didn't have to; I could feel the tension, like he didn't want me there or didn't think I should be there because I was a girl. It didn't really affect me much; I just kept on going how I was, and it was fine, but it definitely made me uncomfortable.

Talk about sinister. And you can see the psychological effect of this old man's glare. But why glare in the first place? Why attempt this nonverbal bullying? Is it simply because this young woman is being reared by her father to be a person who explores her full humanity of interests? I think that is happening more and more. But there is push-back. Another gun-shooting young woman wrote:

Two years ago my dad and I went with my boyfriend, Carson, to hunt doves one weekend. We met up with a few of Carson's cousins and their friends before heading to our spots. Carson and his dad stepped out of the truck and approached the group of men. My dad followed, and I was slipping on my boots in the car. As I shut the door I overheard a guy asking my dad if that was his son. Now, the attire for any sort of hunting is pretty universal. You are dressed in camouflage from head to toe and usually wear some sort of big clunky boots. I also had my hair pulled back and was wearing a hat. With a little laughter my dad corrects the man and states that I'm actually his daughter. The man looked shocked.

I walk up to the group of men and flash an embarrassed smile and say hey. Now I feel really awkward. I try to hide my embarrassment by joining in the laughter.

The man asks if I hunt. I casually tell him I've hunted for a while now. He then asks a series of questions to validate my information. For example, what gun do you use, what do you like to hunt, where, etc. After I've passed my interrogation, small talk fills the awkward silence after he looks as if he's solving a math problem.

After about thirty minutes we disperse and head to our spots. I remember sitting by my boyfriend and not wanting to shoot the rest of the afternoon. I was afraid I wouldn't have good accuracy shooting down the doves and would end up scaring them off or interfering with the other hunters around waiting for the kill shot. I lost my confidence. While sitting out there I only fired my shotgun three times. It was hard to tell if I got anything. I felt defeated by the doves and felt even more defeated by the group of men who couldn't believe I, a female, was out hunting on the same grounds they were.

There is a lot to explore in this one. Analyzing it herself, this young woman wrote:

Neo-diversity: Many years ago, females wouldn't have been caught hunting. It was because of neo-diversity that this interaction even happened. As soon as I stepped out of the truck and the man asked if I was a son, he was experiencing the minimal group effect: automatic categorization of a person as either inside or outside of your group, with a tendency to compete with out-group members (us vs. them). Ah, the rough beast of neo-diversity. The man must have known I was hunting (people don't dress in camouflage just because . . . OK, some do), but he felt he had to make certain I was a part of the group he belonged to.

When my dad stated that I was his daughter, for the man the situation became one of vague interdependence. The man was interacting with a female outside the normal interaction of males while he goes hunting, and there were no clear gender roles for the interaction. Also we had just met, so we had no relationship history. All those factors of the situation add up to vague interdependence.

So he wasn't sure how he was supposed to act. Now you can see the uncertainty. Now you can feel the intergroup anxiety, anxiety that comes from contact with a person you perceive to be outside your group. In this situation of vague interdependence the tension in the situation was gender differences. And his neo-diversity anxiety was exposed by his use of language when his conversation reflected a police interrogation rather than a meet-and-greet.

An insightful, self-educational analysis is what this young woman produced. Still, disturbing to me was the nontrivial impact this social interaction had on her. She wrote:

> As the day progressed and I'm sitting in my spot hunting, I have seemed to take on some of the feelings I experienced about my identity in this situation. After my interaction with that man, I felt as if I no longer belonged in this type of environment. I felt that because I was a female, I did not quite fit the preconceived notion of a "hunter" hunting. The man had clearly expressed his disapproval of me being here when he asked me so many questions. So instead of shooting my gun, which I am most certainly capable of doing, I sat back and felt defeated. I felt that I did not belong in that cornfield, and I was not allowed to enjoy this hobby with them because I have two X chromosomes. All because of this man's language I felt I was not good enough.

Social interaction is powerful. A brief moment between two people can leave one or both carrying a heavy burden. Sinister in this case is the effect called stereotype threat; worrying that you might confirm the stereotype of your group. Again she wrote: "I felt that because I was a female, I did not quite fit the preconceived notion of a 'hunter' hunting. The man had clearly expressed his disapproval of me being here when he asked me so many questions. So instead of shooting my gun, which I am most certainly capable of doing, I sat back and felt defeated." That's the power of stereotype threat; that's the power of social interaction.

Having no doubt of that power, I am troubled that we appear to be setting up neo-diversity, gender-anxiety-provoking situations ourselves. Earlier I asked who is rearing all these males to believe and act not as men but as boys. I have my answer: We are. A male student wrote:

> Now my new thought is this, with everything that has happened in the past, categorizing ourselves into groups is not smart. If we are categorizing ourselves at all, first and foremost it should be a group called "people" or "humans." Sadly though we do not do this at all, we categorize ourselves into groups by race, gender, religion, and sexual orientation, and we are always trying to be better than the people who are not in our "group."
>
> When I was little I was always put into situations where there was some type of competition against another group. The most classic of this grouping is the "boys" versus "girls" approach to playing games. I was not aware of how often this happened until after I worked at a church's kids' ministry. Before the first game that we played with the kids we were trying to figure out how to split the groups, and someone suggested boys against the girls. Immediately after she said that there was excitement in the room; there seemed to be a clear rivalry here. Before we even told the rules of the game boys were booing the girls' team and the girls' team was making fun of and taunting the boys.
>
> What in the world?
>
> I was amazed about what we are teaching our kids in the United States these days. They will have to work with each other in the future no matter what "group" they are in, and this says that competition and splitting the groups in such a manner is okay. I say let's scratch the old way of doing things, clearly splitting groups in such a way has not helped our country before, with racial segregation and today the country is extremely divided on the issue of gay marriage.

We are too casual about what we set up. It all seems so innocent.

In his science fiction novel *Empire of the Ants*, Bernard Werber makes a comparison between ants and humans. He writes:

> In ants and in human beings, sociability is predetermined. A newborn ant is too weak on its own to break the cocoon in which it is imprisoned. A human baby cannot even walk or feed itself on its own.
>
> Ants and human beings are species designed to be assisted by those around them and cannot or will not learn on their own.
>
> This dependence on adults is certainly a weakness but it sets in motion another process, the quest for knowledge. If adults can survive while the young cannot, the latter are obliged to ask their elders for knowledge from the start.

Yet we pretend to be unaware of this. When it is convenient to do so, we act as if we do not know that children follow our lead.

Too much is taken for granted, and even when it shows up ugly in the language of our social interactions we don't seem to grasp how far we will extend the power of this automatic categorization. A female student wrote:

> I came into this class thinking I would only learn about race and its pervasive nature in our society. I thought we would delve into the subject objectively, like scientists studying specimens. Oh, how wrong I was.
>
> This class has definitely changed me. For a while now, I have felt like the way we spoke about things had power. It could divide, it could unite, express differences, find similarities. We refer to people based on terms or slurs, in aggregate, and group form. Little did I know, this was the linguistic intergroup bias. Linguistic intergroup bias is a way of talking about an outgroup member that supports the stereotype of the out-group.
>
> This occurs all the time in all of our social circles and language communities. Use of the word nigger, cracker, even Southerner or Northerner shows how we talk about people as part of a group different from ours. I've been taking a "Race in US Politics" class as well this semester, and I've thought a lot about the terms Black and White in politics. If we continue referring to the represented interests based on race by referring to Black/White interests, aren't we creating a divide by using that language? Why do we have to split

everyone up? Can't we just have politicians represent everyone's interests as citizens and not just groups?

I know the answer isn't that simple, but it's something that I think about a lot, especially because I am in your course, Dr. Nacoste. I also think about how even the use of gender/sex terms could be a way of linguistic intergroup bias. When people, especially men, refer to someone as being a wimp they always use the term "pussy." Um, what? By referring to a female body part, they are implying that the other person, usually a man, is not a full person, but only a body part of the mostly deemed inferior sex, females. It really angers me when people do this.

Football is not for softies. Said that way, the motivation is to not be soft and pliant. But by using the phrase "Football is not for pussies," that language places us in a moment of group categorization and negative evaluation. An attempt to motivate is done by way of differentiating actual groups and demeaning one of those groups.

That kind of language is not innocent. It is not playful. It is not funny. It is not necessary. It should never be used to motivate males for anything because the language is demeaning to women. It's in your face, in the moment, demeaning to women even if no woman is present. When a woman is present, these are attempts to devalue and isolate that woman or those women, not at a policy level but at the interpersonal level.

Look, we carry our social experiences with us to every situation. If a person has adapted to gender situations with behaviors that put down women, that person will try that adaptation again. I am concerned. It would be disturbing enough if this demeaning-to-women gender bigotry were isolated to college campuses, but it is not. That is part of its sinister nature.

Truly sinister is the fact that these are social interactions, which means that what happens between the two people is in the young woman's experience and also in the psychological experience of the young man. Always in social life, which is all real life, each person is building a repertoire of social experiences with (good or bad) adaptations. There is some likelihood that the young man will take this part of his social repertoire into decision-making situations.

How did we end up with a national ad campaign for a car manufacturer that shows women bound and gagged in the trunk of one of its vehicles? How do you think it happens that in the midst of a policy disagreement among school board members a middle-aged male says about a middle-aged female that she's just "a prom queen"? How do you think these things come to pass? The impulse comes from past social experiences and adaptations. We let boys be boys, forgetting that boys will grow into ignorant men.

> *Guardian.co.uk, Sunday 9 December 2012 12.39 EST*: Virgin Mobile US has pulled an advert that seemingly made light of rape after Sir Richard Branson slammed the online commercial as "ill-judged" and "a dreadful mistake."
>
> The offending ad depicted a man holding a gift while shielding the eyes of a woman, an accompanying caption asks: "The gift of Christmas surprise. Necklace? Or chloroform?" (Williams.)

Ad campaigns? What? Are these not vetted? How could this happen? Well, it happens when we let people speak of women in demeaning ways, without anyone challenging that language. It happens when we do not challenge what is offensive; what comes across is that the neo-diversity of our society doesn't really matter.

It's all just a big joke, right? Well, no, it's not. Instead it is prejudice gone outward and public. It is bigotry, and bigotry has consequences.

A female student wrote:

> A friend and I were eating dinner at a restaurant one night. I met this friend at orientation right before freshman year because he was in my orientation group. Ever since then we have always tried to stay in touch. He asked me if I wanted to grab dinner with him to catch up, and he asked where I wanted to go. I told him that I loved this particular restaurant, and he said that would be fine.
>
> At the restaurant we were just sitting at the table catching up with each other and asking questions about each other's lives because it had been a while since we last saw each other. During this conversation my friend said something about how he didn't really like the restaurant, and I asked him why we came here if he doesn't like it. He said that since I suggested going there he did not want to be difficult.
>
> The waiter comes up to the table to take our drink order, and after I said I would like water my friend says, No, she wants a coke (as if he knows what I want to drink). I politely said, No, water is fine with me, thanks! I

remember sitting there confused and thinking why would he try to order my drink for me? He does not even know me that well. The waiter brings us our drinks and takes our food order. I was scared that my friend would try to order my food for me too, but thank goodness he didn't!

Once our food came we ate dinner and continued talking with one another. Then the waiter comes up and asks if the check will be together or separate, and I immediately say separate, but my friend says absolutely not! I am the man and you are the woman, so therefore I will be paying.

I still tried to insist on paying for my meal, but he was making a scene in front of the waiter, and I was getting embarrassed, so I kind of roll my eyes and gave in and allowed him pay for the meal. I think that when a guy pays for the meal it is a date, and I did not want to give my friend the wrong impression. That was why I was so adamant about paying for my meal. I did not think there was any reason for him to say that just because he was a man he was going to pay for my meal.

"I am the man and you are the woman, so therefore I will be paying." Really . . . Me Tarzan, you Jane. Is that the story he is living inside his head? The strength, the vehemence of his statements is quite disturbing. There is something sinister at work here, sinister in a way that can open the door to male violence against women that may have something to do with sexual assaults on college and university campuses.

In 2008, a set of researchers published their investigation of the factors that lead up to moments of sexual aggression in interactions between college-aged males and females. Here is one of the data-based conclusions: "Women were more likely to experience sexual aggression when they were with a man who made hostile, controlling or derogatory comments . . . or caused [the woman] to feel uncomfortable interacting with him" (Yeater, Lenberg, Avina, Rinehart, and O'Donohue).

Sound familiar? "*I was scared* that my friend would try to order my food for me too. . . ." We have seen these factors in all of the stories of gender bigotry that young women in my class have written about their own interactions with males. For too long we have taken for granted our destination on the Wrong-Line train. Now in the twenty-first century we have ended up here in a dangerous gender jungle.

Left to be boys, left in boyhood, not taught how to respect other human beings, we know how boys will behave toward women. We all know that left to themselves these boys will be ignorant bullies.

PART 4

GET ON BOARD, LITTLE CHILDREN, THERE'S ROOM FOR MANY A MORE

CHAPTER 7

THAT'S PRETTY GOOFY

Before my knees went arthritic, for most of my adult life after the military I started my day off in the gym. After my workout I would head somewhere for coffee and something to eat. That's it, that's all I want. Very focused on getting my coffee and eating something, I am not yet ready to engage in a real social interaction. I am pretty much delirious with hunger. All I want is my coffee and muffin. That . . . is . . . all . . . I . . . want.

One morning I was in Global Village Coffee Shop on Raleigh's Hillsborough Street. I was in line waiting my turn to place my order. Soon I feel a presence to my left.

"Excuse me," a voice says.

I turn and look down at a young White female. *I do not want to talk.*

"Yes . . ." I groan.

"Are you a professor?"

With the delirium of hunger aching in my stomach along with my cognitive need for coffee, I continue to look down at this little 5´2˝ White girl.

"Yes, I am."

"I've heard a lot about you," she said.

Oh, god . . . I need coffee.

"Really," I said out loud. "What have you heard?"

"That you're just a great teacher . . . very passionate in the classroom."

"Well, that's nice to hear . . . uh . . . who is telling you these things?"

"Oh, I have friends who have had one of your classes."

"What else have they told you about me?"

"No . . . that's really it."

"I see . . . then how did you know I was *that* professor?"

At this point, the young woman dropped her gaze to the floor, started to shuffle her feet. I waited. Where at first she was bold and almost flirtatious, now she is squirming.

"No, really," I said. "How did you know I was *that* professor?"

Still squirming, something occurs to her. She looks up at me.

"Uh . . . well, they said that you wear shirts like the one you have on now."

Most summers, my best friend, Dr. Craig Brookins, takes students to Ghana, West Africa. Before he goes I always give him a check. Only because we are close friends, with that money he has Ghanaian shirts made for me. I love these shirts: the colors, the textures, the styling. At this point I have quite a collection, and I wear them often. Even so, I wasn't buying the claim being made by this young woman.

"Really . . . so you knew I was *that* professor because of the shirt I have on. That's it?"

Now she is squirming again. I wait for an answer.

"Well, no," she said.

"What else did my students tell you about me that helped you identify me?"

"Well . . . they said . . . you were . . . a . . . big . . . Black man."

"Ah . . . good. I always tell my students that they should give a realistic description of me to their friends and family. Thanks for speaking to me and letting me know what students are saying. Excuse me, though, I need to drink this coffee and eat something before I pass out."

After I tell this story to an audience, I say that I think I have noticed that nowadays people are very reluctant to mention someone's race in a conversation about that person. People seem to want to avoid giving any indication that they notice a person's skin color. "Am I right about this?" I ask. No matter the audience, heads nod yes. "That's pretty goofy," I say.

Look, an accurate description of me must include how I look. Saying that I am a big and tall, dark-skinned, mustached, bald-headed Black man is accurate, not prejudiced, so it can't be bigoted. I look how I look. Trying to avoid mentioning that is just goofy. Unfortunately that goofiness has real interpersonal consequences. In 2010, one of my White male students wrote:

Earlier this year I went to a fraternity house with some friends before an NC State football game. I already knew most of the brothers on a more individual basis, but my other buddies had just been friends with me and a few other guys in the fraternity. One of my boys from back home, Bobby, who came was Black.

Our friend in the fraternity didn't mention to any of the brothers that one of his friends coming was Black. We all walked up to the door without thinking anything about race, only the Wolfpack. As soon as we stepped inside, it felt like all of the air had left the room; everyone became very still and controlled in their breathing. I was stilled hyped up about the football game and didn't immediately notice the change.

The next move was introductions and greetings. Looking around I not only noticed how rigid everyone's bodies had become but felt a stiffness sink into my posture. It suddenly became difficult for everyone in the room to discuss even meaningless football statistics and predictions on the game. It was even difficult for me to think of anything to say; my mind was blank in shock and confusion trying to figure out the next move.

Somehow my friends, including the one in the fraternity, and I were able to isolate ourselves by going to our friend's room at the house. Although it was some pointless excuse to go to his room, it seemed clear that everyone was thinking the same thing. As the door to the room shut, all of our voices became whispers. My friend immediately apologized, stating that he "didn't even think about telling the brothers that one of his friends was Black." Bobby stated that he was unconcerned and not to worry about it but not in the same tone of voice that I thought was typical of him.

Let me interrupt the story here to talk about the obvious. This all happened because, as the storyteller informs us, his friend "didn't even think about telling the brothers that one of his friends was Black." Too often nowadays, people work very hard to avoid dealing with the intergroup tensions in our everyday lives. For any social interaction we go through five stages:

Stage I. Each person assesses the situation: Where, Why, When, Who? Where am I going? Why or for what purpose am I going there? When am I supposed to be there? Who else will be there?

Stage II. Each person assesses possible outcomes for self: How will I be treated? Will I have a good time?

Stage III. Each person tries to find a cognitive, shortcut way of under-standing what might be going to happen (it's a party versus it's a funeral) or what is happening in the moment. We do this to avoid or to solve an actual or potential interaction problem.

Stage IV. Each person experiences large or small identity concerns that can heighten emotion: Am I being myself? How am I coming across? What am I saying?

Stage V. Each person engages in interpersonal behavior: What is said or done. We attempt to interact safely, in a way that is appropriate to the situation or interaction moment.

When a person stands in front of the mirror checking his or her clothes, that's part of Stage I assessment of the situation. It's just a prior assessment. You thinking about who will be there is part of Stage I. You saying it is going to be a good time is Stage II, assessing possible outcomes for self. You wondering whether your experience might change because the friend you are bringing is Black is also Stage II. You skipping over the implications of the race of your friend is made possible by the use of a cognitive shortcut—Stage III.

We get ready for social interactions so that we have some idea of how we are supposed to think, feel, and behave in the upcoming interaction situation. We do these pre-assessments to make sure we don't bring the wrong expecta-tions to the situations. Nowadays, though, when it comes to intergroup neo-diversity dynamics, we avoid the whole racial thing by a quick move to Stage III, where we find a cognitive shortcut.

Avoidance is using the cognitive shortcut "It's 2010, I don't have to mention I am bringing a Black friend; we're past all that." Avoidance that then ignites the interaction as it did in this case at a fraternity house, yes, in the year 2010. Now the whole plan for the day, tailgating and football, is filled with unexpected racial tension. As the story goes on:

When we ended up going back downstairs the house seemed to be back on balance. However there was a stale politeness in the questions and responses as well as body language. Shoulders turned away deflecting communication and interaction at all.

Although the initial intensity of the race differences had somewhat abated by the time everyone got to the tailgate, my friends from home and I stayed more to ourselves, facing each other and talking. As I moved from hometown friends to guys in the fraternity I noticed how both groups had formed these inward-facing circles of communication.

At the end of the day there were sincere good-byes and enjoyable memories as a whole. However, thinking back through all the occurrences of the day, and taking into account the subtle changes that took place, leaves stains on the memory as a whole. The awkward, unexpected, and sheer power of the encounter made my whole thought process muddled and uncomfortable. I have no idea how Bobby, our Black friend, looks back on the situation, but I am certain that he had the social skills and intelligence to feel the swift changes in the interaction.

Should a person always have to announce that they are bringing along with them a Black person, a gay person, and a person with a visible bodily condition? No. But each of us should have the social wherewithal and maturity to know what kind of social situation into which we are taking a friend or acquaintance.

So yes, you should think about potential negative intergroup reactions that might be set off when your friend walks into the gathering. You should assess the situation before you bring someone into that setting. Otherwise, even you will be surprised by how other people you think you know will react.

A White male student wrote:

It was a blistering September Saturday last year, and football was in the air. Opening week of the college football season, and North Carolina State was set to kick off the season opener at home against Virginia Tech. A couple buddies of mine and myself were pre-gaming at a friend's house before we headed out to the tailgate. Needless to say, three hours, one-fifth of Kentucky straight bourbon whiskey, and a Bojangles four-piece Supreme dinner later I was ready to help my team to a victory any way possible. When we arrived at the tailgating location, I remember the sun was beating down terribly and all I wanted was to get in some shade. Luckily, one of my best friend's family and friends were tailgating somewhat close to the stadium and had invited us to come hang out.

I had known this family for years, so I knew they would not mind if I was "slightly intoxicated." When we arrived, my friends and I were welcomed with hot dogs and cigars, so we took a load off and started up conversation. I had only been there for a half hour when my phone rang. I politely left the noisy area and answered my phone. I was excited to hear the voice of my good friend EJ, who I had played soccer with for years (by the way, EJ is Black). He was at his first NCSU football game (since he was only a freshman) and was looking for someone to tailgate with.

Knowing that the family I was tailgating with knew who EJ was, I assured him that he would be more than welcome to come. When I hung up the phone, I went back to the tailgate and told my friend that EJ was on his way. That was when everything went wrong.

Apparently, the friends of the family I was tailgating with did not care for Black people much, which was news for me because they went to the same church as I did, and I never knew they were racist. At this point my friend's father told me that I should call EJ back and tell him not to come. As he was telling this to me, I heard the husband of the other family agreeing with my friend's father, saying, "Yeah, tell that nigger boy to stay away from our tailgate" right when EJ was walking up. The look on EJ's face sent a feeling of hatred through my body that, with the help of the whiskey, I could not control.

I laid into the two families with no signs of stopping. I had already used every curse word I knew and threw up both middle fingers before EJ pulled me away and walked me down the road toward the stadium. Completely embarrassed by the way the families had responded to one of my good friends, I burst into tears.

I have not talked to the family since that day, but I still hear from mediators that they think I was the cause of the whole problem for acting like a "drunk ass." But the words EJ said to me while we were walking down that road remind me that it was not my fault at all. He told me not to worry because "it wasn't the first time it had happened, nor the last," he was just glad to have a friend stick up for what they believed in.

Now understand, just because you anticipate tension does not mean you should not bring your friend into a particular situation. What it does mean is that you should let both sets of people know ahead of time. Your friends who are hosting the gathering can tell you how they feel, and then you can decide whether these are people who are actual friends of yours; people who share your values. The friend you want to bring along can make a decision about going with you. Unless you take these steps, you could be faced with a situation filled with hurt feelings, anger, and resentment. Another White male wrote:

> The most intense interracial interaction I have ever had happened to me last semester. My African American friend RaShonda and I decided we were going to go to a party that one of our friends was going to. We had always been on good terms with our friend, though, at some points I felt he had some prejudice against her. We had had a rough day with schoolwork and were looking forward to a decent party to unwind and relax a little. We did not know the people who were throwing the party but assumed if our friend was on good terms with us we could be on good terms with them. Boy, was I wrong.
>
> We started off to the party looking forward to having a drink or two and just having a good time to relax. The party was out in a field, and we could see a large bonfire already started. We parked where everyone else had parked, and the first thing I noticed was a good amount of pickup trucks with excessively high suspensions and a few Confederate flag stickers on some of the trucks. I couldn't help [but] let the stereotype of rednecks cross my mind, which also made me think about the possibility of some of them having negative prejudices against my friend. I was a bit worried but calmed myself down. We were determined to have a good time, so we headed on over.
>
> Everyone seemed to be having a good time drinking, dancing, and partying around the bonfire. It wasn't until our friend called out to me that everyone noticed us walking up. The change in tone was unmistakably obvious. The loud fun dulled to whispers and murmurs throughout the crowd with some apparent looks of disdain across their faces. I felt bad for my friend, so I tried to play it off like it was nothing, hoping everything would pick back up. I tried talking to my friend [who] we knew were at the party already. Before getting halfway through my first sentence with him someone said it. "Who invited the nigger?"
>
> A wave of anger flowed over me. I grew up strongly believing that everyone was equal. In my hometown there was no outward expression of prejudice whatsoever. To hear someone say something so vile in public pissed

me off. The thought that anyone could say that was just so alien to me that I didn't know what to do. I was mad, confused, shocked, and embarrassed.

My friend's eyes began to fill with tears as she ran back to the car. I locked eyes with my friend from the party, who was laughing as if it was just some funny joke. With anger flowing through every ounce of my body I struggled to control myself. I shook my head in disgust and backed away to help my friend and get out of that place as fast as possible. I couldn't even make it all the way home because of the amount of frustration I felt. We stopped in a parking lot on the way back to my place just so I could walk around a bit to cool off before driving more. I have not talked to the friend that invited me to that party to this day.

Sad as you may feel about bringing up the topic of race, at least everybody knows where you stand and what to expect. Sad though you may feel, it is the mature thing to do.

Americans don't realize how much work they are doing to distance themselves from the issues of our neo-diverse America. "I don't see color" is one of those immature pieces of work. If I don't see this racial stuff, I have no responsibility for anything racial that happens even if it "leaves stains on the memory as a whole."

For my "Interpersonal Relationships and Race" course I wrote a book to be used as the technical reading for the class. When I first created and started teaching that course, I used a social psychology text on intergroup prejudice, but it did not suit what I was teaching or the way I was teaching. There was too much reliance on concepts that implied that White people had just found new ways to be prejudiced; modern racism, symbolic racism. That meant I was spending too much time in lecture debunking such concepts to keep my students on the right track. There are no innocent.

So, for my course I wrote *What Rough Beast: Interpersonal Relationships and Race*. "What rough beast" is a phrase used by W. B. Yeats in his poem "The Second Coming." Yeats was a believer in millennial change, the idea that every two thousand years some great change comes to humankind. He put it this way:

> The darkness drops again; but now I know
> That twenty centuries of stony sleep
> Were vexed to nightmare by a rocking cradle,
> And what rough beast, its hour come round at last,
> Slouches towards Bethlehem to be born?

My answer to Yeats's question is that neo-diversity is the rough beast. The year 2000 is a good marker for the explosion of neo-diversity in America. Neo-diversity has been born, and now it grows and grows. What are we prepared to do? What are you prepared to do?

What Rough Beast, my course book, is based on my extensive review of contemporary social psychological research on intergroup tensions. With it as reference for the technical parts of my lectures, my students get an in depth, research-based review of the social psychological concepts I teach. In the course book I also use stories. One of the stories is part of a discussion about the anxiety some people feel about "what to call" members of other groups. Part of that section reads:

> Right now, let's continue to examine the idea that in an interracial encounter the matrix of possible interactions and outcomes is less clear than in other interpersonal encounters. Why would that be the case? Interracial interactions are being influenced by dramatic changes in race relations themselves and also by changes in communication technologies, gender relations and international relations. It is all those forces pressing on any one interracial encounter that make the possible outcomes of the interaction less well defined and less pre-dictable. "Should I say African American or Black?" Some Black Americans say they prefer African American; some say they prefer Black; some don't care.
>
> One of my former graduate students is a member of the Lumbee Indian tribe of North Carolina. When I used the term "native American" in a con-versation with him, he said, "I don't like that. I'm an Indian. Anybody born in America is a native-American." OK then . . . in an interracial intergroup, interaction the matrix of possible interactions and outcomes is less clear than in within group encounters. (Nacoste, pp. 105–106.)

After doing that part of the reading, a student came to me and said, "I read that David wants to be called Indian."

"Yes," I said.

"Well, but isn't it true . . ."

OK, whenever I hear that phrase I know that the speaker is about to distance him or herself from the neo-diversity issue at hand. Here comes the historical, sociological cop-out. "Isn't it true . . ." is a set-up to imply that it's not about me, it's not up to me; it's about the truth that is up there on the mountaintop in the burning bush.

"Well, but isn't it true," my student said, "that when Columbus . . ."

"Whoa," I said. "You have just shifted the conversation from one person's personal preference to a historical analysis level. David is not making a historical or sociological point. David is speaking from his perspective for himself. He is telling whoever he is interacting with, if you have to bring up my group membership then I am an Indian."

When we try to shift from the interpersonal moment to some burning bush truth, it is a way to interact with the person as a representative of a group. Never do that. Never try to interact with a person as a representative of a group. As soon as you do that, you start relying on stereotypes. From the research on stereotypes, guess what, the person you are interacting with knows that you are interacting with them through a stereotype. Yes, members of stereotyped groups know the typical ways their own group is stereotyped. The person recognizes your reliance on any stereotype of the group; they see and feel the stereotype coming at them. That's when the interaction goes to a level the two people are not ready for.

Funny, though, how people want to shift to the big level to justify how they interact at the interpersonal level. Social scientists know and have known for a long time that when looking at an out-group, we have trouble seeing individuals as individuals. That is why we go to the big level even though we are interacting with one person. We try to wash our hands of our responsibility in this intergroup interaction by going to the historical, sociological, burning-bush-of-truth level. We do Motown proud.

"I heard it . . . yes, I heard it . . . through the burning bush."

"I can't help myself."

We do this because we want the problem to be bigger than us. We want the problem to be big and societal and so out of my, the individual's, responsibility. Racism does not implicate me as an individual; it is just a big damn problem.

Bigotry is close-up, personal, and interpersonal. Any person of any color, religion, gender, bodily condition, socioeconomic status, ethnicity, or sexual orientation can be a bigot toward some group. Bigotry can implicate anybody. That is why that term is so seldom used nowadays. It's all racism and racist, almost never bigotry and bigots. And there are no innocent when it comes to using this avoidance strategy.

To avoid having a real conversation about intergroup matters in the America of today, some African Americans rely on the sociological claim that "Black people can't be racist. Where's the power?" What a muddled argument. All it says is that right now, in this society, the material condition of African Americans is such that, as a group, Black people can't oppress another racial group. That argument has no moral standing. That argument has no interpersonal relevance. The argument says nothing about you, a particular African American, having the potential to be a bigot. Indeed, that is the point of the argument, to avoid the personal, interpersonal level of accountability.

To claim someone is a bigot, to call out bigotry when we see it, means to draw our attention to our own hidden prejudices. That is hard to do because it is hard to handle the self-focus that the moment activates. Holding the mirror up to look at yourself, becoming the object of your own observation, to see the potential in you to be a bigot, makes you run from the moment (Duval and Wicklund). We run, highly motivated, to find a strategy that lets our potential bigotry go by unanalyzed.

Now in this neo-diversity era of American history, before the darkness drops again, it's time for us to stop playing these games of avoidance. Any person can be a bigot, and bigotry can come in a number of forms.

"Go do what a woman's supposed to do for her man and go cook up something nice." That is bigotry. No, it's not racial, but it is based on a prejudice toward a whole group of people—women. And it is bigotry of a certain emotional type—it's primal. Primal bigotry is, yes, simple and crude, but its main characteristic is that it is so ingrained in the person that the person has no social filter for it. No matter the stage of the relationship of the person being interacted with, the bigotry comes out in a very matter-of-fact way. For example, "Who invited the nigger?" If someone even seems to have a negative reaction to the verbal or nonverbal bigotry, the person who showed the bigotry would be puzzled. That is primal bigotry.

A White female student wrote:

> After living in a dorm freshman year, one of my friends and I decided to live off campus. We couldn't find two other girls to live with that were available, so we didn't really have a choice but to sign up for random roommates. We go inside the office, talk to the manager and fill out our leases. A few moments later, she informs us that we are living with two girls, Ebony and Janae. I take the paper, which has their information on it so that we can contact our new roommates.
>
> As I am beginning to walk out of the office, my friend says, "There is no way in hell I am living with these two."
>
> In complete and total shock, I turn around and see the confusion on everyone's face that works in the office.
>
> "I am not living with two nasty Black girls." She speaks another cruel sentence.
>
> I couldn't even speak; little did I know how she really felt about living with girls of different race. Not to mention, the part-time employee at the front desk was Black. She storms out by me, and I am left standing there apologizing to him and explaining with frustration how shocked I am.
>
> This left me in a difficult position. I had my friend that stormed out, leaving me with these people that just heard such a racial and nasty comment almost as if it were up to me to fix this. Not only did she assume they were Black because of their names, but she acted on her thoughts. I cannot even begin to describe how hurt I was to hear someone I call a friend say that to people that we do not even know. This was awkward, hurtful, and hard to process.

Hard to process, she says, but by the end of the class she was able to use concepts from my course to analyze that interaction moment. Analyzing it, our storyteller came to this conclusion:

The minimal group effect is an automatic categorization of a person as either inside or outside of our group, with a tendency to compete when outside our group (Nacoste, chapter 3). My friend put Ebony and Janae into a category of "us" verses "them," assuming that they are Black by their names because the office manager never informed us of their race, just their names. So my friend assumed they were Black, put them in an automatic out-group, and then mentions that there was no way in hell that she was going to live with those two, which is the result of anxiety. She panicked, felt frustration and uncertainty. Clearly I had no idea of her opinions towards living with anyone of a difference race, and was in complete shock as I had mentioned, which is explained by correspondence of outcomes.

Correspondence of outcomes is the degree to which two people find their interests or preferences in or out of alignment (Nacoste, chapter 1). My preferences for who might be my random roommates were very open, while my friend's preferences were limited, and I had no idea. At the moment she burst and was overcome with anxiety, the entire interaction went downhill. That one comment was filled with hatred, and then she decided to tack on another comment that was caused by her high level of uncertainty and said, "I am not living with two nasty Black girls." At the time, the room fell silent.

To speak loud and proud, "I am not living with two nasty Black girls" in the presence of not just the White female friend but an employee who is African American means this is a primal reaction. No social filter at all. It's primal bigotry. That can be a reaction to any group.

An East Indian American student wrote:

Here is what happened—I am an Indian girl, born and raised in America, the child of two immigrant parents. I am all of 5'2" short, and as such, fairly harmless in my appearance. I also love ice cream.

On this particular day, I stopped by at the ice cream shop on a whim. I walked in, and the shop was empty except for two well-dressed White ladies standing at the register. One was fairly young and the other significantly older—grandmother and granddaughter, I presumed. As I waited for the granddaughter to pay, I noticed the older woman staring at me. I looked to her and smiled, thinking to myself it was nice to see a grandmother and grand-daughter on an ice cream date. She smiled back but didn't quite look away.

The cashier finished their transaction, and the young woman went to set the ice cream down on a table. As I turned to order, I saw the grandmother reach out and say, "No, honey, let's get out of here before the Paki blows up the place."

The cashier's eyes widened, as did mine. I stopped mid-sentence and turned. Shocked, I could do nothing but stare at their backs as they walked out the shop.

Grandma, what big eyes you have!

Talk about primal. Our storyteller had this to say in her analysis of what happened. She wrote:

I am a first-generation immigrant child—Indian in ethnicity, Hindu in my beliefs, but nonetheless AMERICAN. I have watched as the war on terrorism has grown. I have been saddened by both the loss of our soldiers and the loss of innocent lives overseas. I, too, felt the shock of the attacks on our country on September 11, 2001. And after this experience, in a small ice cream shop in the comfort of my own hometown, I can say, I have also felt the other side.

I was in disbelief at the multitude of implications in the seemingly sweet old lady's simple statement: "No, honey, let's get out of here before the Paki blows up the place."

WHAT!

At the time, I was stunned into silence, stunned that I could be so easily alienated in the place I was born and raised. Granted, I had been witness to subtle and outright bigotry between Blacks and Whites, and sometimes Hispanics. And I'd also been victim of the "smart-Asian" stereotype. But never had I experienced such twisted hatred directed towards me. Even now, thinking back to that afternoon fills me with an unprecedented mix of emotions.

I will perhaps never truly understand the thought process or justification behind that statement. But the levels-of-interdependence hypothesis does help me understand it a bit.

The hypothesis states that whenever the situational conditions surrounding a social encounter between two people creates or intensifies interpersonal uncertainty, the interaction between the two people is more likely to shift from a behavioral level of interaction (I looked at her and smiled; she smiled back) to a dispositional-identity level of interaction (No, honey, let's get out of here before the Paki blows up the place) making the encounter more volatile. Volatile, indeed.

It is important to note that the elderly lady and I did not go through this process at the same time. My interaction was quite frankly over after I smiled and as I turned to order my ice cream. I had decided that she posed no threat to me, even that she seemed sweet. She, however, was mulling over the fact that I appeared Paki, so she was likely stuck in the emotional stage-four before she made her comment. However, after her statement, I was also thrown back into the interaction, with feelings of shock and offense. To this day, I am still likely stuck in the stage-four dispositional level, as those feelings erupt every time I think back to the situation.

No situational filter, no common courtesy of social interaction. The older lady's comment was primal.

Members of any group can be bigots. There are no innocent. A White male student wrote:

So this happened last year during the weekend. One of my best friends is Black and said he had some plans for us to go out that weekend. He decided to go to a fraternity party (I cannot recall which one), and I reluctantly agreed, as I'm not a big fan of the frat party scene. But I thought it would be a fun little switch-up from the normal parties I attended.

Well, we arrived and I won't lie, I immediately realized something. I was the only White person there. At first I was nervous because I stood out so much. But then that faded as I knew I was just there to have a good time and that I probably wasn't going to be called out about it.

Well, we walked in, and this place is super crowded. At least 100 people in this tiny house. But everyone seemed to be having a good time. Me and my friend Anthony walked over to the bar where there was a guy offering drinks. I walked up to this guy, and nothing seemed to be wrong at all. He asked me, "What's up?" and told me to have a good time.

At this point I had pretty much forgot that I was the only White guy. Until I felt a tap at my shoulder. I turn around, and two Black guys were looking at me. That's when one of those guys flat-out asked me "What are you doing here?"

I was utterly shocked. Immediately I wanted to leave, of course. But I replied with "I'm just here to have a good time, man."

They then looked at me and smirked and walked away. As soon as they walked away I went outside and chatted with a few people that seemed a lot more "cool with me being there," and then I left.

I didn't understand. I wasn't being stupid or causing any problems. I was just White. At least my friend was pissed off about it too. But it was still pretty hurtful to hear those words.

Primal bigotry can really be let loose in the company of "my own." Already unlikely to be filtered, primal bigotry can be emboldened by raw numbers. In his analysis, this White male student of mine wrote:

The interaction described was a blatant example of vague interdependence and neo-diversity. Vague interdependence as described by Dr. Nacoste are situations in which the requirements of the interpersonal-interaction are unknown. Neo-diversity anxiety is the new social uncertainty brought about by the rapid and substantive changes in the spheres of communication of technology, gender-relations, race and ethnicity, and international relations.

Personally I did harbor a little bit of social anxiety, uncertainty of one's ability to deal with the possible evaluation focus that is unique to the situation in which the person is located at the moment, and the fact that I knew I was probably being categorized by the minimal group effect. This effect occurs when people take the most obvious things about a person at first glance, such as race, clothing, behaviors, and composure and categorize them into a group. Since I was the only White person there, I stood out. Therefore I was probably very noticeable, and it is possible that many generalizations and stereotypes where made of me.

A situation like this can cause the interaction to shift from a behavioral level to a dispositional level that causes the people in the interaction to search for the appropriate identity or attitudes to display. It also contains the affective consequences such as emotional and evaluative reactions. So when the man said, "What are you doing here?" I had an emotional reaction to it. I felt hurt, confused, and like I did not belong at all.

It was obvious they wanted social distance from me, a White man, at their party. Social distance has to do with the preferred types of interactions between groups. Obviously these two preferred not to have a White man there. I responded with "I'm just trying to have a good time, man." The obviously snide and disapproving smirk was enough to show me that they did not want me there at all. So once being asked the question and responding, it pushed the interaction into the dispositional-emotional level of interaction. They sneered and walked away, obviously still not wanting me to be around and holding resentment towards me simply because I was different. My behavioral response was avoidance.

Quite bold. Quite primal to walk up to someone and say, "What are you doing here?" when the only point can be "What are you doing here, White boy?" Said out loud with a smirk, that is bold in an informal social setting where a person, this "White boy," has arrived by invitation. My student learned from this, and, well . . . here are his analytic conclusions:

> Overall the interaction was one that definitely exemplified neo-diversity and the vague interdependence that it causes. Intergroup relations are hard to manage due to the ensuing interpersonal anxiety caused by these two things, which leads to interactions that can quickly lead to an interpersonal crash. As this story shows, negative stereotypes and out-group evaluations still exist and will probably always exist. However, it comes down to acceptance that others will always be different and about finding the maturity to cherish and accept those differences that will end situations like this one.

Some might ask, "Why could this not just be two Black guys having fun?"
"We were just kidding."
"We were just having a little fun."
"We were just joking."
Turn it around. Let two White guys walk up to the only Black guy in the room and say, "What are you doing here . . ." and then evaluate that. Still, I am aware that the "just having fun" excuse is used all too often today. "We were just having fun. What's the big deal? Why are they so sensitive?"

Hidden under all those excuses is the social fact that something has drawn the attention of the people who are "just having fun" to the person who is now the object of the fun. In the neo-diverse situation, the person who is the target of fun stands out by race or gender or by having a short left arm or by wearing a hijab or tattoos and piercings. Whatever factor about the person that turns the situation into a neo-diverse one has activated the anxiety of some, even though they are in the majority. Whatever factor makes the person different in the situation makes someone assume this person to be uncomfortable, to feel awkward in the situation. But that feeling may only be a projection and certainly is not one to be acted on to gain social advantage. Nonetheless, based on the assumption that the person must be feeling out of place in the situation, rather than approaching that person humanely to make that person feel more at ease, the decision is made to have a little fun with that person's vulnerability.

Why would it be fun to pick on someone you assume is already uncomfortable? To bully, that's why. Bullies target and pick on the vulnerable. And in this case because of the racial composition of the situation it is racial bullying motivated by two people who could not control their own neo-diversity anxiety about having someone different in their midst.

There are no innocent. Not even among the religious. A White female student wrote:

> It was during my first semester as an undergraduate student. I was living in the University Honors Village, and I was going through the process of meeting new friends. One day, I was invited to dinner with a new group of people, and I readily accepted. There were fifteen of us in all. I sat at the end of the table, across from a girl we'll call Tiffany.
>
> Tiffany and I started talking about generic college-type things. When we had finished exchanging information about our hometowns, majors, family pets, and siblings, she asked me what denomination I was.
>
> That was something that caught me off guard. "Denomination" was a word that I had heard before, but definitely not a word that I used very often. At first, I thought she was talking about money.
>
> While I was mulling it over, I must have given her a strange look because she followed that question with "I'm Baptist. Back home we have Baptists and Methodists. I'd like to meet people from different parts of the church."
>
> "Oh," I replied. "I don't claim a denomination."

"So you go to one of those new-age contemporary churches?" Tiffany asked.

There was a sneer in her voice. I remember breaking eye contact, pushing the food around my plate, knowing that my answer wasn't going to sit well with her. But I wasn't going to lie either.

"No." I eventually said. "I'm not a Christian at all. I don't really believe in any god; I'm agnostic."

She fell silent for a moment; her face turned bright red. I quickly tried some damage control, desperate for a way to move past the religious discussion. "I don't disrespect people who have religion. But it's not something that I want in my life."

"How can you say that?" she asked me. "That is so disrespectful."

I was taken aback. I meant no disrespect to her faith. I tried to explain myself better.

"I'm sorry if you feel offended," I said. "I respect that you have faith; it's a great thing to have."

I hoped that that would be enough to diffuse the situation. I was ready to talk about something more appropriate for the dinner table. No such luck.

"Well, you just need to come to church with me this Sunday. You haven't heard the word of God from the right people," she said.

It made me very angry. I had just as much of a right to my beliefs as she had to hers. I was appalled that she thought she could so readily dismiss my point of view in such a condescending manner.

"No, thank you." I replied. "I appreciate that your faith is that important to you, but I am not at all interested in joining that club."

Tiffany sat back in her chair for a second, then stood up very quickly. It felt like the entire dining hall was staring at us. I had never been more uncomfortable in my entire life.

"You seemed like such a nice person," she spat, picking up her still-full plate of food.

"But I am a nice . . ." I started to reply.

"No, you aren't!" she shouted. "People like you are the reason the world is so messed up. You are a sinner, and you will burn in hell."

I felt my face go cold. I had just been condemned to eternal damnation by a girl I had only just met.

"Who are the 'we' and who are among the 'they'?" is the neo-diversity interpersonal struggle of the twenty-first century (Appadurai). Sometimes when a person butts up against that question, primal bigotry is activated and something dreadful is said: "She fell silent for a moment; her face turned bright red. . . . 'People like you are the reason the world is so messed up. You are a sinner, and you will burn in hell.'"

Ugly as her behavior was, I feel sorry for "Tiffany." No one had prepared her. No one in her church, no one in her family, no one in her school had prepared her for the real world of university life. Somehow "Tiffany" came to a university with the expectation that most of the students at the university (or at least in the Honors Village) would be either Baptist or Methodist. How will she survive at a neo-diverse university with faculty, staff, and students who are Jewish, Buddhist, and atheist, not to mention Presbyterian and Catholic? With one new surface-contact interpersonal encounter that should have been simple, her expectations were so violated that she shouted in primal pain. I feel sorry for her, for the way her community put her on the Wrong-Line train and then left her to travel unprepared to experience a psychological discomfort so disturbing that her soul is in agony.

She turned red at the very idea that a college colleague did not care about or go to church. She shouted at a colleague, with condemnation to hell. It turns out that this can happen to anyone whose ideas and beliefs have never come in contact with a contradictory set of ideas and beliefs. It can happen to anyone—religious, pious, agnostic, or atheist. It's primal.

But how does primal prejudice and bigotry get established in a person? Remember, what makes it primal is that it is a prejudice so much a part of us that we do not even try to stop it from going public. It is so much a part of us that we have no social filter with which to stop it from coming out in social interaction. This type of prejudice and bigotry could only have been set in place in childhood. There is no other social psychological answer.

CHAPTER 8

WE TEACH CHILDREN

People often say that today's young generation has no trouble living with diversity. Yet the evidence to support that claim has never been strong. Oh sure, these young people live in a more desegregated America than has ever existed. But for a long time social psychologists have warned us about over-interpreting the meaning of the contact experience. Even before systematic, societal, desegregation efforts began, social scientists pointed out that desegregation is not the same thing as integration (Allport). Desegregation means contact. Integration means acceptance of, embracing of, enjoying that contact. Contact leads to integration as acceptance only under certain situational conditions (Pettigrew). Telling young people, any people, that they "just have to be more accepting" is not a situational condition that leads to acceptance of intergroup contact. So, it should come as no surprise that contact by itself does nothing positive when there are social forces telling young people the contact is wrong.

I am always working my students through false teachings from the Wrong-Line train. "Children don't see color" is a classic. Any psychologist, especially one who studies sensation and perception (Kalat), would start to choke and spurt if he heard anyone say that. Unless something is very, very wrong with a child's visual system—with the occipital lobe and the rods and cones of the eyes in particular—children do see colors, including skin color. I get my students to understand that what people are trying to say is that children don't seem to automatically give another person's skin color social meaning. No, it's not automatic. As with all things in the social world, children have to be taught social meaning.

A White female student wrote:

145

It all began with an innocent friendship. Danny and I were both in elementary school. We had met because we had class together and because we rode the same bus to go home each day. It quickly became apparent over the year that Danny and I were going to become good friends.

Danny and I chatted in class and always sat beside each other on the bus ride home. Danny was the coolest guy that I knew. We stayed to ourselves on the bus and sat near the back. I did not know any other children on the bus, and never paid them much mind; as long as Danny was there, I was happy.

One day on the bus ride home there was an incident. Some children on the bus, kids that I did not know, begin to pick on Danny. The children all started saying that Danny smelled bad. I was sitting right next to him, but I could not smell anything at all. The children were laughing and teasing him right to his face. Then I heard it, "He smells bad because he is BLACK!" I just sat there in awe; Danny was also silent. I did not know what to do in the situation. After the "Black" comment was made, the teasers busted into laugher and shouted other racial slurs.

How do elementary school children learn to associate skin color and negative judgments? How, indeed. It is certainly not because it's natural. It is certainly not because "children are mean." Children learn to be mean. Children learn to be bigots. But from whom? Well, "if adults can survive while the young cannot, the latter are obliged to ask their elders for knowledge from the start" (Weber). Adults teach children to be bigots.

A White female student wrote:

My best friend from kindergarten until fifth grade was Schar. We were ridiculously alike. We both loved to read, had Winnie the Pooh backpacks in kindergarten, smartest in our class, and we even liked the same boy at one point. The only thing different was our appearance. She had braids, I had pigtails. She had no freckles, I had a small colony on my face. She was Black, I was White. It was pure and unfiltered.

Looking back on our friendship I remember so many things that meant nothing at the time. People looked at us strangely on a daily basis. This tall, curvy (even in first grade) Black girl was glued to the hip with a skinny shrimp of a White girl.

One day when we were in fourth grade, after school Schar and I were playing outside at her house. We were swinging, and Schar looked at me and said, "Momma says I'm getting older and I should get more friends that are Black like me." I stared at her, continuing to swing and said, "But I'm not Black like you." She looked down and said, "I know." Schar's mom was the epitome of a smart Black woman, and what she said was law to us both. We looked at each other, searching for the differences that everyone else seemed to see. We brushed it off that day, but things began to unravel not long after that.

Please understand that children learn from us in many ways. Our writer points out that "people looked at us strangely on a daily basis. This tall, curvy (even in first grade) Black girl was glued to the hip with a skinny shrimp of a White girl."

We teach children by what we do with our eyes. A stare is not just you taking a long look at another person. A stare delivers an evaluation; it's a long and hard look. And when that stare, that hard look, is aimed at children we begin to teach them that something is wrong with what they are doing. In this case, something is wrong with you being friends with one of "them." Yes, all that through nonverbal interaction. Never forget that the child is constantly seeking information from the adults around them.

Nonverbal communication that can go on around interracial friendships among children is in this story, but also in the story is the verbal directive. Our writer tells us that Schar's mother was law to them and when she said that her daughter should find more friends her own color Schar had to take it seriously—this was mom talking. The law of the land had been spoken to two children who really liked each other. No matter their feelings, because the law, the mother, says there is something not quite right about your friendship. Not quite right comes across to these two eleven-year-olds, and they are left to their own devices to try to figure out what makes that the case: "We looked at each other, searching for the differences that everyone else seemed to see."

About her own story, our analytic writer said:

When you were young, little mattered. Your biggest problem was wanting to play longer, but dinner was already on the table. If you're lucky, you knew nothing about race or skin color, and it didn't hinder the way you made friends. This was at least my experience with my dear friend Schar. Not only were we inseparable; we were one soul in two bodies. Our brains worked the same, whether it had something to do with the books we were reading or the boys we were chasing. We were one, but we were young. When you're young (if you're lucky), you're blissfully ignorant of things meant to hurt you. Something like perceived race to categorize people into "us" and "them" don't yet exist. Schar and I had a wonderful friendship, and it wasn't until race was pushed upon us that our relationship began to crack.

A good way of describing the evolution of my relationship with Schar is to use interdependence theory, which describes and analyzes the different stages of the relationship from zero contact to awareness, to surface-contact to the levels of mutuality. Before we met, before that day in first grade, Schar and I had zero contact. We were unaware of each other's existence. The day we met was on the first day of school. We were five years old and in awe of our new surroundings. No longer were we in the preschool building—we were with the big kids, but we were alone. The few friends I met in pre-school were no longer in my class.

Schar sat beside me, and I noticed we had the same Winnie the Pooh backpacks. She smiled at me, and I at her, and this was our first sign of awareness. We saw each other every day and after the first week, bravely introduced ourselves. Our first move into minor mutuality was the day Schar offered me some of her pretzels. I had forgotten my snack on the bus that morning. I didn't say anything, but Schar noticed that I wasn't eating anything and slid her pretzel bag over to me. I took one, and we began to talk. We carried on this way for months, neither really knowing much about each other but enjoying our contact immensely.

Self-disclosure is the force most likely to be the engine for relationship development and evolution (Altman and Taylor). In this case, the self-disclosure was nonverbal. She "slid her pretzel bag over to me." It was a self-disclosure of concern for the other. "I care that you might be hungry." A friendship begins to evolve. Our writer goes on:

Then came my birthday. I invited Schar, and she accepted and she had the first glimpse into my life. This moved us into moderate mutuality because she met my parents and I met hers. We started telling each other about stuff that hurt our feelings, or how we felt when her grandmother and my grandfather died. We were only five and six, but this seemed very important. Throughout the rest of our grade-school years, we grew and learned together. We shared everything, not worried about paying each other back. It wasn't always peaceful; we fought sometimes but always resolved things and moved on.

This is classic relationship evolution where now the relationship has developed stability and depth. Maybe that's what brought it out. Maybe seeing her daughter developing a strong interracial friendship sparked anxiety in the mother, and that anxiety was what activated the African American mother's primal bigotry. Yet we must understand that when such bigotry is discharged onto children, it reverberates through the children. Our writer says:

Now that we've analyzed the nature of our relationship, we can move on to analyzing the actual interaction. To do this we will use the model of interracial-interdependence, which states whenever the situational conditions surrounding a social encounter between two people intensifies interpersonal uncertainty, the dyadic interaction is more likely to shift from a behavioral level of interdependence to a dispositional-emotional level of interaction, making the encounter more volatile.

In Stage I Schar and I assessed the situation, and this is when we recognized that we were different colors because Schar's mom suggested that she should find Black friends, friends not like me. This makes way for vague interdependence (without clear roles and norms and its unfamiliar territory) when neither of us are sure how to deal with this comment.

Do I agree with her mom because she's a grown-up and knows best? Or is she wrong, and Schar and I are fine being friends? Does Schar follow her mom's instructions or does she rebel?

That's Stage II: Assessment of Possible Actions/Outcomes of Self. This stage affected Schar more than me because she was weighted with the responsibility of whether to disappoint her mom and family and stay friends with me or do what they wanted. She was worried about negative evaluations of an in-group.

In that moment our interaction did shift to the dispositional level. This happened to us because we were worried that we would no longer be friends, which prompted us to move onto the next step, cognitive shortcuts (Stage III). We were just trying to get through this conversation with an appropriate answer. I had mental shortcuts, like "of course they don't like me, I'm White and they're Black." This may have not been true, but I felt disapproved of.

The next stage, which is the dispositional-identity stage (Stage IV), was when we were trying to figure out what each of us thought about this comment. I didn't know whether I should be mad. I didn't know whether Schar was mad or had she accepted it? Did she agree with her mom? She might have been subjected to more disapproval than me and was more actively searching for a solution.

This is when I said, "But I'm not Black like you." I was trying to figure out if I was the right kind of person for Schar, for our friendship. This was ultimately the unraveling of our friendship, which was partially due to lack of contact, but also due to external social opinions.

Real friendships are hard to find. Children start off doing it pretty well. Until, of course, grown-ups tell them to stop. That's when adults introduce children to the typical anxiety so many adults experience in trying to make real friends. It is an anxiety that comes from those adults' own childhood experiences that introduced the child, now an adult, to uncertainty and anxiety about being judged by other people.

A Black female wrote:

My intense interracial-intergroup experience was at age 10 when I was in about sixth grade. My friend CP, a White female, with whom I had been friends since first grade, was having her birthday party soon. This specific day she was passing out cupcakes in class and her party invitations. As I sat waiting for my invitation, I noticed the pile getting low. As she came over to me I realized that she actually had a gift for me. I sat puzzled but she quickly began to explain.

Very nervous and reluctant-sounding she began with "Hey, girl, this is for you." She continued with "I'm giving this to you because I cannot give you an invitation to my party."

I sat flabbergasted. Shocked, I asked why not, and she explained to me that her father didn't like Black people at their home. She went on to say that "I'm allowed to be friends with Black people at school, but bringing them home is another story."

I must add that I was the only Black child in my class and this was not the first time I had been rejected, but I had never really been "bought off"!

As you can see, this young Black woman was, at the time, quite confused. That's part of what happens to children who are suddenly confronted with primal bigotry from adults. Now we have seen this in two stories. Here is how our writer put together her analysis. She wrote:

CP and I moved on past this incident not being really good friends anymore but still cordial (autistic friendliness); we went on to be on the same dance and cheerleading teams in high school with no real altercations. However, I must say that I did learn a lot from this situation.

For me this was the first blatant racial discrimination I had ever encountered, and at the time I was not sure how to react. I did not know whether to be upset, angry, hurt, or accepting of what I was told. Should I not be mad because these were her father's beliefs and she couldn't change them, or should I be upset that a close friend of five-plus years did not stand up for me? Confusing as this was for me I chose to not be upset or angry because as a ten-year-old you do not have much power and adults are the center of your universe. When you have no job, money, or any means to take care of yourself, what the adults say goes. This interaction did not discourage me from interacting with other-race children, and I actually now still have friends that one parent is not supportive of them having friends or dating of someone of another race.

Too many adults do not seem to understand the power of their own bigotry to influence children. Or those adults actually want to have their bigotry influence the child. A White female student shared this story as her most intense interracial experience:

I had two very close friends when I was in our United Methodist Church after school care from first grade to fourth grade, Melissa and Robert. Melissa went to a different school from Robert and me, but we were both in the same Girl Scout troop, so we were fast friends. Robert and I met on the bus to after-school care, and we too were fast friends.

Robert was Black. This didn't bother Melissa or me, and the three of us were inseparable from the moment we arrived at the church to the minute our parents picked us up. Robert was one of two Black children in the after-school care program, and the little Black boy playing with the two little White girls was something that stood out.

Here's what happened: one day when we were 8, one of the attendants asked me to help prepare snacks to give out to all of the kids. Being Southern, the only thing I could do was to say, "Yes, ma'am," even though all I wanted to do was to play. This woman, her name was Ginger, was very quiet as I poured animal crackers into small paper cups, but I could tell she wanted to say something. She kept opening and closing her mouth like a fish out of water. Finally just as I thought I could go back outside, she bent down so she could look me in the eyes and said, "You know, you, Melissa, and Robert can't be friends. He's Black and you're White. You can't be friends with him."

I was literally speechless, and this is highly unusual if you know me, but I eventually managed a "Yes, ma'am" before I walked out of the kitchen and headed toward the playground. Out there I immediately found Melissa and told her what Ginger had said. We both looked at each other, looked toward where Robert was saving us a tire swing, looked back at each other, and we both knew what we had to do. We walked straight over to the tire swings, got in, and Robert pushed us. We could see Ginger turning red and getting upset, but we ignored her and kept right on playing.

Here we have a form of adult bigotry that puts two forms together. "Ms. Ginger" turned red, was upset at seeing the interracial group of children playing together after she told one that this was inappropriate. That's primal bigotry. What set up this interpersonal moment and intense experience for our writer was maternal/paternal bigotry. With that form of bigotry, the bigot tries to present himself or herself as not being hateful but simply informing you for your own good, something true from the burning bush.

Analyzing the maternal bigotry of the moment, our writer said:

When Ginger told me that I could not be friends with Robert because he was Black and I was White, I was expected to "yes-ma'am" her and never play with him again. Ginger's assertion that Robert and I could no longer be friends and her assumption that I would do as she said caused our interaction to shift from the behavioral level of interdependent interaction to the dispositional level of interaction. The interaction shifted from simply preparing a snack, behavioral, to Ginger suggesting that she knew more about my friendship with Robert than I did, dispositional (identity).

That shift pushed us into concerns about dispositions. This stage (four) is where members of the dyad search for the appropriate identity or attitude to display. This is also where members of the dyad experience affective, or emotional, consequences of the interaction.

Upon deciding to use a cognitive short-cut to get through the interaction I then had to handle my emotional reaction to Ginger's disclosure. I experienced hurt and anger that was amplified because it was on a dispositional-identity level. Ginger, an adult, had told me that my friendship with Robert would not or could not survive because of our racial differences, and this made me incredibly angry.

Before in my previous encounters with adults I had never been addressed about a racial issue that concerned me personally, but I was old enough to know this wasn't right. I was angry not only because of what she said, but because I felt that she had insulted my intelligence by assuming that a simple statement from her would convince me that her assertion was correct. I realized that if I were to express my anger to Ginger in that moment, I would cause myself to be caught in another interaction with her as she responded to my reaction, which is why I chose to use the cognitive script of "yes ma'am."

As I exited the kitchen and headed to find Melissa on the playground, I entered the final stage of the model. In this stage members of the dyad must deal with the behavioral consequences of the interaction. I immediately sought out Melissa on the playground to tell her of my encounter and to decide what we should do. We both knew that nothing Ginger could say would keep us from being friends with Robert, but we did not know how to move forward. We would have to continue to interact with Ginger every day after school regardless of how we felt. I had to act in a certain way in order to create new norms for interacting with Ginger. I decided to let Ginger know immediately that I did not agree with her statement, so we went to play with Robert when we knew she would be looking. When she saw us playing she turned red and was visibly upset by my behavior; I knew she got the message.

After this encounter Ginger never approached me or Melissa about Robert again, in fact she rarely spoke to me again, which was just fine with me. Twelve years later that interaction still shapes how I begin my interactions and how I develop my relationships. No one other than myself can tell me who I can and cannot be friends with, and if I decide not to be friends with someone it is never on the basis of race.

So that didn't work out quite the way Ms. Ginger had hoped. Backfiring is, I think, one of the dangers of maternal/paternal bigotry. If that is not warning enough, understand that just plain anger and outrage can also erupt in the backfire. A Black female wrote:

Recently, while on a retreat with my co-workers (orientation counselors) a common topic arose. We were all sitting in a large circle of 45 people or so, a mixture of race and color, 9 Black people, all holding a script for one of our skits we will have to present to incoming students this Summer. The weekend had been going great. We were all bonding, and as we were told to review the script before we began to read it aloud, a friend of mine and I noticed something.

Now, mind you, this skit is intended to dispel negativity as it concerns race, sexual orientation, social groups, and athletic groups, and so on and so forth. So, as I'm reading there comes a section where there is a list of about 50 words that are thought to connote negatively or "unacceptable" to be used here at State. Why were my eyes looking at the word "Black"?

Yes, I know that may seem simple or irrelevant to some, but to me and my Black friend sitting next to me, we were offended that what we are—BLACK—is considered to be something negative to say here at the institution we attend. Needless to mention White was nowhere to be found amongst the list of words like "Fag, bitch, cow, Jew, towel-head, etc."

I was furious to the point it drove me to tears because I didn't feel like that should be something for me to feel uncomfortable saying. I am not African American, no matter how politically correct it may be. I was not born in Africa, I was born an American. I am a Black American young woman who is of African descent/ancestry.

Moving forward, when my friend and I addressed the issue we were told that it has a lot of negativity behind it. As a rebuttal we said if you want this script to be uncensored and most importantly realistic and forthright, then the word that Black people find offensive should be "Nigger," or we could go so far to say, "Them, they, or those people."

All eyes were on us. "Oh, well, we can see about changing it," says the woman who helped write the script draft. "Yeah, well, make sure you do that" was my response. How dare a White woman speak for Black people to say Black is not a positive word?

Oops. Again backfiring is, I think, one of the dangers of maternal/paternal bigotry. In her analysis, our writer picked up on the bigotry that rested on the idea that the speaker was "just trying to be sensitive to *your* situation." She wrote:

Examining the situation from the beginning we can see the group composition had already set up an atmosphere which created vague interdependence; situations in which the requirements for interacting are unknown. There was a room with forty-five people in it, only nine of whom were racial minorities. This set the stage for intergroup anxiety; uneasiness brought about by uncertainty of how to interact with an out-group.

Also, the language in the script we were reviewing was an external force which contributed to the tension that filled the room. A list full of intergroup-biased phrases and words that is, ways of talking about an out-group that supports the stereotype of the out-group.

The leader of the discussion, a woman, and I had only made surface contact, and we never moved beyond that area according to the relationship-development model. Clearly this woman and I had two different ways of dealing with problems concerning race. From my point of view I simply wanted to make sure that my in-group was not misrepresented. She and the other scriptwriters may have thought they could see these issues from both sides, which was incorrect because instead of appeasing those who were a part of the racial group by including what they thought was a slur, they actually offended the authentic members of that group. This is possibly connected to the woman and the draft-writing staff trying to have a communal response to that group: Person-A acting on what Person-A believes to be needed by Person-B. Maybe this is how the woman and the draft-writing staff saw fit to try to alleviate negative racial slurs for Black people.

Once I read the script and saw that "Black" was being understood as negative, seeing "Black" included as a derogatory term, I knew there would be only negative outcomes if I wasn't to speak up. Now I was working through my own cognitive short-cuts and identity concerns based off simply reading something I felt like this woman had something to do with, when in reality she may not have had any input into the script.

But when I brought to her attention that the inclusion of a word that refers to my ethnicity was offensive, along with my increased self-aware-ness and emotional reaction, the interaction now fell subject to the levels of interdependence hypothesis: whenever social interaction creates or intensi-fies interpersonal anxiety, the interaction dynamic is prone to shift from a behavioral level to a dispositional-identity level of interdependent interac-tion. Because I was unsure about the intentions of including "Black" in the list, I was immediately thrust into dispositional concerns making the situa-tion about self-identity rather than it being a normal behavioral encounter.

In the woman's case, when she said that the word "Black" has a lot of negativity behind it, I believe she was speaking in reference to the conno-tative history it carries. But I took into consideration the unintentional yet impactful psychological influence that putting the word "Black" on the list would have on other people. I was concerned about the stereotype threat, the sense of threat that can arise when one knows that he or she can possibly be judged or treated negatively on the basis of a negative stereotype about one's group. I thought that this stereotype threat would be activated because of the racial tension the script created; the script says the work "Black" is negative when you came here thinking that there was nothing wrong with referring to yourself as "Black," which there isn't. How uncomfortable or awkward would it be as an orientation counselor to tell a new student "I'm Black" when that new student has just been told during orientation that "Black" is a racial slur and inappropriate to use? Very uncomfortable, is the answer.

There was an obvious disconnection between language communities as well. The woman thinking that saying "Black" was offensive may have been normative in her language community. As for my language commu-nity, many in that community find offense in more historically consequen-tial words like "nigger," "spook," or "jigaboo." Language communities and the language used within the communities are things that must be agreed upon by the people who are members. That's why I believe it would have been hard for the woman to understand that there are words that actually are derogatory and demeaning, and that should have been the guide to building the script rather than just throwing a person's culture onto a sheet of paper and calling it a slur.

In conclusion, there were many misunderstandings and inferences that should never have happened or been made. In this case, the woman wasn't informed of what constitutes a disgrace and what doesn't for certain ethnicities. That is why it is better to ask and be sure than to assume and be completely wrong.

It is always better to ask, if asking is necessary. I say it that way because I am finding that this kind of maternal/paternal bigotry is far too prevalent. Even in my own life.

I get myself in trouble by giving presentations to groups away from campus. People in nearby communities find out about my presentations on neo-diversity, and the next thing I know I am asked to speak at the UNC-Hospital-sponsored 4th Annual Dimensions of Diversity Conference, presenting "Delivering Care on the Neo-Diversity Frontier" on October 19, 2012. Now on the radar of yet another new group of people, I got an e-mail and a phone call asking if I would be the keynote speaker for an event for hospital staff. In January 2013, I was the keynote speaker for the UNC-Hospitals Martin Luther King, Jr. Memorial Celebration. Leading up to the MLK celebration, something odd started to happen.

I got this e-mail from one of the MLK celebration organizers:

Dr. Nacoste, I have attached the bio we have for you from the conference in October. Do you want us to use it for your introduction at the UNC MLK Remembrance on Friday? If not, please advise. Thanks again for being our keynote speaker.

I thought that a little odd since this person was letting me look at the bio that I had sent to them. In fact, this was the very same bio I had written for and that had been used to introduce me at the October conference. Odd, but it gave me a chance to add in a line about my new book, *Howl of the Wolf*. Updated, I sent in the "new" bio I wanted used for my introduction. That bio read:

Dr. Rupert W. Nacoste is Alumni Distinguished Undergraduate Professor of Psychology at North Carolina State University, where he has been on the faculty since 1988. He served in the US Navy from 1972–1976. Beginning during his service in the Navy, Dr. Nacoste has worked on diversity issues as a facilitator of racial discussions and as a scholar of interpersonal and intergroup relationships.

A native of Opelousas, LA, a Louisiana Black-Creole, Dr. Nacoste is always on the hunt for a bowl of good gumbo. When that search fails, he makes his own. No surprise, then, that the title of his published memoir is *Making Gumbo in the University*. His new book is *Howl of the Wolf: North Carolina State University Students Call Out For Social Change*.

A small matter done.

When I arrived for the event, I ran into the person, a White man, who had e-mailed me about my bio. We sat and started to chat. Then he said:

"Dr. Nacoste, I wasn't certain if you understood my question about the bio you sent us. Someone on the committee asked if the wording was appropriate; they wondered if you really wanted it to read that way."

"What are you talking about? It's the bio I sent you. Of course it's what I want used."

"That's what I said, but the chair wondered about the phrase 'Louisiana Black-Creole' being offensive."

My whole body went rigid. He noticed.

"I'm sorry . . . I told her that you were probably doing that just to be humorous."

"Humorous? That is my self-description, with no humor intended." My deep voice now close to a growl.

"I'm sorry about that, sir," he said. "I don't think . . . oh, here she is now, the person who was concerned."

"Call her over here," I said.

I did not stand to greet her.

Introductions made, I asked about her "concern." A White woman, she said she worried that her having to call me Black might offend me. Keeping full control of my anger, I said, "You are overstepping your bounds. I wrote and sent in that introduction. That means that is what I want said, verbatim."

From my sitting position, my head upturned, I looked directly into her eyes as I spoke.

"And by the way, your concern is not about protecting me. It is about you protecting yourself from being perceived a certain way. You might want to take a close look at yourself and figure out why you are so worried about using the word Black to refer to a Black man."

Although she was still standing there looking stricken, I was done. I shifted in my seat and turned my back to her. When the time came, she went up and read my introduction as I had written it, verbatim.

I walked to the podium and started my presentation by singing the first stanza of "America the Beautiful." Eyes of focused attention, smiles, and head nods were evident during my keynote. With that and the warm handshakes (and a few hugs) after, I felt that the forty-five-minute celebration of Martin Luther King Jr. was big success.

Understand that maternal/paternal bigotry is a shield for a person's self-concerns. And understand this, too: Black people do not all agree on a label. Some Afro-Americans prefer "African America." Me, I am of the James Brown "Say it loud! I'm Black and I'm proud" generation. In all groups there is variability of opinions. That is why no one should try to interact with a person as a representative of any group. If you do, that will mean you are interacting with that person as the group is represented in your head. That cannot be accurate for anybody you are interacting with.

So my student is only partly right when she says, "It is better to ask and be sure than to assume and be completely wrong." That only applies if there is a real question. It doesn't apply if the person tells you and hands to you the way that person wants to be spoken about. Not unless the language is that of group slurs, and calling myself a Black and proud Louisiana Creole is not a racial slur.

Americans get into this kind of trouble by trying to avoid talking about bigotry. We do not want to face our own potential bigotry. Well, as long as that is the interpersonal strategy we take, as long as we keep a distance from our own primal or maternal/paternal bigotry, we burden our children. We keep trying to wash our hands of our racial history by acting as if it's all outside of our control. Racism, it's just so big; I'm not part of that. The burning bush told me so.

We stay away from the interpersonal level where bigotry implicates us all. We leave it to our children to carry our baggage on their backs. Baggage they cannot see, but heavy baggage they can feel as we put them onboard the Wrong-Line train; baggage that can get so heavy our children's souls shout out in psychological agony.

We hope that the rocking of the Wrong-Line train will lull bigotry to sleep. That is why it can surprise us so much. Although it is we who have kept it safe and cool as the train travels along, we are stunned when something happens to awaken that resting, hibernating bigotry.

PART 5

I HEAR THAT TRAIN A COMIN',
SHE'S COMIN' ROUND THE CURVE

CHAPTER 9

HIBERNATING BIGOTRY

"Yeah, my family's struggling right now."

His comment came out of nowhere. We had been discussing teaching and teaching techniques. By way of an emergency in his department, an undergraduate himself he had volunteered and now was assigned to teach a lab section of a course. He was taking my general social psychology course (Psych 311) at the time. Having seen my teaching, he had come to ask me for teaching pointers. When I get that chance I always say, "Humanize the material."

I have seven principles of effective teaching in the college classroom. Principle 1: Violate expectations. Principle 2: Set a pattern for social interaction in the classroom. Principle 3: Assume that the students are engaged by your lecture; that they are really listening. Principle 4: Humanize the material; make the material connect to their lives, not just be relevant to the discipline from which the theories come. Principle 5: Show how work in the discipline can help to organize students' life experiences. Principle 6: Be provocative; based on the knowledge base of your discipline, make an argument that your students will disagree with, let them try to convince you that you are wrong, then demonstrate why and how it is that your position is supported by systematic research. Principle 7: When you teach, where appropriate use your personal talents and skills. I can sing, and there is a lecture in which I do so.

Humanize the material is the topic I talk about in a one-shot opportunity. It is the one thing that can immediately change a lecture and the lecturer. And for someone teaching a college-level physical science course, Bernoulli's Equation is the example I use.

$$\frac{P}{\rho} + \frac{1}{2}V^2 + gz = constant$$

P = Pressure

P = Fluid Density

V = Fluid Speed at a point on the streamline

G = Acceleration due to gravity

Z = Elevation of the point

Bernoulli's Equation.

I don't know squat about Bernoulli's equation. I have read that it describes fluid dynamics, which I also know nothing about. All I know is that somebody has to teach it to undergraduates. How do you humanize an equation? I suggest two things.

First, show a picture of Bernoulli. It's amazing the things we can find in the age of the Internet. The Victorian male wig is priceless.

Daniel Bernoulli.

Second, talk about the fact that Bernoulli had to rebel against his father to study mathematics. Having to go against family, I say to teaching-workshop audiences and I said to this young man, is something to which any young person can relate. That is how you humanize Bernoulli's equation. Doing that will change the lecture and the classroom dynamic. Bernoulli rebelled against his father . . . in order to study . . . math. That is when he said, "Yeah, my family is struggling right now."

"Oh . . . how's that?" I asked.

"My sister, who I've always looked to because she is so discerning about her relationships . . . well, she has found the guy she wants to marry."

"And that's a struggle for your family?"

"Well . . . it turns out the guy just happens to be Black. So now all the bigotry in my family is coming out; bigotry I had no idea was even there."

"Well, how could you know," I said. "I bet you didn't know it because everybody acted liberal and open."

"Yeah," he said. "They did until now."

"What looked like openness had never been tested until now," I said. "And now with a roar, that racial prejudice that was always there has awakened from its quiet slumber. That is hibernating bigotry."

It's not an unusual story. A White American female of Cherokee descent wrote:

> In high school I dated a lot of different types of guys during that phase where everyone's trying to figure out what they like and what they're looking for in a significant other. Some of these guys were real losers; they were awful boyfriends back then and have become less than upstanding citizens today. Another one, on the other hand, is now training and hoping to become a Navy Seal. He is one of the most caring, compassionate people I've ever met as well as one of the classiest and educated for his age. He also just so happens to be African American.
>
> So, one night my parents call a family meeting during my freshman year of high school, around the time that I had really started to get to know my aforementioned African American boyfriend. Unfortunately, I immediately recognize it's not a true family meeting because my younger brother had been sent upstairs and told not to come down. At that point, I know

I'm in big trouble—however, of all the stupid things I had done and could potentially have been busted for I never anticipated why I was about to be grounded. My parents, having heard that I had been dating a Black guy had hacked into my e-mail and AIM accounts and found evidence confirming what they referred to as "an embarrassment to the family" and "their worst nightmare." And that was it—I was grounded for almost a year for dating someone of a different race.

They told me I had destroyed their trust and they were so disappointed. I lost Internet privileges; if I had a class assignment my father would sit over me and watch to make sure I didn't use my e-mail to get in contact with Erik. I couldn't ride the bus to or from school because this guy was on my school bus route. Instead my mother would take me and drop me off and pick me up. When they found out I had purchased one of those pay-as-you-go cell phones in an attempt to call Erik, they took both the phone and my bedroom door away so I would have no privacy at all.

Eventually my parents started to feel bad, so they decided to hook me up with the son of a family friend, who just so happened to be a heroin addict. My parents would rather me date a heroin addict than an African American.

Yikes! This young woman writes, "Of all the stupid things I had done and could potentially have been busted for I never anticipated why I was about to be grounded." From that we know that this bigotry had not been shown before. It had been asleep. But now in this young woman's life, that hibernating bigotry awakened, roaring with anger, slobbering with hunger.

One of the things we are struggling with in America is what to call what. Some people are so desperate to be racially innocent that they see and hear things that aren't there. Stephan Pastis points that out with his "Pearls Before Swine" comic strip episode on the "Tie-Dye" problem.

> Pig asks Goat, "Do you think it's wrong to single out someone because of their nationality and tell them you no longer want them to live?"
> Goat: "Of course it is, Pig. That's very racist. Why?"
> Pig: "Because I saw a man doing that to Thai people."
> Goat: "What?? That's horrible! Lead me to him right now."
> Pig and Goat take off at a run. Then, suddenly, Goat has a thought and stops running.

Goat: "Pig?"

Pig: "Yes?"

Goat: "This guy didn't happen to be selling t-shirts did he?"

Pig: "Yeah. He was doing that too. Look . . ."

A bearded man, dressed in a way that some might describe as Hippie, is behind a make-shift counter covered with t-shirts. The man is holding up a t-shirt and yelling, "Tie-Dye! . . . Tie-Dye! . . . Tie-Dye! . . ."

Goat: "Boooo! Racist t-shirts! Boooo!!"

We have become so confused that we have jammed three concepts together and created a wrong-headed one. Prejudice is not bigotry; bigotry is not racism. Racism should not be used as a catchall term for prejudice and bigotry. But that is the way we are operating right now, confusing our attempts to label and deal with intolerance.

Prejudice is inside the person: negative feelings, negative evaluative attitudes about groups and persons who are (actual or perceived) members of such a group. It's prejudice because it is a prejudgment. It is a prejudgment because no one can know (or have an experience with) a whole group of people. But when the group is mentioned or a person who is a member of the group comes around, negative feelings rise up in the individual.

But that does not mean the person with those negative, judgmental feelings acts on those feelings. The well-socialized person can be in the presence of the stimulus for their negative feelings and not show any outward reaction. When, however, those negative feelings are expressed in behavior (word or action), that is bigotry.

Your aunt has always seemed a polite, open person. Then on a casual evening visit, you bring up the Defense of Marriage Act because it's in the news. A female student wrote:

My Aunt-B came over to my house for dinner one night in the summer of 2013, as she sometimes does. This particular night, the nightly news was on in view and loud enough to be heard clearly in the dining room and kitchen area. Brian Williams of NBC was discussing the Supreme Court's decision to strike down a key part of the Defense of Marriage Act or DOMA, a decision that had been announced earlier that afternoon and was making rounds in the news. It was a decision I was quite happy for, as it was a small step toward gay rights—a cause I support.

I was setting the table and pouring the tea while my aunt sat listening to the news program. I sat down happily, and we began eating and continuing to watch the coverage. "Pretty big decision that came out today," I noted, before putting a forkful of spaghetti in my mouth.

Aunt-B said in a distraught tone: "Oh, that is *disgusting*."

Silence. I didn't know how to respond.

Aunt-B looked slightly more uncomfortable now after I didn't immediately follow up in agreement. She followed: "Well, isn't it, though?" Her words took on a deep and slow tone, as if waiting for a nod of approval.

"The court's decision?" I asked to clarify, confusion bubbling inside me.

"Yes! *Obama* is letting *all the gays get married* and it's *ruining* the country. I can't believe how far down the world has gone. What's next?"

I sat there awkwardly for a few seconds—mouth slightly agape and a sense of shock running through me—before I could recover and calmly explain that the decision did not allow all gays to get married and that Obama was not on the Supreme Court and thus did not have a part in this matter. I felt my anger build inside—anger and confusion as I didn't know my aunt felt that way and certainly did not think she would express it that way or use the word disgusting to describe it.

Aunt-B didn't say anything—and now looked embarrassed for the comment. Head down, focusing entirely on the food. The rest of the meal was mostly silence, with a few mumbles about how good the food tasted, how it was prepared even though we already knew—and other awkward attempts at conversations. When dinner was over she hurried out. I didn't hear from her for at least a week after the encounter—and it was never discussed again.

You didn't even know that prejudice was in your aunt. Out of nowhere, it seems, you now are confronted with your aunt's primal bigotry. And though it is not brought up again in conversation you know that her negative feelings about gays and lesbians getting married is in her, hibernating.

So, although related to each other, prejudice is not bigotry. Yet today someone says something about those "damn Chinese," and somebody else cries out, "What a racist!" Racist? Wait . . . what is racism? First, racism is never inside a person. Second, racism is institutional; racism is in the laws and enforced customs of a group or society. We cry out "racist" when we see the old pictures of the goings-on of the civil rights movement. We cry out "racist" to label those Whites whose primal bigotry we see in those pictures; Whites screaming at, spitting at, and swinging bats at peaceful Black protesters. But we should be asking, how was all this bigotry in public allowed? How? Simply because the law supported that bigotry.

As I've said, I grew up in the Jim Crow South. Nowadays, because of hearsay teaching about that period in American history, too many Americans are not able to think through what that really meant. It meant that I did not go to school with White children of my own age because it was against the law. It meant that when I went to the movies, I had to sit in a balcony with other Black people, because the law prohibited racial mingling. If in the movie house any Black person tried to sit any place other than the balcony, the police would be called and would come and take that Black person away, beating that person with billy clubs. Bloodied by the beating, that Black person would be arrested and jailed for disturbing the peace. That's what it meant.

Gene Smith, an editor of North Carolina's *Fayetteville Observer*, writing on the fiftieth anniversary of the assassination of civil rights worker Medgar Evers, had this to say:

> The line inscribed by Evers' blood is important because it marks a point at which many people go astray and end up missing the point. Evers' murderer, Byron de la Beckwith, belonged to the White Citizens Council, which, like the KKK, was just another incarnation of the lynch-mob impulse. But here's where you need to let go of something you might have long held as true: The Klan, even in its heyday, was never White supremacy's great driving force. It was a bit player.
>
> The culprit was the law.
>
> The Klan didn't make it all but impossible for 20th century Blacks to vote in Mississippi or bar non-Whites from public universities. The law did that.
>
> Medgar Evers gave his honorable service to the United States in an Army segregated by law, not by night-riding goons. It wasn't the Klan that stacked the deck against Evers' parents, consigning them to discrimination and endless struggle against steep odds.
>
> It was the law.

Racism is what we see in the pictures of the police setting loose police dogs to maul peaceful Black protesters. Racism is institutional and organizational and operates at the level of law and societal authority. Racism is never in a person. Racism authorizes and supports prejudice and bigotry. Racism is what the civil rights movement was successful in making illegal. Old laws were voided and new laws enacted that provided Black citizens and all citizens with "equal protection under the law."

Despite hearsay teaching, few have come to understand this. It was because he came to that understanding that in March 2013, that the chief of police in Montgomery, Alabama, issued a formal, public apology to Congressman John Lewis, who had been a Freedom Rider coming through Montgomery in 1965. Freedom Riders were Black and White college-aged young people who boarded a bus together and took that bus into the Deep South, where, according to the law, Blacks had to sit in the back of the bus. To protest those laws, these young people rode the buses with Whites in the back or at least with Whites and Blacks sitting together throughout the bus.

Chief of Police Kevin Murphy apologized to Congressman John Lewis for the fact that in 1965 the Montgomery police force had allowed the Freedom Riders to be attacked and beaten with bats when they arrived in Montgomery. Murphy apologized for the police enforcing "unjust laws" that made the attack on the Freedom Riders legal (Giammona).

Today, when providing public customer services (e.g., movies), and in housing, restaurants, schooling, hiring, or getting your car repaired, bigotry is prohibited by law.

"Attention, Walmart customers: all Black people leave the store now."

That announcement came over the loudspeaker of the Walmart in Washington Township, New Jersey. Before the success of the civil rights movement, African Americans would have been forced to heed that announcement, because to not do so would bring the law down upon them. In March 2010, within days of the occurrence, the following report was in the newspapers and online:

POLICE: BOY, 16, MADE RACIAL COMMENT AT NJ WALMART
By BRUCE SHIPKOWSKI

Associated Press Writer

The Associated Press; 9:35 p.m. ET, Sat., March 20, 2010

WASHINGTON TOWNSHIP, NJ—A 16-year-old boy who police said made an announcement at Walmart ordering all Black people in a southern New Jersey store to leave was charged with harassment and bias intimidation, authorities said Saturday.

That is the success of the civil rights movement. That was the aim of the civil rights movement. Yet today some people seem to believe that the movement was about changing, even fixing, the hearts and minds of *all* White people. If that was the aim, then the movement was an epic fail.

But I say again, changing the hearts and minds of all White people was not the goal of the movement. Its goal was to force our government to recognize that the US Constitution protects all of its citizens from discrimination, from bigotry at the institutional and organizational level. That did not require Supreme Court justices and members of Congress to drop their racial prejudices. What it required was that we got those officials to enforce the Constitution.

Having served in the military, I swore the same oath that the president, vice president, members of Congress, Supreme Court justices, and other federal justices do, to "defend the Constitution against all enemies, foreign and domestic." It was the goal of the civil rights movement to get officials of our government to understand that racial discrimination against US citizens is an enemy of the state, an enemy of the US Constitution. Using that, the goal of the movement was to get those federal officials to repeal unjust racial laws and to write and enact new laws to prohibit American institutions and organizations from engaging in bigotry. It required that our institutions and organizations be held accountable in affording to all citizens opportunities to live out the American Dream.

Was individual racial prejudice and bigotry eradicated? Don't be ridiculous. But because the story of the magnificent changes that have come to our multiracial, now neo-diverse society is told in such a bland, bad, and hearsay way, Americans are confused and cry out, "What a racist!" when they encounter bigotry they don't go along with.

Our interpersonal expectations are confused. We fail to understand that there can be prejudice (potential bigotry) all around us that we cannot see because it does not show itself until the conditions rouse it from sleep. Without realizing you are doing it, you take the quiet that surrounds inter-group matters to mean that there is no prejudice on the train.

Then something is shown on TV, or a friend of the family sees a picture of you holding hands with someone on your Facebook page, and there is a temperature change in the intergroup situation of the train. A Puerto Rican American female wrote this:

> During the month of August in the year 2012, my grandfather passed away. Being very close to my family, I decided to skip the first week of my junior year of college to spend time with them, especially my dad since it was his father who passed. During my grandfather's funeral—and, yes, I mean mid-burial—my grandfather's sister, who is a Catholic nun, called me over to talk to me. She is a very big part of our family, as is our religion (we are all Roman Catholic). I am always pleased to see her since I do not get to do it very often.
>
> My grandfather's sister was sitting next to her niece, my dad's younger sister, my aunt Ivel, an artist and art professor at a major university in Puerto Rico, definitely on the more liberal side of everything. When my dad's aunt, the nun, called me over she asked me a very curious question. She asked about a picture that I had posted on the Internet, on a social network website called Facebook.
>
> On Facebook, I have various pictures uploaded with my friends and about my life. The particular picture the nun was asking about was a picture of my current boyfriend and I. She was curious to know if the boy (or should I say, man) in the picture with me was my boyfriend. My reply was a simple yes, to which she hesitated, and then said: "Oh . . . but he's Black."
>
> My boyfriend is a 26-year-old, 6´8˝ Black military man. However, I was talking in the moment to a Catholic nun. This is the person who is supposed to override prejudice and bigotry for the love that God has for everyone in the world. Or so I thought.
>
> My aunt quickly jumped into the conversation and clearly stated that

she supported my decision for dating whomever I wanted. Yet, the nun pressed the subject of WHY I was dating a Black man. I explained to her that I did not believe the color of his skin made a difference, since it does not make him a bad human being, does it? I do not think so, and while I was trying to keep my cool, I tried to explain this to the nun.

I felt myself getting angrier and angrier, extremely frustrated with most of my family for questioning the values of a man just from the color of his skin. I felt even worse about the fact that this was coming from a Catholic nun! The one person who, again, is supposed to override these thoughts and actions. I was not really sure of what else to do or say, so I simply walked away to watch my grandfather's casket be dropped down to the earth.

Temperature in the coach cabin of the Wrong-Line train can get warm really fast. Suddenly you hear the snores you have been ignoring grow louder. You sense the person next to you moving. "However, I was talking in the moment to a Catholic nun. . . . This is the person who is supposed to override prejudice and bigotry for the love that God has for everyone in the world. Or so I thought."

Sometimes you are real sure that there is no prejudice in your family's car on the Wrong-Line train. You are so sure that your only focus is to make sure that the visitor you are bringing over behaves the way a nice boyfriend should. You even give those instructions to your boyfriend. Then the moment is here and . . . well . . . let her tell own story. A White female wrote:

I had been dating my Filipino American boyfriend for about six months, and my parents finally convinced me to bring him over to meet the family. The only things they knew about him at the time were that he was two years older than me and a double major at NCSU in mechanical and aerospace engineering with a double minor in French and German.

So here is what happened: I drove him over to my parents' house in Cary to go out to dinner and have a chance to talk. As I pulled up I gave him the pep talk every girlfriend gives her boyfriend before he meets her parents that goes along the lines of "Don't say anything stupid and I'm sure they will love you."

We then got out of the car hand in hand and walked up to the front door. My mother greeted us there with a confused look on her face and yelled for my dad to come to the door. She opened the door and gave me a big hug and kiss. Then paused as if trying to force herself to say, "And you must be B." She then stuck out her hand to shake his as we all stood in silence. (This was interesting because my mom is what you would call a "hugger.")

We then walked inside and began small talk at the table, which was all about my life and ignoring my boyfriend. This began to annoy me because I see my parents several times a week, so they didn't need an update on my life. Trying to get away from the awkwardness, I offered to show my boyfriend the house. I led him to the backdoor but before I could follow him outside my mother grabbed me and asked to speak with me for a moment. I politely asked if she could do so later so I didn't have to leave my boyfriend unattended. She then blurted out that we wouldn't be going to dinner after all and that she thought my boyfriend should leave. I then looked to my dad and said, "What are your thoughts on this?" to which he replied, "I'm gonna have to agree with your mother."

I was hurt. I really had feelings for this boy, and he was the first one I had ever brought home, and my parents chose to hate him based on skin color. As I packed up my stuff and began to walk out with him I told my parents if they couldn't have dinner with my boyfriend they could forgo spending any more time with me, hoping they would reconsider. My father then said, "We would rather not see you until you learned how to choose a suitable boyfriend anyways." Right in front of B. I could see the pain in his eyes, but he kindly said, "It was a pleasure to meet you both." And walked to the car. I followed with tears beginning to fill my eyes.

Growing up in my house I was brought up thinking that EVERYONE should be treated equally no matter the skin color, so I was shocked that my parents could be so cruel. I was furious and embarrassed to be put in that situation.

Her boyfriend B was "a double major at NCSU in mechanical and aerospace engineering with a double minor in French and German." He was also Filipino, not White. No matter his other qualities, that difference was quite enough to activate "us versus them" neo-diversity anxiety. That difference was quite enough to awaken her parents' hibernating bigotry.

Hibernating bigotry is bigotry that sleeps until the situational temperature rises and revs up its metabolism. It might awaken slow and soft to ask a crafty question, "But why are you dating a Black man?" But it might awaken with a roar so loud it scares everyone in coach; so loud it scares even people in the private sleeper cars. "You are an embarrassment to the family. You dating someone of a different race is our worst nightmare. My parents would rather me date a heroin addict than an African American." It might awaken with a roar of manipulation. Trying to avoid having to eat its own young this once-hibernating bigotry uses its giant snout to move the cub's behavior in the right direction. "We won't be going to dinner." When that manipulation doesn't work, it rises on its hind legs to its full grizzly height, roaring and threatening with its giant arms and paws: "We would rather not see you until you learned how to choose a suitable boyfriend anyways." What was once hibernating bigotry is now a slobbering beast trying to trap you in a corner.

Hibernating bigotry can awaken crafty, primal, and manipulative. All the quiet has fooled you. Even worse sometimes, loving voices have fooled you with what seemed to be a clear message: "Growing up in my house I was brought up thinking that EVERYONE should be treated equally no matter the skin color." Suddenly, with a temperature change, right next to you, it begins to stir from its sleep. You react to the movement, turn and see that what you thought was just another person is in fact a monster, growling and slobbering with anger and hungry bigotry.

CHAPTER 10

SURPRISE, SURPRISE

Surprise is the usual response to hibernating bigotry—surprise, shock, realization, and hurt. A White female wrote:

The most intense racial interaction I can recall was one that involved myself and an ex-boyfriend of mine. Honestly he probably would be shocked to know that his comment hurt me so deeply.

First, it is important to know a little background information. He is one hundred percent Italian American, whose family originated from Sicily. I have been told I am Scot Irish, but my surname is English. My family has really not kept up with our heritage, so, therefore, I barely know for sure what I am, but at the time I was convinced we are mainly Irish.

He was at my apartment one day, and we were discussing things like food and family, and how they are connected. We got on the subject of how Italian families operate. He made it extremely clear to me that in an Italian family, a mother would never allow her children to be raised by someone else (i.e., daycare). He even went as far as to say that if it came down to it, his sister who has children would live in a cardboard box before she would put her kids in daycare so that she could work. And he was not saying all of this to me objectively as to just casually talk about the Italian culture; he very much felt like this was the only way a family should operate. He could not even fathom the idea of his hypothetical wife putting their kids in daycare to go out and work, and that was the point of him relaying the message.

His next comment was something along the lines that Irish families do not think this way, and that they basically do not mind putting their kids off on someone else for them to raise them. I felt like he had just knocked the breath out of me, I was so insulted.

The conversation ended with me saying, "Well, I put Leo (my son) in daycare because I have no other choice. I have to go to school so I can get a degree, so I can get a career started, so I can support him."

My boyfriend knew my situation (I am a single mother), and he tried to tell me that my situation was different, but his comments still put a horrible taste in my mouth.

Keep in mind that although my course is titled "Interpersonal Relationships and Race," race is only the prototype for intergroup tensions in America. In our neo-diverse America, national heritage can become a tension point (just as race can) that reveals hibernating bigotry during an interpersonal encounter. Using concepts from the class to understand what happened, our analytic writer said:

The Nacoste levels of interdependence hypothesis states that "whenever a (social) interaction creates or intensifies interpersonal anxiety, the dyad becomes prone to shift from a behavioral level of interdependent interaction to the dispositional (identity) level of interaction." That hypothesis could explain why this interaction went the way it did. Being that this was such an important topic to him, and to our relationship, really, there is a distinct possibility that the interaction created some interpersonal anxiety within him that caused him to blurt out the remark about Irish families.

For both of us, there were dispositional needs and goals in both people, and his need at the time was to convey to me how much he disapproved of women who allowed other people to raise their children. My goal and need at the time was to, yes, listen to the message with the intent to show respect to my partner, but once he made the remark he had infringed on one of my needs, and that was for my partner to show respect to me and to the culture I grew up in.

The neo-diversity effect is that because the interaction involved two people from different groups, the possible outcomes of the interaction are not well defined, making the interaction somewhat unpredictable. It is clear that this neo-diversity effect was present in this situation because it was an intergroup encounter that bred social uncertainty. The social uncertainty was not that we were uncomfortable with one another; after all we had been dating for a significant amount of time. The uncertainty was evident in how he was unable to know that by insulting Irish families, he was insulting me and how I was raised; he had insulted my ethnic group.

By the way, once the hibernating bigotry has awakened, you better pay attention. Carolyn Hax is a newspaper advice columnist. Almost every time I read her responses to letters she receives, I come away feeling that she was trained in interdependence theory. She wasn't, but that's how her column comes across to me.

Ms. Hax reported this letter on July 10, 2012:

Dear Carolyn: I recently discovered that my boyfriend has some religious and political beliefs that differ wildly from my own. This normally wouldn't be an issue except that when he met members of my family, he proceeded to make highly inappropriate and bigoted comments about them.

We discussed some of his views and he agreed to keep the comments to himself, but now I'm nervous about introducing him to friends and family for fear of what he might say. Is there any way to recover from this, or is it a deal breaker?

I was quite struck by the letter writer's statement that discovering the bigotry of her partner "normally wouldn't be an issue except that when he met members of my family, he proceeded to make highly inappropriate and bigoted comments about them." Only when it pertains to her own family, only when it's about saving her own, does bigotry appear to matter to this woman. Ms. Hax caught that as well, and responded:

So, if I think all (people of targeted demographic) are (stupid/lazy/bad drivers/cheap/dishonest/greedy/violent/dirty/suspiciously good at math), you're OK with that, as long as I don't say it out loud?

Slightly different question: Is there any way to recover from soft-pedaling bigotry as "some religious and political beliefs that differ wildly from my own"?

People with bigoted views are bigots, even when their mouths aren't moving. Unless your boyfriend said in response to your discussion, "Wow, I never thought of it that way; I'm wrong to believe all (whoevers) are (whatever)," then he's still as much of a bigot as he revealed himself to be when he met your family. And if that isn't a deal breaker for you, then what is?

That's what I mean when I say that Ms. Hax sounds like she's been trained in interdependence theory. To the letter writer Ms. Hax said: "People with bigoted views are bigots, even when their mouths aren't moving." I love the conceptual clarity of that sentence. If you understand the concept of bigotry, then you must understand that quiet hibernating bigotry is still bigotry.

We interdependence theorists and researchers do not mince words. We admit that people make mistakes in their social interactions, but we do not excuse such mistakes saying, "Oh well." We say that mistakes can have major consequences for relationship formation and continuation. We say that interpersonal mistakes can be deadly to the relationship.

Early in their full statement of interdependence theory, Harold Kelley and John Thibaut (p. 4) say:

> It must be emphasized, though, that when two persons are placed in a given interdependence relationship . . . their respective actions and their interaction may not be predictable from the properties of that relationship. One or both may misunderstand their interdependence and therefore make inappropriate decisions and one or both may respond with an inappropriate habit. . . . In the long run, if the inappropriate decision or habit is not deadly, we would expect it to be replaced by one more appropriate. Thus we expect behavior to be moderately appropriate to the interdependence problem [the interpersonal situation] of the moment.

Regarding the relationship between our Irish American writer and her Italian American boyfriend, his bigoted statement about Irish families was a serious interaction mistake. Our writer stated: "His next comment was something along the lines that Irish families do not think this way, and that they basically do not mind putting their kids off on someone else for them to raise them. I felt like he had just knocked the breath out of me, I was so insulted." His nationality-based hibernating bigotry had awakened and been let loose. For his girlfriend, our writer, his bigotry was a deal breaker, a deadly mistake.

Actually, the number of intense intergroup stories for the 2012–2013 academic year that involved nationality as the intergroup variable surprised me. In one instance, surprised confusion was what that led to. A White male wrote:

> I come from an interesting family—a mother from Kentucky, so down-south home cooking is pretty familiar, and a father from England, so I watch

futbol, not "soccer" (or "football"), and a biscuit isn't always something you'd eat at breakfast. So here's what happened.

I was talking with some of my friends, when another friend of a friend joins the group. I've never met him before, so I introduce myself. Fred and I shake hands, and then Joe asks where I'm from. I tell him I'm from here (Asheville, at the time), and he says, "Well, you don't sound like you're from around here."

So I say, "Well, my dad is from England and my mom is from Kentucky, so I think the accents just kind of evened out to nothing" in a joking manner. Fred responded, "Oh, you're from England? How's the queen?"

I wasn't really sure what to say to that. I moved away from him a little and tried to determine whether Fred was simply joking, or if he seriously thought I was on a personal level with the queen. So I simply corrected him and ignored the other part: "No, my father is from England—I'm just a dual citizen there."

At this point, I thought the conversation was over, but this guy insisted: "Oh, so you aren't an American?"

"Yes, I am an American. I was born and raised in North Carolina. I'm a citizen here and there."

I could see that Fred couldn't understand. His confusion manifested itself in some form of staring contest.

That was pretty much the end of that conversation—he fidgeted around for a while, and then Fred and my friend left after we finished talking about what we had been discussing before he arrived. But the entire time Fred remained, I could tell he was still unsure of what to think of me and anxious of how to treat me.

We no longer live in an America where anyone can identify another person as a citizen by the way they look or sound—if we ever did. That is part of the social interaction problem in this interpersonal situation. Another part of the interdependence problem of the moment is one person being so arrogant as to challenge another person's self-stated group identity.

Identity issues are always hot. Interdependence theory takes formal note of that in order to analyze how identity issues can burn into a social interaction. About the importance of identity in social interaction, Harold Kelley points out that "we have goals for the kinds of persons we are, the attitudes we have toward our partners, and the values we express in interaction with them. It is because of this fact that the partner's negative attribution [or interpretation] of our behavior, if communicated and credible, can effectively constitute a sanction, making us feel ashamed, and a challenge to live up to our standards" (p. 109).

Our writer's identity goals are to be true to the citizenships of both his mother and father. Mom is an American Southerner and Dad is a British citizen. To have that dual identity challenged is unnecessary in this particular interaction and in general in America today. To have that dual identity challenged is also not credible. No one can tell someone else who they are or tell someone that the ethnicity they claim is not right (Oxendine and Nacoste). Trying to do so makes the interaction awkward: "I could see that Fred couldn't understand. His confusion manifested itself in some form of staring contest." A staring contest? Awkward and deadly to the interaction and potential relationship is that moment, since challenging someone's stated identity makes no sense.

Analyzing his interaction with Fred, our writer says:

> For this interaction, the Nacoste levels of interdependence hypothesis hold true. As soon as Fred said, "Well, you don't sound like you're from around here," we were both stepping into the dispositional-identity step of the interaction. For Fred, I was challenging what he felt a member of Asheville's community should be like, as well as simply a member of the South. For me, Fred was not only challenging my identity as a Southern American but also my identity as a British citizen. Our interaction then began to burn more ferociously in the dispositional-identity matrix as we discussed in what ways I was both Southern and English.
>
> The whole interaction with Fred could have been interpreted better from both sides, and I still hope to one day meet "Fred" again, and potentially smooth things over—or at least understand his "How's the queen" comment.

Nationality as the intergroup dimension played a role in a number of my students' intense interpersonal-intergroup experiences. Whenever it was present and active, that intergroup dimension activated hibernating bigotry.

A White male student wrote:

Here's what happened. My girlfriend is from Sweden. That is probably the first thing I ever learned about her. She is extremely proud of her ethnicity and it shows. Over Christmas break she learned that her and her brother would get to go to Sweden to visit her family and old home and everything in January because she had that month off. She was unbelievably excited, and I heard about it for weeks and weeks. And that got really old.

So one night about a week before she left we were sitting in my car and I was listening to her go on and on about how amazing Sweden is and how much better it is than America, which annoys me to no end, and she knows it. She has always gotten upset when I don't get as excited about her ethnicity as she thinks I should. I just don't care that much, and I told her that. I said to her, "I don't get why you're so attached to a place you lived in for a few years of your childhood; you're an American."

I had no idea that this would boil her blood as much as it did. You would have thought I just told her I was cheating on her with her best friend or something. She snapped.

For the next hour she absolutely blasted me about how I would never understand and that Sweden was one of the most influential things in her life and the culture is so amazing and the government is perfect and every inhabitant is wonderful and happy and it's just the best.

Then I started getting defensive because I'm tired of hearing about how great it is and how much America sucks. What made her even angrier was that I wasn't getting angry and yelling like she was, so she could hardly choke out cuss words through tears. And boy, was she crying.

Then she started to push me away (I kept an arm around her, mainly in case she decided to hit me I could hold her back) and get out of the car. She said she was going to walk home, which would have been awful at 1 a.m. and a few miles away from her house. So I held onto her and tried to reason with her and apologize and ask her to just talk to me when she calmed down. She explained that Sweden was part of what made her, her.

To have an ethnic group is to have a sense of shared peoplehood. I am a Louisiana Black-Creole. Every morning Daddy (Mr. Nacoste) would turn on the radio to listen to Creole Cajun music and the news in Cajun French. With various people around town, my father only spoke in that Creole Cajun patois. Then there was the food we ate (and that I still eat): gumbo, crawfish-étouffée (a-too-fay). Not to mention mudfish and garfish. You put a little sauce on that, you got yourself something. Fans of the New Orleans Saints football team have stolen a phrase from Acadiana when they chant, "Who dat say they gonna beat them Saints. Say who dat?" I am of that "who dat" nation.

Visiting my Acadiana-Louisiana heritage can shake people up. Down-the-bayou way in Breaux Bridge, Lafayette, Opelousas, you hear a different language and you see a different language used on some signs. Language can wake up hibernating bigotry. That, at least, is what one of my students came to believe. In her one-new-thought paper, a White female wrote:

> I think a big problem today is that some Americans believe that people coming into "our country" need to learn to speak "our language." For example, I was with someone in a department store and there was a laundry detergent bottle that was completely in Spanish. She looked for the English side, but it turns out there was no English on the container at all. She said, "This is America. There should never be products in our stores that aren't in English. I wouldn't care if this was the best and cheapest detergent in the store, I would NEVER buy it."
>
> This shows how opposed people can be to different language communities that are unlike their own. Instead of letting the minimal group effect ("us" versus "them") take over, we need to embrace the diverse language communities that are present in our country. We need to take the time to understand others for who they are and not discard a potential relationship because someone looks or sounds different from us.

The language used to label a product means there are people in "my" community who may prefer that language. For some that raises the neo-diversity specter of "who are the 'we' and who are among the 'they' in "my" community. No wonder that hearing a person speak a language other than English in America can also set off the neo-diversity anxiety that "this is America; speak English." But trust me when I say, please don't go down-the-bayou way and tell some Cajun or Creole they are not American because they speak Cajun French. Don't ask a Cajun and Creole about their "funny-sounding" names just because you haven't heard these names before: Semien, Lazard, Fontenot, Nacoste, Mouton, Boudreaux. Don't do it. Just remember, some of those Semiens and Boudreauxs use their bare hands to hunt gator, and the gator loses.

American through and through, I haven't lived in Louisiana since 1972, but I cried in anguish as I watched the scenes of the flooding of New Orleans after Hurricane Katrina when the levees broke. If you speak to demean Creole Cajun culture, because of my sense of peoplehood with that culture, I will walk away from you because I am well socialized, and so I know that there are times to simply end a social interaction. Not everyone, everywhere, is well socialized. I will walk the hell away from you because my daddy taught me not to waste my time on bigots.

In his story of his interaction with his Swedish American girlfriend, our writer says, "She has always gotten upset when I don't get as excited about her ethnicity as she thinks I should. I just don't care that much and I told her that. I said to her, 'I don't get why you're so attached to a place you lived in for a few years of your childhood; you're an American.'" This is a stunning interaction mistake: it's not how long you live somewhere; it's socialization, how you have been shown you should feel about the group. I am sure that her parents talked to her about her ethnic group, her Swedish sense of peoplehood. No doubt there were symbols of old Sweden in the house and Swedish dishes were prepared and eaten, Swedish music was played, and Swedish-language books were read. An ethnic identity, a sense of peoplehood, was all around her in the home she grew up in, and there is nothing wrong with that. America has always been made up of people of many different ethnic groups, all of whom are proud to be American.

Our storyteller, this young White man, learned something from this intense intergroup interaction. He learned something surprising about himself. In his analysis, he wrote:

> Even before the explosive argument took place, we had been in a long-running conflict over our different nationalities. Generally this is a light-hearted back-and-forth, but sometimes one of us takes it too far and things get nasty. This quick shift is perfectly explained by the levels of interdependence hypothesis: whenever interaction creates or intensifies interpersonal anxiety the dyad becomes prone to shift from the given level of interdependent interaction to the dispositional level of interaction.

At the dispositional level things get very intense because we have emotional reactions. This is what happens when someone goes too far. We go from joking around to an emotional argument in a flash.

The conflict in my story however was not because of joking around. It was entirely a challenge to identity. That is what I did.

I challenged Jamie's identity as a Swede, and that identity is one she holds very close. I never understood why she continues to call Sweden her home, even though she lived there for a couple of years out of her life, and these few years were in her early childhood. I always wondered why, even though she was young and could not have understood or appreciated where she was or how it was that different from her true home, America. Of course this is not a fair or true thought process, but it was true to me at the time. And I told her all of this, and I just continued to dig myself into a hole trying to justify my thoughts even though what I thought did not matter at all, because I wanted to be right. I wanted power.

Power is the range of outcomes through which one person can move the other. Of course this begs the question, why did I want power in the first place? I was worried she was going to leave me; I thought she had alternatives. At this point in time she was looking at her comparison level for alternatives, meaning that if we have better alternatives then we will leave the current relationship. Truth is I was unsure as to whether she thought she would have a better life in Sweden. So I tried to tear down something she really loved because at the time I believed that I could gain power and be right and pound my chest in victory.

This conflict really came about due to the fact that when Jaime and I interact, it is an intergroup interaction. Intergroup means any interaction that occurs between people of a different race, religion, sexual orientation, nationality, ethnicity, et cetera. She is of a different nationality, so this creates intergroup anxiety. Intergroup anxiety is anxiety stemming from contact with a person we perceive to be in an out-group. While this is not one of the more extreme examples of intergroup anxiety, there are times when it is definitely felt, and during our argument the anxiety was very tangible.

She was so frustrated that she just broke down and cried and actually tried to get out of the car and walk home. This was where I had to come in and try to console her and make up for all my transgressions, transgressions that were very personal and cut deep, so it would take more than a simple "I'm sorry."

I became very apologetic, and I used language that conveyed respect for her and her culture. She calmed down enough to explain how she felt, and she told me that I needed to respect how she felt about her country, and that this was not about being right or wrong; it was about a need to feel respected, because everyone deserves to be. She said I had no right to tell her how to feel.

She was right.

I had no understanding of her situation because it was all so foreign to me, yet I tried to convince her that the way I felt and what I understood was right. In the age of neo-diversity that cannot happen. If I tried to limit my interactions to what I understood, I would not be with her, and I would not have many interactions, especially not in college. But this is difficult to work through because it is so hard to break from the cognitive-shortcut (ways of thinking) we have spent our whole lives forming.

It was unfortunate that stereotypes and motivational biases caused me to disrespect my girlfriend on such a deep personal level. Anxiety and power are surprisingly compelling motivations. That night before we started talking about Sweden, we were laughing and talking and having a good time. But once we got on the subject, the interaction shifted in the blink of an eye. I experienced the (stage four) dispositional level of interaction at its most intense, and it is interesting to learn about these concepts and think back to that night and see many of them in action. It is shocking and somewhat scary to see these concepts in the real world, but a deeper under-standing of why we do what we do has helped prevent something like this from happening again in my life.

The clear-eyed way this young man looked back on this intense intergroup interaction and drew out lessons about himself is impressive. To admit his feelings of vulnerability to the possibility of losing his Swedish American sweetheart was the only way to educate himself. It was not just that he admitted he was so in the wrong but also that he was willing to work to figure out why he acted in such a bullheaded, insensitive way. His analysis was impressive—and a good thing, too, because his relationship mistake was ever so close to being deadly to the relationship.

In our relationships we too often try to run away from our vulnerability. That is a vain attempt. Being vulnerable is a natural, unavoidable part of the human experience.

In her one-new-thought paper, a female student wrote about the way we try to handle our human vulnerabilities. She wrote:

> There are so many social forces at work, pushing on our relationships, our perceptions, and our social life that we sometimes try to deny the vulnerability. "Denying that vulnerability doesn't change the fact that sometimes we have been, can be, and will be interpersonally anxious, scared and hurt" (Nacoste, PSY491 textbook).
>
> Interpersonal anxiety can lead to the use of cognitive shortcuts and motivational biases when dealing with a person of another race, ethnicity, gender, sexual orientation, or religion. This is the basis of the push hypothesis: when the addition of an intergroup variable to the interaction pushes the dyad to interact in ways that do not fit the current stage of the relationship existing between the two people.
>
> Dealing with neo-diversity in the 21st century is something everyone must accomplish to lead a productive social life. While not everyone will be able to readily accept other people not like them, tolerance and education can eventually lead to acceptance and openness. Even people who live sheltered lives will feel the need to reach out to others, and when those people happen to be different, we will crash into each other with interpersonal anxiety and it will hurt everyone involved, unless:
>
> We interact with each person as a person—a human, live-in-the-interaction-moment, and interact with all new people in the same way—no biases, no stereotypes, no avoidance, no hostility. Neo-diversity requires people to interact with each other, learn about each other as a person rather than a group, and interact with that person based on the relationship status. If we have a protocol for interacting with new people, no matter who it is, our interpersonal anxiety will begin to fade and our attempts to achieve good outcomes for the interaction will become more positive.
>
> We are all vulnerable when it comes to new intergroup-interpersonal interactions, and there are no innocent—we all make mistakes, we all have prejudices, and we are all vulnerable to our behavioral and psychological consequences. But if we become more aware of such social forces that affect our interactions and work towards interacting with another HUMAN BEING, we—as a global community in the 21st century and beyond—can begin to understand our relationships more, become more positively involved in our social world, and be able to rid ourselves of intergroup anxiety.

Personally, with this education and new thought process I will be able to work towards equal and just intergroup-interpersonal interactions with all humans. There are no innocent, and everyone is biased, but knowledge is power that can be converted into social clarity and strong relationships.

Too often we do not look back on our own behavior to see how and why we have surprised or hurt other people. Too often, with interpersonal arrogance, we say hurtful things within the hearing of, and to, other people about groups to which those people have a strong sense of peoplehood. A Mexican American student wrote:

This happened when I was in high school in Asheboro, NC. I do not remember if it was in my history or English class. We were in class discussing/talking about (how and why) people migrate to other countries in search of an opportunity and a better life.

Someone brought up the topic of the vast amount of Hispanics that are seen migrating to the United States every year. Some people commented and said things such as many Hispanics come here because in their home country they are not able to find jobs that will support their family or because there is much violence in many of their countries—many caused by the fact that they are not able to support their family, so the lack of money can lead them to deviant ways to get the money needed.

This then led to where someone made a comment about Hispanics saying, "They come here to get free health care for their children and whatever other benefits they can get." Someone also added, "Those Mexicans just come here to steal our jobs."

After this comment was made I was shocked to hear what some of my classmates said and to learn what their thoughts were. I felt my face getting red, my anger was through the roof, and I could also feel the tension in the room.

The teacher then said, "Settle down class," she tried bringing the conversation back to the original topic, changed the topic, and eventually steered the conversation in another direction. But no matter what the teacher said, the anger and tension could still be felt in the room even until the end of class.

It is one thing to have a guided discussion about immigration in a class-room of young people; quite another thing it is to not anticipate that the topic might heat up and awaken the hibernating bigotry of your students. And it is even worse not to be prepared to manage the bigotry when it wakes up in your classroom.

Worse than hearsay teaching, the teacher in this student's classroom was not even attempting to teach. And that was a deadly mistake because now, those students are not likely to learn any real lessons about intergroup matters in America, at least not in that class. Bigotry has been enabled in that class (and possibly the school). With such attitudes expressed, we should not be surprised by some of the odd attempts Americans make to stand up for America.

A Muslim Latina female student wrote:

This is what happened to me three years ago. It was Sunday, and I needed to do some shopping. I went to the shopping mall. Once I finished, I thought I deserved a special treat. I decided to get an ice cream.

I was just walking, looking at the stores, watching people back and forth with their shopping bags, and enjoying my ice cream. I saw in the distance a young White and well-dressed man who was passing by. As he approached me, I noticed by his gesture that he was going to ask me some-thing. I kept walking and as soon we were face-to-face, his face turned so angry and his body got so tense at that moment that I thought he was going to hit me. I remember that I stopped eating my ice cream and tried to listen to what he had to say: "You should be ashamed of being here today, at least respect our grief."

What?

The time for me stopped. I threw my head back and frowned at him. I could not say anything, because I did not know what he was talking about. Why was he so angry at me? What did he just say? I tried to understand the situation and the reasons behind this man's behavior, but none of them made sense. I got my phone to call my husband and tell him about what happened. Then right there, when I saw on my cellular screen and I read September 11, 2011, I just realized his anger and frustration. I felt so sad that I threw my ice cream in the nearest trash can and left the shopping mall as soon as I could.

Once I got home I cried a lot, because I did not comprehend why I was to blame for the others' wickedness. Why did I have to be verbally assaulted just because I am a Muslim? I do not know what is worse, when people look at me with hate or pity because they believe I am an oppressed woman due to my veil.

Here was a person doing what so many Americans do on a Sunday afternoon. Here was a human being trying to make her way through another day, strolling through the mall, eating an ice cream. And then, out of nowhere, primal and bullying bigotry.

Analyzing her own story, our writer pays close attention to the power of stereotypes. She wrote:

The media plays an important role in this context, especially when the information provided to its audience is overloaded with linguistic-intergroup bias. That means the way of talking about out-group members "that supports the stereotypes of the outgroup" (Dr. Nacoste, 229).

As an example, I will talk about the language used by the media when some attacks are committed. In the case of Timothy James "Tim" McVeigh, who detonated a truck bomb in front of the Alfred P. Murrah Federal Building in Oklahoma City on April 19, 1995, his religious background was not the main point or even related with the horrible attacks. I am wondering if McVeigh were to be a Muslim would his religious denomination have been named and written in every piece of information about this unfortunate incident.

Talking to other members in the Muslim community about this tendency to blame Islam rather than the individual is a pattern in the media. It is so deeply embedded in people's minds that when I talked to non-Muslims about their idea about Islam, their first word that comes to their mind is terrorism. The recent Boston bombing incident where innocent people were killed by alleged Muslims is the most recent example of my position.

The disinformation and bias aired by some news channels about the religious background of the suspects confirm my idea about the linguistic-intergroup bias. I heard an "expert" about terrorism in a news program who said that it is so clear the extremist ideology of the first suspect's family in the Boston attacks, that he was named after a Muslim warrior that "killed millions and millions of disbelievers." I have been studying Islam for almost 10 years, and I never have heard about this man. I have been lately researching about this information, but I have not found anything. There is no evidence that corroborates the "expert's statements" declared in the news.

This kind of misinformation not only perpetuates the conflict but generates hatred among all sectors in our society. The influential role of stereotypes that took place in my story is relevant because they were the cause of the man's prejudiced behavior. According to the definition of shared impression, it is an interpersonal expectancy for individual members of a group and the group as a whole. What we think and believe strongly depends on the social environment in which we live. So, in my social environment I carry with me stereotypes that are shared with others of my in-group about/against the out-group. Then, more of our conversations would be loaded with stereotypes when we discuss about the out-group. The power of the group and the need to be liked may have a strong reason for a dyad to bring more stereotypes to the conversation, agree on those attributes, and come to shared impressions, making it more difficult to change people's beliefs. I assume from my encounter with the man at the shopping mall that probably in his social network people blame Islam for the 9/11 attacks, then whosoever follows Islam is at blame.

After that man's words, I felt assaulted, insulted, and feeling wobbly because I immediately thought: "Are the others looking at me in the same way today?" After this encounter at the shopping mall, I felt how the man's words pushed me into vague interdependence and sent me to search for safety.

Sometimes I forget about my Hijab or veil, and I feel like any other person around me. However, incidents like this one drag me to the concerns about my religious practice and how stigmatized Muslims are. In moments like this, I try to be self-protective and react proportionally to the nature of the threat. At this particular day, I felt harmed and decided to go back home. There was not the space or opportunity for me to answer this man's assumptions and make him know about what Muslims think and feel about what is happening. This so-called war on terror sometimes resembles more a war against Islam.

Finally, I may conclude that something must be done, because the stereotypes are holding us back from knowing people and having peaceful and positive intergroup relationships. This country is a mix of wonderful diversity. When I came to visit the US for the first time, what made me love this country was the diversity. People of different colors, different ethnicities, different religious practices, and different languages made me feel that I did not need to travel the world. However, after twelve years I sense that neo-diversity is becoming a huge challenge for us.

We do not know how to interact with out-group members or how to be tolerant with others' differences. We are not free from in-group norms, and we are not innocent of the discrimination and prejudice prevailing in our society. That is why it is a general obligation to work together and build a more tolerant and less prejudiced society.

One of my personal goals after taking your class, Dr. Nacoste, is that I am already giving myself the opportunity to sincerely meet and know people without stereotypes and deal with them without prejudice. I want to deal with a person as an individual, not as a member of a group; the same attitude I desire toward me.

Sometimes we are at fault because out of fear we prefer to isolate ourselves and avoid any interrelation with others different from us, and this is a great mistake. We are giving away the possibility to know more about others and learn about different things and become wiser and learned. There is so much to learn about others, so much to understand about others, and so much to accept about others that I hope I could live to see a country joined for a common goal, which is the well-being of its people; peaceful lives and prosperity.

No one can stand up for America using stereotypes. That is the lesson. Stereotypes are not patriotic. Stereotypes are not the armor of patriots. Active use of stereotypes is not just bigotry but an enemy of American patriotism.

I took the oath in 1972. And since then I have carried that oath in my mind, and in my heart. The oath serves as part of my motivation in my work. What oath? I speak of the oath to "defend the Constitution against all enemies, foreign and domestic." Prejudice, bigotry, and racism are domestic enemies of the American way of life. Our Declaration of Independence says that all "are created equal, that they are endowed . . . with certain unalienable rights, that among these are life, liberty, and the pursuit of happiness." Eating ice cream and walking the mall is one of the simple, pleasant ways to pursue happiness. All are entitled to a walk in the mall eating ice cream, without fear of being accosted and demeaned for the racial, gender, ethnic, religious, bodily conditioned, sexually oriented group they happen to hail from. Violating that is a violation of our shared values in the United States, and I will fight against this evil and domestic enemy of the state. I took the oath, so I fight stereotypes in my life and with my teaching. Stereotypes are an enemy of the state, an enemy bent on preventing our attempts to build a more perfect union.

Stereotypes are the whistle announcing the Wrong-Line train. Listening to that loud whistle makes it hard for us to hear and accept the true nature of America. Listening to that loud and misleading whistle is how we end up doing and saying things that make all Americans look ignorant and shows some Americans to be bullies in the face of their own neo-diversity anxieties.

CHAPTER 11

THINE ALABASTER CITIES GLEAM

Until the e-mails started to come in, I had not heard about it. Keeping up is never a problem, though, because my students are out there scanning the social environment. Whether they are taking or have taken my class, the experience puts my students on alert for examples of neo-diversity dynamics. When something happens related to neo-diversity, they send me word. So, no, I hadn't heard about the reaction to Marc Antony singing "God Bless America" at the Major League All-Star Game, but word came to me in an e-mail.

July 18, 2013

I was interviewed yesterday for the food access educator position at. . . . I am assuming that the next week will be contacting references. Below I have attached the job description and the cover letter. I have given them the University e-mail address and the phone number for the office. Thank you so much for everything, and I am glad that I was able to meet up with you!

I have lots of stories to send you about race, for example this:

http://publicshaming.tumblr.com/post/55715208108/baseball -fans-super-angry-hispanic-american-superstar

An example of social media used the wrong way. . . . Hope you're doing well!

N.

I clicked on the story and first saw the headline:

BASEBALL FANS SUPER ANGRY HISPANIC AMERICAN SUPERSTAR
SANG "GOD BLESS AMERICA" AT ALL-STAR

Some of the comments on the article included:

> Welcome to America where god bless america is sung at our national pastime
> by a mexican.
>> Another disgrace. Marc Antony singing God Bless America. Is he even
> an American citizen?

These are two of the cleaner comments. So I understood what N meant when she wrote: "An example of social media used the wrong way. . . ."

But now I needed help. It's just that I have seen so many online stories where the comment sections are filled with ignorance and bigotry that I wondered what such comments are telling us about the state of America today. Are these comments diagnostic?

The previous April a young Black man who had taken both of my classes e-mailed with the subject: "Bigotry is rampant." He wrote:

> I read these very short pieces attached to these photos and was just amazed,
> Dr. Nacoste. It is a shirt that Jamie Foxx wore to the MTV Awards this past
> week with Trayvon Martin and the Newtown Kids on it. Just speechless
> with the audacious responses that people have created. Bigotry is rampant
> and unapologetically professed.

I clicked but could only stand to read a few of the responses:

> Comment A: "F*** that nigger with the Trayvon Martin shirt on."
> Comment B: "Jaime foxx arrives at the MTV awards wearing a shirt with a
>   dead nigger criminals on it. Sad."

Profane and filled with racial slurs, these remarks were raw, primal bigotry that had been hibernating. I asked myself, does being online and anonymous make it easier to let the monster loose? I wondered. I responded to my student N, an American of Dominican descent.

> I just said to the "Interpersonal Relationships and Race" class, "I believe
> with all my heart that the major problem for America is intolerant language;

language bigotry. If we don't get this under control, we are all going down."
Yes, it is rampant, it is sad, but it is dangerous; very dangerous for our neo-
diverse America.

Still, I struggled with how to think about the online profanity and
bigotry. How much is there to worry about? I wonder about the goals of those
who commented. What was the point of writing that kind of reaction? Can
those who wrote with such vitriol believe that their expressions would stop
the neo-diversity change going on in America? Are these comments meant to
intimidate and bully?

At this time I was also in the midst of reviewing my students' submis-
sions of their most intense interracial-intergroup experiences. I received this
comment in a paper from a White male student:

> Here's what happened. . . . My friend and I were playing "Call of Duty" on
> Xbox Live one afternoon. Xbox Live is live gaming with other individuals
> from all over the world; therefore, these are more virtual interactions. People
> communicate through headsets and are able to talk to people on the other
> team, as well as teammates.

My students are usually kind to me in this way. They know a few relevant
things about my limitations. This young traveler was giving me enough
information to understand the setting and nature of the interaction so I could
follow what happened. He did this because he knew that I know nothing
about video games. He went on to say:

> There is no modesty on Xbox, people curse and throw around racial slurs
> like it's nothing; mostly because it isn't a face-to-face interaction. So my
> friend Dylan and I were randomly paired to play with some Black guys from
> New York. The reason I knew they were from New York is because they told
> me they were from Brooklyn.
>
> So the situation is, Dylan and I (both White) interacting with two Black
> guys. Someone on the other team said something racial to the Black guys,
> probably something like "Shut up, you dumb Ni**ers." So after the game
> had started, the Black guys proceeded to respond to the other White players'

racial malice. Unfortunately you can only talk to players on your team when the game starts, so it was just Dylan, me, and the Black guys. The Black guys turned to Dylan and me to trash talk because we were clearly White.

They said that White people were so stupid and were the reason the world was going to "shit." If White people would just get out of Obama's way, every problem would be solved. They said that Black people dress nicer, spend money on better things, make better music, and that White people were just a bunch of rednecks. They went on and on, and it was actually kind of funny because they were obviously mad. Then, one of them said, "The world would be better off without White people. Black people may commit crimes, but at least we aren't serial killers. You only see White people doing that crazy shit; like shooting up movie theaters on the premier of batman, or shooting up schools with little kids. Ya'll are crazy, that's why we don't have rights anymore, because of White people."

So I began to get a little offended at them blaming all White people for mass murders. Dylan and I began to respond in the same manner, by generalizing the Black race. Dylan said, "Ya'll don't dress better, at least we actually wear our pants on our waistlines. We talk more proper and don't say "nigga" every other word. And ya'll spend ya'll's money on stupid stuff like rims and superhero vinyl's for your cars." So as you can imagine, the Black guys began to get angry again and started to say more bad things and generalize White people even more. When talk of serial killers reemerged, I had to add in my own generalization. I said, "Well, the reason Black people aren't usually associated with mass shootings is because ya'll hold your guns sideways and probably couldn't even afford a machine gun to use in a shooting."

Some of the things that were said were down-right hate talk, while some of it was to try to make your buddy laugh. At the same time, it was pretty heated and nothing but complete generalizations of different racial groups. I have been in other interracial encounters (not confrontational ones), but this one just kept coming to mind, not to mention it was pretty recent. None of us playing that day would have ever said anything like that if we were face to face, and that's what makes this encounter interesting.

I was thinking about all this because of the e-mail from N. She had asked me to read the story about people's responses to Marc Antony singing "God Bless America" at the All-Star game. In response to her e-mail I asked N for her thoughts.

So, about the online response to Marc Antony singing "God Bless America . . ." Everything I see from commentators online when it comes to race is really awful. My question is, who does this represent? I ask that so that I can also ask, how seriously should we take such responses? What are your thoughts?

In reply N said:

> In terms of who is saying these things, I think it represents the average person's thoughts regarding this issue . . . it is just crazy to me just how much ignorance there is and how to overcome that. Rather overwhelming . . . that's how I feel. . . .

I replied:

> Sadly, I think you are right. Which means we all have to pay attention to this crap. Take a breath . . . I always have to.

The same day, while I was reading the Marc Antony story and interacting with N online, there came another e-mail. The subject line read, "I thought this would interest you." L, a Puerto Rican American, wrote:

> I'm not sure if you've heard about this recent incident, but I thought I would write you about it. I really think you could use it in your classes.
>
> Knowing you aren't really very interested in sports, I wasn't sure if you would already know about it. The MLB [Major League Baseball] All-Star game was last weekend, I believe, and the person who sang "God Bless America" at the game was Marc Anthony . . . a New Yorker of Puerto Rican descent. I think you should read these articles about the "American" public's reaction to this. The first link is a completely serious article, the second link is a comedic (of sorts) article—it plays a lot on sarcasm.
>
> http://nbclatino.com/2013/07/17/baseball-fans-take-to-twitter-to -protest-marc-anthony-singing-god-bless-america/
>
> http://publicshaming.tumblr.com/post/55715208108/baseball-fans -super-angry-hispanic-american-superstar
>
> Let me know what you think. I don't even have words to express my anger towards this right now.

I replied:

> I was stunned when I heard about this. I was also angry, so I completely
> understand your anger. All this stuff is about neo-diversity anxiety. Keep
> your head about you.

You would think that some Americans have taken as reality the third
stanza of "America the Beautiful." In part, that stanza reads:

> *O beautiful for patriot dream*
> *That sees beyond the years*
> *Thine alabaster cities gleam*
> *Undimmed by human tears!*
> *America! America!*

Alabaster . . . White . . .

Of course "alabaster" does not have to refer to skin color. The reference to
gleaming cities could be literal. But our American racial history is the context
that makes it seem to me the lyric could be taken to also refer to a racial ambition. I could be wrong, but look at the history of our language about race. I
grew up hearing, "If you're White, you're right; if you're Brown, stick around;
if you're Black, get back." The racial ambition is the idea that White is the
right American. But, as we know it turns out, that was never America, and
it certainly is not America today. Today we live and travel in a very colorful,
neo-diverse world. But something is up.

Native New Yorker, to say again, *native* New Yorker Marc Antony sings
"God Bless America" and attracts comments of dismayed bigotry like "*Why is*
this spic" allowed to sing "God Bless America." Are we really rearing a generation of people who believe that to be American means to be White or at least
nonethnic? Referring to "White Americans" is not a reference to ethnicity but
a reference to race; race is also what we are referring to when we use the phrase
"African American." Ethnicity is a sense of group-ness; a sense of peoplehood.

That is why we should really pay attention to the research evidence indi-
cating that being identified as American is psychologically associated with
being White. In a 2005 article published in a leading social psychological

research journal, Thierry Devos and Mahzarin R. Banaji drew this conclusion from their systematic work: "At the outset . . . a simple yet unexplored question was raised: Do people differentiate ethnic groups in their inclusion into the category 'American'? The conclusion that can be drawn on the basis of the six studies presented here is [clear]. To be American is to be White" (p. 463).

Imagine that. American citizens are walking around with the assumption that to be "classic" American is to be White. I'm sure you can understand what that means. It means that in our country there is a hibernating bigotry about who are the "we" and who are among the "they." Does that have consequences?

Just two months after the silliness about Marc Anthony, we crowned a new Miss America: Ms. Nina Davuluri. At NBC.com, I saw the headline "MISS AMERICA CROWNS 1ST WINNER OF INDIAN DESCENT." Then I saw another: "MISS AMERICA CROWNS FIRST WINNER OF INDIAN DESCENT, AND CRITICS SLAM HER AS ARAB TERRORIST." Given my expertise in the field of neo-diversity, given what I teach, I have to keep up with these kinds of stories. But trust me, I get tired. I clicked the link, read a few reader comments: "How the f--k does a foreigner win miss America? She is a Arab! Idiots," one man tweeted just after the first winner of Indian descent was crowned Sunday night. "If you're #MissAmerica you should have to be American," another woman wrote. "9/11 was 4 days ago and she gets miss America?" chimed another man.

At that moment, I couldn't go on. I stopped. I was not in the mood. In that moment, I did not have the psychological strength. I closed the link.

I should have known I couldn't get away that easy. The e-mails began to come in. The first was from a young White male who grew up in Garner, North Carolina. While at NC State "J" took both of my classes, and after that he was an undergraduate teaching assistant for my "Interpersonal Relationships and Race" course. Now in graduate school, J's e-mail subject heading read: "Even Miss America can't escape." All J put in the body of his e-mail was a link to a news report about the bigoted Twitter reactions. All I could say was: "Yes, J, I saw this today. We have got so much work to do to save the soul of America."

Minutes later came an e-mail from a female student of Southeast Asian Indian descent. K, too, had been a student of mine at the same time as J and was also one of my undergraduate teaching assistants for the "Race" course. K wrote:

> I can't even put into words how upset and distressed I am as an Indian American young woman. Dr. Nacoste, I hope you are able to bring this up in PSY 491. I know I would have A LOT to say. Speechless.

Like our new Miss America, Ms. Nina Davuluri, this student is an accomplished young Brown woman. She graduated from North Carolina State University and is now off in the world, embarking on her own career path. Yet some would say she is not American because she is of India-Indian descent.

That is a problem for our democracy. Not only are too many people not accepting the neo-diversity of our nation; too many feel that anyone other than a White person is not a legitimate American. And far too many people are reacting like bullies to anyone who doesn't "look American," however they may interpret that term. Far too many want us to go backward: "Let's go back to the old racially controlled, gender-controlled ways," they say. All of that (primal-bullying) bigotry is being activated by neo-diversity anxiety.

But look, we ain't going back. No, we are not going back, yet we have not prepared our children for an America that continues to evolve in this twenty-first century. We are definitely in trouble as a nation.

Trouble spelled with a capital T. We ain't going back because our demographics continue to evolve. With each rising sun, America's racial and ethnic mix continues to change and expand.

> White Americans No Longer a Majority by 2042
> The Associated Press updated 8:23 p.m. ET, Wed., Aug. 13, 2008
> WASHINGTON—White people will no longer make up a majority of Americans by 2042, according to new government projections. That's eight years sooner than previous estimates made in 2004.

For a person who has bought the sales pitch, finding out that the racial demographics of America are changing into something more colorful and ethnic is quite disturbing. Neo-diversity anxiety might be pushed even further when the person learns that multiracial, mixed-race Americans are the fastest-growing neo-diversity demographic group. This will make it even more difficult to just look at another person and answer the question "Is this person a 'we' or a 'they'?"

That old, outmoded strategy is a sinister legacy of racism. It is a legacy of our decades of American apartheid: laws (both local and regional) and customs that pushed individuals to use some difference to identify the "we" versus the "they." Taught these cognitive shortcuts in childhood, many Americans struggle to classify other people's race (other difference) as if it is a necessity for social interaction. My students tell me that it is not unusual to hear someone ask another person, or to be asked yourself, "*What* are you?" A White female wrote:

> I think Tim Tyson is right that we need to focus on how much we have grown instead of pretending we have never made any mistakes. Pretending there were never race riots didn't help my generation at all. I believe the race drama is better now, or at least quieter. But now it's different, it's ambiguous. It was easy to tell then who was Black and who was White. Now there are so many races, and mixed races. Everyone wants to know what you are; asking strangers on the street what race are they. Which is really weird, people really need to stop doing that. Who cares what race that random person you don't know is? You have to deal with them for 2.5 seconds. No need to get race involved. Who cares who's White and who's Black and who's purple and who's rainbow? Let's just all be people and call it a day.

Asking someone you just met "*What* are you?" breaks all the rules of decorum for social interaction in the moment, not to mention all the rules of relationship formation and development. In their interdependence theory, John Thibaut and Harold Kelley make it clear that "any failure to communicate adequately and fully *in the initial stages of the relationship* will affect the representativeness of the outcomes sampled" and so will influence whether one or both persons is willing to continue the interaction (p. 72). "*What* are you?" is an inadequate communication anytime, but is especially so as part of a first-time interaction. It is inadequate, to be sure, but still it communicates enough to say to the person asked, "This is not someone I would have fun getting to know." The question is inadequate to the point of being deadly to the interaction and any potential relationship.

The rules of social interaction say that self-disclosures should come slowly anyway, as if peeling an onion (Altman & Taylor, p. 27). Just because your neo-diversity anxiety is a fever burning in you, it does not give you the right to ask a person, "*What* are you?" That is offensive in any social interaction, let alone one with a new acquaintance—a person with whom you have only had surface contact. If you are struggling to pin down a person's race or ethnicity, maybe you should ask yourself why knowing this is so important to you. As my student wrote: "Who cares what race that random person you don't know is? You have to deal with them for 2.5 seconds. No need to get race involved." This level of neo-diversity anxiety is worth some self-examination. If more people took the time to do that, there would be fewer of these stories. An African American student wrote:

I was in the ninth grade, and it was the end of the school day on a Friday afternoon. I was in my Physical Education class, and we were rewarded with a free period in which we could just sit and talk or play the various games that were set up. I chose to talk to some new friends I had made in the class and get to know them better. I was having fun when a girl, who I had only talked to a few times, came up from behind and ran her fingers through my hair and proceeded to ask, "What are you mixed with?"

This is not the first time I heard this question, being a fairly light-skinned girl with jet-black straight hair down my back, but it was the first time it was to be debated as if I were part of a forum.

I simply smiled and said, "No, not with anything other than Black," and I thought that we would go back to our conversation.

But then she replied, "You're lying. You can't have hair like that and not be mixed with something."

I just sat there and looked at her because I could not believe she thought I was lying about my race. But before I could respond, a boy said, "Yea, you have to be mixed with something; look at you," which made the debate begin.

Everyone began to point out features such as my light skin and my "valley-girl voice," and they all came to the conclusion that I could not possibly be "just Black." I sat there amazed at how, because of the way I looked and talked, they could define me as Black or not. I could not say anything but rather I just smiled and let out small giggles during this debate, which felt more like 15 hours instead of 15 minutes.

Finally, I managed to get out the words "I doubt I am but maybe I will look into it or whatever." I couldn't believe what I was saying, and I was ashamed that from that simple conversation I began to question who I was.

The above interaction spells trouble. What happened in that interaction is deadly and it's bullying. A self-identified mixed-race student wrote:

High school, a time where teenagers think they know everything, and the words they utter are pure genius, how could they be wrong . . . they know EVERYTHING! Everyone has been there, including me and the guy I met my freshman year of high school. I remember coming into my biology class and on our desk was our names, ahhh, the joys of assigned seats.

Instead of having individual desks, there were tables that sat two at each. I soon found my new biology partner I was to spend the next few months with walking through the door. He was a White male, and admittedly he was cute. We proceed with our usual introductions, "Hey, I'm Erica."

"Hey, I'm Ethan" . . . the usual.

Then here it comes, he asks me, "What are you?" Little did I know this was definitely not the last time I would be asked this question, yet it was my first.

"Huh? What do you mean?"

He looked at me as if I were stupid in not understanding his question, "I mean what race are you?"

"I'm mixed, I'm Black and White."

I am not sure how long he stared at me. After an uncomfortable moment, he commented that he could not believe that my mother married a Black man. Then it was like a switch in his demeanor happened in an instance, "Well, you sure are the prettiest Black girl I have ever seen. If I dated Black girls, I would definitely date you."

Now it was my turn to stare; unsure of how to react I said, "OK? But I said I was mixed."

His response, "You know what I meant."

Class started soon after by the grace of God.

Apparently, too many of us just can't let people be people and call it a day. Neo-diversity anxiety, that worry about how to interact, pushes some of us to a social clumsiness that becomes offensive. Too many of us seem to think we have to be able to put other people in a racial category in order to know how to interact in the moment. We get huffy about it too: "His response, 'You know what I meant.'"

Another mixed-race student wrote:

I work as a part-time server at a bar and grille and am often subject to a variety of comments (most of the time alcohol-induced). Some are hilarious, some rude, and some just completely off-the-wall strange. This past weekend, Saturday night, at about 11:30 p.m., a table of about five men stopped me on my way to attend to one of my tables.

"Excuse me," two or three of them said at once, "we have a question for you."

"Sure," I said, both curious and afraid of the inquiry that was coming.

"We have a bet running," one man said. "What are you?"

I paused. "What am I?" I asked. "What do you mean, what am I?"

"Your race, or ethnicity, or whatever you want to call it," they responded.

I don't know my entire family tree, but I know the general ancestry of at least the past few generations in my family. I was perplexed by this question because it was the first time anyone had asked me this, especially on a first-time interaction.

"What do you think I am?" I asked.

"Now, I don't mean to *offend* you, by any means, but this half of the table is betting Asian and this half is betting Native American," one man said.

In truth, my mother's side is a combination of French and Cherokee Indian heritage, and my father's side is Scotch-Irish. I explained this to the men (why I don't know, because it was clearly none of their business), to which the "Native American" voters cheered in exclamation.

"Why would that offend me, being Asian or Native American?" I asked.

"Well, I don't know, I mean you look mostly White, but I could tell you had a little 'foreign' in you, and I know some people get pissed when you question their Whiteness, you know," the man said, chuckling.

"I see," I said, and went back to my duties, disgusted by the ignorance and bigotry I had just enabled. I told a couple of my fellow servers about what had just happened (they were White, as well) to which they replied, "Well, I can see the Asian, I guess. It's probably the way you do your makeup that makes you look Asian. Maybe you should try doing it differently."

You think that might get old for the person being asked this crass question? You bet it can. Relationship development is delicate; fragile. If Person-A acts as if they can ask Person-B anything right in the beginning, Person-B will be put off. And if the interaction is not personal but in the context of business, personal inquiries are not appropriate and are off-putting. That is why the young woman was confused and felt awkward. While she is trying to be professional, she is receiving questions about her racial history.

A mixed-race student wrote:

Sometimes I wish that I could be either White or Black because it's disheartening to not be considered a race or an ethnicity. Growing up, I have always felt like an outsider; even when I was in elementary school. The group of Black girls would call me "mud-blood" and "mutt." It seemed that I was an outsider to the White girls because I do not look like them, but the Black girls always said that I talk "White." I don't really understand how we consider speaking in proper English as being "White."

Even the standardized tests and surveys do not identify with being a mixture of races. I have to color in the choice for "Other." It makes it seem as though it is wrong to be considered another race. This also translates to typical questions that I get asked on a daily bases. Are you Dominican? What are you? Actually, a Mexican individual started speaking to me in Spanish because she thought that I was a native Spanish speaker. It's annoying because at times, the first question I receive is "What are you" instead of "Hello, what is your name."

I still feel like an outsider.

No, the problem is not that she is mixed-race. Too often I have heard people object to interracial dating and marriage by saying "What about the children?" as if the children are doomed to a life not worth living. For a long time Americans from a variety of racial and ethnic groups have argued that mixed-race children will suffer too much. But is having a Black and a White parent really the problem?

There is nothing wrong or dooming about being mixed-race. To even suggest this seems to me to be saying that there is some biological deficit that goes with having parents who are from different racial groups. Being mixed-race is not the problem. Being in a society so riddled with the legacy of racism that says you must belong to one racial group is the problem. And just because some African Americans (and some members of other non-White groups) also object to inter-racial dating and marriage using the excuse of doomed children does not validate the claim or reduce the bigotry in the claim. And what about the children?

No doubt, in a society still struggling with the leftover psychology (a legacy) of forced racial segregation, some mixed-race children will be asked the question "What are you?" But some of the most recent research shows that having to negotiate that question does not doom the child. In fact recent research shows that mixed-race children who accept being "multiple" turn out to be well-adjusted (doing well in school, for example) (Binning, Unzueta, Huo, and Molina). So what about the children? Well, I say, maybe one of them will become president of the United States. Mixed-race, multicultural Barack Hussein Obama did.

Even so, we must pay attention to how we treat all our fellow travelers on the neo-diversity frontier. How we treat people always matters. And mistreatment based on neo-diversity anxiety can create neo-diversity anger. A White male student wrote:

> This interaction took place about a year and a half ago during the beginning of my sophomore year. My roommate freshman year was unavailable, and I, not knowing of anyone else to room with, had been assigned a random room-mate. The day I moved in my roommate, who had moved in the previous day, greeted me at the door and shook my hand. His name was Drew, and he was slightly taller, slightly tanner than me, with dark hair, as I observed. He was friendly, very friendly in fact. He seemed to always have a constant grin on his face. I asked him various questions to help me get to know him such as "What year are you? What's your major? How many siblings do you have? What kind of music do you listen to? etc." We got to know each other and then went and ate some lunch later and then rode the bus to Target where we bought whatever things we forgot to get before we moved in and selected a rug for our room. We were both getting along very well.

The following day, which was a Sunday, we went and hung out with some of our suitemates and attended a concert that was being held for the students at Lee Field. I retired earlier than Drew and headed back to the room. He had stayed out and mingled with other people who had been at the concert.

Later that night we were both in the room lying in bed in the dark chit-chatting about our day and how it had been fun. I said that I thought all our suitemates we hung out with were nice, and he agreed. Then the next thing that came out of his mouth really surprised me, to say the least.

"I hate White people."

I had no idea where this was coming from.

He repeated: "I just hate White people."

I had no idea how to react. I thought: "I am a White person. Did I do something to offend him? Why was he saying this? What do I say now?"

This cold sweat had swept over me at that point. I asked, as he repeated a few more times "I hate White people," why he felt that way. I was some-what offended that he said this because I am White but more so because I would be offended that anyone would say something like that about anyone. Not wanting to be judgmental or overreact, I tried to understand why he said and thought this.

He told me that every time he is with a group of strangers who are White they always ask him what his race is or assume that he is Hispanic.

I had to admit to myself that those questions of what race or ethnicity he was had crossed my mind when I met him, but the thought wasn't so important or pressing that I would blatantly question him about it after just meeting him. He also said, "Anytime I'm with a group of Black people or any other minority they don't even ask 'cause it doesn't matter." I said, "I think of myself as being fairly open-minded and tolerant and try to avoid judging others based on appearance." I could see what he was talking about and thought I understood.

Feeling confused a bit because I could not think of what race he could be, I asked him, "Well, what exactly are you?" He said, "I am Indian, Native American." From there the conversation led to us discussing our parents, and the subject was changed. I never asked him about how he felt about me or if he thought I treated him in a biased way, but for the rest of the year we seemed to get along well, and there weren't any other awkward conversa-tions like that between us.

There can't be any justification for hating a whole group of people, nor can there be any justification for hibernating bigotry. Yes, to ask a person "What are you?" is intolerant. It says to that person "I have to know whether you are a 'we' or a 'they.' I have to know so I know how to treat you." Such an intense push to know, such a strong disposition toward the interaction fuels intergroup tension but does not justify hate.

I wonder, though, if this particular legacy of American apartheid is still quite so strong. Can we not get through a brief social interaction without being pressured to reveal racial or ethnic information when it is not obvious? What are we so afraid of? Are we trying to put up roadblocks to what in our hearts we believe will be the awful eventuality? Is this hibernating bigotry about who has sex with whom?

A White female wrote:

Last year I was on my way to the first football game of the season with some of my friends. My roommate and I were the last to get picked up, and by the time our friend got to our building there was only one seat left. I agreed to sit in the trunk of the SUV, and when I opened the door to get in, there was a boy already sitting there. I introduced myself and apologized if it was a tight squeeze. He said he didn't mind, and as we got to talking, we hit it off right away. So, we stayed by each other at the game and hung out afterwards as well.

We exchanged numbers and texted each other all the time. We went out on a few dates and would hang out until the early hours of the morning. It all seemed to be going well for about a month and a half; he was sweet and polite and good-looking as well. Then one day we stopped talking, and things seemed strange when we hung out. I asked him if we could talk, and I went over to his dorm to ask him what his intentions had been. He replied saying that he had just gotten out of a relationship a month earlier and did not think he was ready to start another one yet, so we agreed to be friends. I had been hoping for a different answer and was a little hurt to hear this, but I went on with my life.

For the remainder of the school year we talked every once in a while and would hang out when all of our friends got together, and sometimes it even seemed like things could be starting up again. However, summer came, and we went back to our hometowns and hadn't talked again until we moved back into school in August of this year.

When we all hung out the night we moved in, he and I found each other and hit it off again, but only for that one night. We hadn't really talked much after that until we all went out to Tobacco Road to watch a football game, and even then it was just casual conversation.

When I got back to my apartment I was talking to one of our mutual friends, and he said something that shocked me. He asked me if I thought there was a chance that the boy and I would start talking again. I said I wasn't sure and asked why he wanted to know. He replied saying that he had talked to the boy on the ride over to Tobacco Road and asked him why he didn't date me last year. His reasoning was that it was because he found out that I had dated a boy who was half Black. At that moment my perception of the boy completely changed as I was utterly shocked at the fact that this was even an issue in our day and age.

What is the problem here? Is this really about the fact that this young White woman dated a mixed-race young man? I think this legacy of American apartheid goes deeper than that. I think it is about people trying to avoid an eventuality that in their hearts they themselves believe they would have trouble managing in their everyday life. A White female student wrote:

After I finished sixth grade, my family moved from New York to North Carolina. I attended Sun Valley Middle School for 7th and 8th grade, and then moved on to Sun Valley High School, but only for my freshman year. Sun Valley is located in Indian Trail, North Carolina—a small town on the outskirts of Charlotte, North Carolina. Just as in stereotypical movies where the schoolgirl falls head over heels for the most popular guy in school, I found myself crushing on the most popular boy at Sun Valley Middle School. I had several classes with Tony, and we always flirted with each other, and I really started to like him. Looking back on it now, I was not ready to have a boyfriend in 8th grade, but I wanted more than just flirting and being friends. As my crush got more serious, I wanted to tell my mom about the way I was feeling. My mom is my best friend, and I've always been able to tell her everything, so when I realized how much I liked Tony, I wanted to tell her because I was excited and knew she would be excited for me.

I remember the exact moment that I told her about Tony. We were driving on the road right next to our housing development, and she asked me if I liked any boys at school. I was hesitant at first because I do get embarrassed when I talk about my feelings, but I went ahead and told her that there was this boy Tony that I liked. She asked me all about him: what he was like, if he played sports, if he had any siblings—she wanted to know everything. I knew I had to tell her, but I didn't know how to bring it up. After I answered all of her questions, I said, "There's something else, he's Black." At that moment, her entire demeanor changed. She got very cold, and the excitement she had vanished. She was not angry, but she was conflicted. The main thing I remember her saying was, "Think about if you brought him home to meet our family, all of your aunts and uncles and cousins."

I think concern over what other people will think, about how about people will react, goes to some deep part of hibernating bigotry. A mixed-race student wrote:

I remember the first time I ever had the chance to visit my great-grandma, on my mother's side, at her house instead of her coming to mine. It was summertime; I had just turned ten years old. I always wondered why we could never go to grandma's house. My mother always told me it was because an eight-hour drive with her six daughters in one car would be a disaster. I never accepted that answer, but I played along. Then finally, my mother decided that she wanted us to finally meet her grandmother, my great-grandmother. Along with my five sisters, I was packed into the SUV.

My mother was right. That eight-hour drive was exhausting, which is probably why I slept for the majority of the time. I was awake enough to see the welcome sign that read, "Morris."

Morris is a small southern town at the edge of Georgia, almost touching the Alabama border. I never knew this fact when I was younger, and I never knew that people there would act the way that they did.

It was Sunday morning when we arrived. My mom left late Saturday night in hopes that her six daughters would sleep the entire trip. Then she planned to sleep while my great-grandma took us to church.

The church was beside my great-grandmother's house. It has been in her family for centuries. My great-grandmother, just like her mother, is a very Christian woman, or so she says, but that's a different story. My great-grandma was asked to bring us to church, but she told us to go ahead and walk over there ahead of her. We begged her to walk with us because we didn't know where to go, but she just told us to go and to sit in the back.

We arrived at the church, and the woman holding the door looked at us in shock. She asked us if we were lost. We told her otherwise and proceeded into the door, but she blocked us and asked us where we were going. We answered, "To praise the Lord at our great-grandma's church." The woman's face filled with shock.

She said, "There aren't any African Americans that attend this church."

I answered with "Oh, our great-grandma isn't from Africa. She's from Morris, Georgia."

The woman continued to try to keep us from entering until a White man came up to her and told her that he had just seen us get out the car with Sarah, our grandma. She let us in and whispered to the man, "They must be the children she works with in social services."

We went into the chapel, found a row in the back, and sat down. We saved a seat for our great-grandma, of course. Time began to fly by . . . five minutes turned into thirty, thirty into an hour, until the service ended. I spotted my great-grandma sitting in the third row from the front. She had been sitting there the whole time. I ran to her and asked her, "Grandma, why didn't you sit with us?"

I immediately saw all of the White faces around her turn a pale pink. One woman questioned, "You let them call you grandma?" and my great-grandma replied, "They have big imaginations," and she shooed me away, but before I left she whispered in my ear for me to get my sisters and hurry over to the house.

I did what I was told, with no thought in between.

My great-grandma came home. She was mad at me. She told me that I made her friends mad at her. I didn't understand. She told me that they thought I was her granddaughter. I said, "But, Grandma, I am." My great-grandma turned away and sighed, "That wasn't my choice."

I haven't seen my great-grandma in ten years. This was my choice.

Grandma, what big teeth you have!

Big, yes, but it turns out Great-Grandma made a deadly mistake with the position she took in this interaction with her great-granddaughters. Drawing on her memory of this interaction with her White great-grandmother, in her analytic writing assignment, this mixed-race young woman paints a picture of the forested community she found her great-grandmother living in:

> Let's talk about Stage One—Assessment of the Situation. The structure of the situation played a role in the interaction because we were no longer in North Carolina; we were in Morris, Georgia. This was my first time traveling to another state. The group composition probably played the biggest role in Stage One. Through my eyes, the group composition was all White people. This didn't bother me that much because my White family was all that I knew. So I was used to my sisters and I being the only people with more pigment to our skin. I didn't feel the need to compete like in the Minimal Group Effect, but I did categorize into the "we" and the "they."
>
> This was always a problem for me because I always experienced vague interdependence; uncertainty about where I "fit in." I also didn't know the rules, nor did I know my role in society. Was I Black? Was I White? I was both, but I always felt pressured with social anxiety to choose one or the other; however, I was usually forced into whatever out-group was present. In this situation, I was Black.
>
> This social uncertainty and vague interdependence activated intergroup anxiety within me, so I started to assess the possible actions and outcomes for myself. I reached Stage Two; everyone was staring at us as if we were aliens, so I was fearful of out-group evaluations that were being made. I felt out of place without my great-grandma being there because we didn't know anyone else. Also, we were younger, so no one would really listen to us like they would have listened to an adult like my great-grandma.
>
> I tried to solve the problem by finding my great-grandma. I used a cognitive shortcut to explain why she didn't sit with us. I thought that maybe she couldn't find us. I thought that maybe the really old people had to sit in the front so they could see more clearly. My assumptions led me to believe that she did not choose to sit apart from us of her own free will. This was my mistake. I assumed.
>
> I was in Stage Three until my great-grandma returned home from church. She was angry with me. She told me that I made her friends mad at her. This elevated my anxiety. Whenever a social interaction intensifies interpersonal anxiety, the dyad becomes prone to shift from the behavioral level of interdependence to the dispositional level. Feeling my great-grand-

mother's anger, I started to slowly move into the dispositional level. Then she said the four words that picked me up and threw me fully into the level of dispositions: "That wasn't my choice."

I was ten years old, but I was not an idiot. I knew exactly what she meant. That's when the whole situation played back in my mind, every detail clear and precise. It all made sense. My emotional reactions were amplified; I was furious. How could my own family try to disown me like that? I yelled, "I hate you" just like any other child would do, and I ran to my mom.

For the rest of the trip I was stuck in Stage Five: held hostage as I avoided my great-grandma at all costs. I couldn't let go. I didn't let go.

Four years passed, and I still wanted nothing to do with her. Where before we had had a warm relationship, now our relationship returned to a simple surface-contact relationship. She always tried to apologize, but I wouldn't accept. I refused to go on family trips that she would be present at. I avoided her, for years.

The neo-diversity effect in an interracial encounter makes the possible interactions and outcomes more unclear than in other social encounters. This makes the interaction unpredictable. I never would have guessed that my great-grandma would leave me out to dry in the out-group so that she could be in good standing with the in-group. In a recent conversation, with my new knowledge of neo-diversity, I listened as she told me she had to live in her town year-round and she couldn't handle negative in-group evaluations for that long, but she said she never meant to hurt me. Neo-diversity anxiety got hold of her.

I never stopped loving my great-grandma. I knew that she grew up in a different time than me where different things were and weren't acceptable. Our language communities were different. Language communities are a set of people in interaction who assign unique meaning to words and symbols as a way of establishing group membership and mutual understating. Language can be a display of intergroup power because the intergroup character of language has a history. This history can be so powerful that all members carry it.

My grandma's language community was that of her all-White peers. They all shared the same history that White and Black should never be mixed. They all shared the same history that if a child had one ounce of Black that he/she was Black. They shared the same history that if a White person was helping a Black person, it was through charity. That is why everyone saw us as Black. That is why the woman assumed that we were some case in the social work office. My great-grandma knew the language. She knew the history. This kept my great-grandma silent. Silence allows people to go on automatic, not thinking about what their words really mean.

My mother always taught me that blood is thicker than water, and you keep your family first no matter what. It hurt that my great-grandma would choose her "friends" over her family. Her silence hurt.

All things considered, I understand why she did what she did. I understand that she felt the neo-diversity anxiety build up within herself. I accept that she was taught different things in her time than I have been taught in mine. Blood is thicker than any grudge that I may have held. I have forgiven her. However, I do not have to put up with her if that is her frame of mind. I didn't argue. I didn't tell her what she can and can't do. I just simply made my preferences known through honest self-disclosure, and we will see where it goes from there.

We live in a world of neo-diversity. My whole existence is neo-diversity. If she can't deal with the anxiety that it creates, then we may never have a relationship.

How could the mixed race of these children be a problem for Great-Grandma? After all, the mixed blood was mixed with her own. No, the problem was that Great-Grandma did not want to be seen as connected to her pigmented great-grandchildren in a family way. Hibernating bigotry, you see, is sometimes kept alive by our relational concerns. Sometimes our bigotry is kept strong because we do not want to lose friends or family.

Each of us has a need to belong. We need other people in our lives. It's just that now, as we travel within neo-diverse America, there are many more people to whom we can be connected and ways to connect. If we just go on automatic, we will not hear the neo-diversity diesel humming. If we just do what others expect us to do, all we can hear is the loud whistle of the Wrong-Line train. We just continue the legacies of American apartheid.

And so I worry about all the self-segregation we live with today. I think we are on the verge of making a deadly mistake for our nation.

PART 6

LOOSENED ALL HER STEAM AND BRAKES, STRAINING EVERY NERVE

CHAPTER 12

LET'S GO TO THE RODEO

OBAMA WINS

A RACIAL BARRIER FALLS AS AMERICA ELECTS ITS FIRST BLACK PRESIDENT

(*Raleigh News & Observer*)

W hen the November 2008 election results flashed and thundered across the night sky, some Americans celebrated in joy, and some Americans cringed in fear. People cried, laughed, threw up their arms, danced, collapsed, shook hands, hugged each other, held their mouths, all in pride, shock, disbelief, joy, and fear that this had happened in America. A Black man had been elected president of the United States.

With the election of President Barack Hussein Obama, the Neo-Diversity train went roaring across America. But not all train stations across America were ready. Have you noticed since then the frequency of local and national stories about neo-diversity miscues, misfires, and oddities? Just sitting at my desk, reading news webpages, I have collected hundreds of stories that show too many Americans having trouble adjusting to what the Neo-Diversity train brings to town.

INTERRACIAL COUPLE DENIED MARRIAGE LICENSE

La. justice of the peace cites concerns about any children couple might have

HAMMOND, La.—A Louisiana justice of the peace said he refused to issue a marriage license to an interracial couple out of concern for any children the couple might have. (MSNBC, 2009)

HAWAII FOOTBALL COACH USES HOMOSEXUAL SLUR

IN REFERENCE TO NOTRE DAME (Hinxman)

NJ GOP LAWMAKER QUITS OVER WIFE'S RACIST EMAIL

TRENTON, NJ—A freshman Republican lawmaker resigned because his wife sent "an offensive and racist" email to the Democratic state Senate campaign of nine-time Olympic gold medalist Carl Lewis, a GOP official acknowledged Monday. (MSNBC, 2011)

MORE MEN FILING SEXUAL HARASSMENT CLAIMS

Percentage of complaints filed by men has doubled over last 20 years (Hananel)

POLL: YOUNG PEOPLE SEE ONLINE SLURS AS JUST JOKING

WASHINGTON—Is it ever OK to tweet that a girl's a "slut"? How about using an offensive name for gays on Facebook? Or texting a racial slur? Most young people think it's all right when friends are joking around with each other, according to a new poll. (Cass and Agiesta)

PENN STATE SORORITY APOLOGIZES FOR
HAVING OFFENSIVE MEXICAN-THEMED PARTY

A sorority having a Mexican-themed party seems harmless. But a Penn State sorority party photo surfaced Monday showing a group of girls wearing sombreros, ponchos and fake moustaches and holding signs saying "will mow lawn for weed" and "I don't cut grass, I smoke it," reports the Onward State. (NBC Latino)

ANCHOR CALLED TOO FAT FOR TV IS NOW INTERNATIONAL ROLE MODEL

Wisconsin news anchor Jennifer Livingston made headlines around the world in October when she spoke out on camera to a viewer who said she was setting a bad example for her community because of her weight. (Coffey)

ESPN APOLOGIZES FOR LINSANE HEADLINE

February 19, 2012 8:49 AM

NEW YORK (AP)—ESPN has apologized for using a racial slur in a headline for a story on Knicks sensation Jeremy Lin the NBA's first American-born player of Chinese or Taiwanese descent. ESPN ran the headline "Chink in the Armor" after Lin had nine turnovers in New York's loss to the New Orleans Hornets on Friday night on its mobile website that could be seen on phones and tablet computers. (CBS New York)

US JUDGE FORWARDS RACIST EMAIL ABOUT OBAMA

A federal judge acknowledged forwarding a racially charged email about President Barack Obama, saying he isn't a racist and apologizing while adding that he sent it "because it's anti-Obama."

I could keep this up for quite a while. Let's just admit that when the Neo-Diversity train left the station with Barack Hussein Obama onboard as president of this great nation, we weren't ready. Since adults weren't ready, heaven help the children. A White male student wrote:

> During this current (November 2012) Presidential Election that we have had, Barack Obama was just reelected for the President of the United States. Last night as I was watching the results on television I was also watching what people were saying on Facebook and Twitter, and I will provide some postings here that I saw from last night after the results of the election were announced to the nation.
>
> "WOW . . . four more years of this bull shit. I bet the White house smells like shit."
>
> "I'm movin' to Canada!"
>
> "It'll be a cold day in hell before I take orders from a NIGGER!"
>
> I saw that on Facebook, that one of my "friends" wrote, as were other numerous postings that I saw similar to this one. I was upset to see this. I personally did not vote for President Obama, but he won the election and I will support him because he is our President. I am ready for people to come together, and end this foolishness.

America still has a long way to go.

Moving down the line, making stops in every metropolis, city, town, and hamlet, is the Neo-Diversity train, and some of us still aren't ready. Nobody was ready, for instance, when the Neo-Diversity train made its stop at the Missouri State Rodeo. Nobody in charge was ready or knew neo-diversity had arrived at the rodeo. Those in charge thought, it's just us, and we all agree that Obama is a clown. It's all just a big joke anyway, right? But then it got unfunny.

According to the Associated Press, "A clown wearing a President Barack Obama mask appeared at a Missouri State Fair rodeo this weekend and the announcer asked the enthusiastic spectators if they wanted to see 'Obama run down by a bull.'" Going on with the story, the article quotes Mr. Perry Beam, a White man who has attended this rodeo every year since he was a child. According to the story, as the clown wearing the face of President Obama ran around, everybody screamed and went wild. That was the point at which Mr. Beam was reported to have said he began to feel frightened. Mr. Beam was at the rodeo with his wife and a student from Taiwan. He said he was shocked as the announcer kept talking about "our Obama dummy." He said he began to feel like this was some sort of Klan rally you might see in a documentary on television (Sudekum).

Mr. Beam was very upset. He felt that this display was distasteful and showed disrespect for a sitting president of the United States. But some of his upset was because he has a neo-diverse family; both his wife and their guest are from Taiwan. In the article Mr. Beam is quoted as saying, "I've never seen anything so blatantly racist in my life. If an old country boy picks up on something like that, imagine what a person of color would think."

Criticism of this event has come from national figures. But I find Mr. Beam's critique and outrage to be the most important. He is no outsider. He is no national pundit. Mr. Beam is a local White man who had come to an event he has cherished for most of his life, and he brought his family. Yet he was quick to recognize something was very wrong, that somehow he had gotten on the Wrong-Line train. He remarked that he had never been witness to such a dreadful display, especially one that received financial support from the state. Mr. Beam was certain that this was all about the race of our president. If that was the case, this state-sanctioned, institutional support for bigotry is racism.

Mr. Beam's reaction is also important at the interpersonal level of neo-diversity. He was upset, he said, because his family is multicultural. Yes, he is a White man, but his wife is from Taiwan, and they were hosting a student from Taiwan, so Mr. Beam's social world is neo-diverse. When the Neo-Diversity train started its trek across America, we weren't ready for these kinds of mixed relationships and complex, neo-diverse sensitivities. We weren't ready because so much had been left unsaid and unaddressed about race and the many other social differences we experience in America. With race as the prototype for all things intergroup in America, we were unprepared for all the new tensions about group membership that the Neo-Diversity train activates as it treks across the country.

We elected a multiracial, multicultural man to the presidency of the United States. With that event a significant portion of the hibernating neo-diversity anxiety in the nation awakened, all that neo-diversity anxiety being about that all-too-pervasive question: "Who are the 'we' and who are among the 'they'?"

A White female in one of my classes told this story:

It was the day after the 2008 election when Obama had won; obviously it was a really big deal for the country, and I knew that the next day at school would not be a usual one. I gathered myself to walk into the hallways because I knew it was going to be crazy, and boy, I was right.

I walked into my high school, and the halls were stuffed with people of all races and with them they had posters on large yard sticks and T-shirts and they were all chanting "My President Is Black." I was slightly annoyed by the behavior because I felt as though when a White president had won an election, people didn't chant like this and make a scene at school, but I knew that it was a big deal and people were excited about it, even if they showed it in rather obnoxious ways.

As I was walking to class, I was approached by a Black student, Joe, who I had had a few interactions with before. Joe threw an Obama T-shirt at me. He then proceeded to say, "Hey, White girl, bet you never thought your president would be Black. Your White guy didn't stand a chance."

This bothered me because, first of all, he approached me by throwing a T-shirt and saying "Hey, White girl." Secondly, he automatically assumed that since I was White, I wanted the White candidate to win. He threw me into categories of being closed-minded and other negative things when it came to the race aspect of it. Instead of giving in to this, I handed him his shirt back and simply walked away, fuming mad.

An African American female student had this experience to relate. She wrote:

My freshman year at North Carolina State began with a bit of a culture shock for me. I'm from Charlotte, as metropolitan as one can get in North Carolina, and I was used to going to a school with majority Black and Hispanic cultures. I was in a residence hall with hundreds of people from all over the state, the country even, and expected to at least get along with all of those personalities and opinions.

In 2010, around Thanksgiving our campus was shaken by images and words painted in one of the tunnels students use to go from one side of campus to the other. [Through the use of the racial slur] that our President Barack Obama was called, the campus was in frenzy about the situation. Coalitions were formed, clubs focused on social justice were very upset, and everyone had an opinion.

Now to our story, I was living on a floor with a majority of Caucasian students, as per usual at NC State; our resident assistant called a hall meeting to talk about procedures for leaving for break. I reluctantly went with my suite mates, who were all Caucasian. As we were sitting there my suite mates were making small talk, but my attention was pulled from the conversation to one being had by a group of young men who lived in the suite next door. They were speaking about the incident in tunnel.

I heard things like, "I don't know why THOSE PEOPLE are upset, if he was White no one would care" and "I didn't think it was that bad."

They went on to talk about their opinions in a very rude and demeaning way. I heard it all but said nothing. Looking back, as a more confident person, I still don't think I would have said anything. I was in an uncomfortable situation of again being the "only one," and our RA was in on the conversation!

No, with the election of President Barack Hussein Obama we were not suddenly and forever post-racial. Since we had not dealt with the intergroup tensions of race, the intergroup tension of neo-diversity hit us with its fast-moving locomotive strength. In her third and final reaction to the assigned book *Blood Done Sign My Name*, one of my students wrote:

> I feel like I was very ignorant about the real past of the United States, but I don't want to be ignorant anymore. I want people to know the real, unglamorous, and the swept-under-the-rug truth. More than anything, though, I want people to finally be able to face our history. It's a part of who we are: why do we keep running from it?

As an American Latina, I sometimes feel as if I'm watching from the sidelines, but then I realize that I am just as much a part of it. It's crazy how White paternalism seeps into our culture, even among those of us that aren't "White." I hate admitting to it, but I have participated in prejudiced, and sometimes bigoted, thoughts and actions. I will say this though: I refuse to stay ignorant and will use this new knowledge to be a better person and not commit the same mistakes.

We can't afford to refuse our history anymore. We can't pretend it didn't happen because we can still feel the anxiety and pressure, remnants of a history we would like to forget but can't seem to forgive. I think we all need to recognize our shameful moments, own up to them, learn from them, and not fall into the same trap. History should serve this purpose, and we can't really complete that process if we are not aware of the whole truth.

In his third and final reaction paper, a Black male student wrote:

In short, this book has really underlined the problems that we as Americans face with the "Rough Beast" known as neo-diversity. Back in the beginning of the book when Tyson was writing, you could see the clear "racial" segregation that gave everyone in society a clear understanding as to where they were in the social world, with Whites at the top of the hierarchy followed by everyone else in society.

After the civil rights movement came to pass, the roles were not as evenly/easily defined by both sides who struggled to gain an understanding of the new social structure that had come to pass, because the legal separation that had occurred in the past was gone. These new interaction opportunities have led to the unclear motive on how to approach the other race, and since America just swept everything that happened under a rug, society became lost on how to adapt to the new situation. That problem plagues us today, because we choose not to try and gain an understanding of "where the other is coming from." We'd rather pretend that we "don't see color," which is an insult to those who have struggled to gain their independence and freedom.

We are left to struggle with our own biases as we try to deny that we have biases. How do we try to pull that off? Self-segregation, that's how. Too many Americans avoid interacting with "them." That self-segregation is what lets stereotypes live in us and sometimes control us.

I worry that my university is supporting and authorizing bigotry. Students come to colleges and universities with all kinds of attitudes toward neo-diversity. Some come with primal bigotry, while others come with hibernating bigotry that has been nurtured at home. All come with stereotypes. There are no innocent.

A White male student writes:

> I grew up in Johnston County, North Carolina. I knew about Mule Days; it's hard to ignore when you get a day off of school because Mule Days is happening in the county. However, I had never been to Mule Days, I had only heard about it from friends who had attended in the past. So, my junior year of high school, which was about four years ago when I got my license, I decided to drive through [the county] to go to Campbell University, since I was looking into their school anyway. As I drove through the town of Benson I became amazed at the sights that I saw. There were so many pickup trucks (not a surprise for Johnston County at all) that were flying Confederate flags.
>
> I decided to stop and eat at a fast-food place in town and try to overhear conversations so I could figure out what this Mule Days thing was all about. While there what I heard told me that Mule Days for most people was not about the history of Benson but about excluding the Black population from what could be a good time.
>
> I had to do a project on Mule Days in middle school, yes, a project on Mule Days; it's a big deal, but the purpose of Mule Days is to celebrate the history of Johnston County and how agriculture is a big part of who we are as a county. Clearly the younger generation did not get the memo because all they were talking about was how glad they were that no Black people were around. I was shocked. This celebration was something for everyone to enjoy and take part in. I had to leave and go back home. I still have never participated in Mule Days except for that one time.

Johnston County, North Carolina, where the town of Benson is located, is a rural community. It has a long history of racial intolerance. Traveling to a navy duty station in 1974, it was in Johnston County that I encountered the billboard that read "WELCOME TO KLAN COUNTRY." Not far away, the town of Cary has no such history. It is an affluent bedroom community in the heart of what is known as "the Triangle," made up of Raleigh, Durham, and Chapel Hill and the three associated major universities. A White female student had this to say about growing up in that town:

> I grew up in Cary, North Carolina, near Preston Country Club. There were no race problems in our neighborhoods because there were no interracial interactions. That's when I first realized nothing was "fine." If everything was "fine" then a Black family would've moved into my neighborhood at some point. No matter how many houses went up for sale, no other race but White moved in.
>
> When I started school I got my first culture shock. My elementary and middle schools were filled with students of all races and backgrounds. Some of the students had been bussed in through Wake County's bussing program. They were from intercity neighborhoods and didn't have much. My mom, the PTA president, called them "trouble children." I don't know if they actually caused any trouble or not.

Segregation breeds group stereotypes. Legal segregation that gives one group more benefits than another group breeds implicit stereotypes that say one group is superior and the other group is inferior. Going from legal segregation to ensuring that groups have equal status under the law is beyond important. It is nation-saving. America did that. And to that extent we saved ourselves.

But removing the laws of legal segregation did not eliminate the group stereotypes that have been bred and nurtured over hundreds of years. Stereotypes about "others," or "them," or "those people" live in groups. These stereotypes live in families and are one way or another passed on as family heirlooms. "We are better than them" is powerful in the individual's network of stereotypes. Group stereotypes that say "they are not like us" are the most powerful because they capture the idea of perceived dissimilarity in beliefs among groups. They motivate self-segregation by group. A White male student wrote:

I find the concept of the social psychology belief congruence hypothesis to be quite intriguing. The hypothesis is that based on a person's group membership, like race, we make assumptions about other people's beliefs and that those assumptions influence who we are willing to interact with. To me this theory takes the old saying "Don't judge a book by its cover" a couple of steps farther.

I went online and researched the theory a little more after class, and the thought that keeps popping into my head is one that shows how much our own assumptions hold us back. The perceived dissimilarities that the theory makes reference to actually prevent us, or at the least slow us, from discovering the similarities we actually share with people of a different race or ethnicity.

By assuming that we are different from another person, especially based on race, we typically choose not to make an attempt to learn about the similarities they may in fact have with us. This revelation makes me think about how we, as individuals, hold ourselves back more than anything when it comes to choosing who to associate with. Before we even meet a person we already assume certain things about them based on their physical appearance (race usually being the main factor); it is almost like the chances of a bond forming are doomed before any words are spoken.

These perceived dissimilarities also greatly affect our responses to certain groups we encounter. Every day on our campus assumed dissimilarities prevent people from joining clubs, creating friendships, and even asking for assistance. Many times these assumptions go beyond just "they are different than me" to "I wouldn't fit in with them." People take these assumed dissimilarities and then relate them back to themselves in a way that they convince themselves that trying to form a bond with said group is futile.

Relating this to my personal life, I can say that in the past I have gone into situations holding unjustified beliefs. This theory has made me realize that I've actually held myself back multiple times by focusing on myself as the "out-group" in many situations. I've gone to parties where I was a part of the racial minority and allowed myself to have a bad time because I convinced myself that others would not want to associate with me. As the previous statements imply these are things I did to myself. These are perceived dissimilarities that I chose to have, so with that in mind I feel like I can also choose not to have them.

I've made a plethora of friends that are not of the same race/ethnicity as me, and looking back on the situations like I described about the party (i.e., letting racial dissimilarity convince me that somebody wouldn't want to associate with me) seems silly now. I feel like after studying this concept I'll learn to not judge a book by its cover and actually flip through the pages from now on.

Have no doubt that "They are not like us" motivates the tendency in individuals to stay away from "them." Combine that with the belief that others in your group, friends, and family would disapprove of your interaction with one of "them," and you get group self-segregation. You get self-segregation even in a free and open environment. A Black female student wrote:

I have always said that I wasn't consciously aware of race (in terms of ethnicity) until I moved to the South. I lived in California up until the age of ten years old, and throughout my entire childhood there I had friends of many different ethnicities. Of course I knew they were different in terms of appearances, but to me that's all it ever was and it never mattered to me. I'd thought one of my grandmothers was White up until the time I was eight years old, and I never questioned how it was possible—to me it just was.

So, in the middle of my fifth-grade year my mother decided that we were going to uproot and move to North Carolina. After being in North Carolina for two weeks I finally started my first day at elementary school, assigned to my fifth-grade class. As a means of getting acclimated to my new school and routines I was assigned a buddy. Her name was Brittany, and she was a smaller girl (smaller than me, and I was considered one of the taller girls at the school) with long brown hair and a mousy face. I came to find out later that she was one of the "popular girls." I sat next to her in class, and we played together at recess with her friends from other classes.

We had one of the later lunch periods; the time slots were assigned by grade, and thus the fifth grade was last to eat. Up until this point I had spent my day with Brittany and our classmates, so naturally (to me at least) at lunch I sat down to eat with them, too.

Everything was going well, and it was now the middle of the lunch period. Everyone who hadn't brought their lunch had gotten their choice of pizza or nuggets from the serving line and was now enjoying their meal. I was busy trying my best to keep up with the conversations of my peers around me, and suddenly a hefty Black girl sitting at the table in front of me shouted out, "Hey, why are you sitting over there, with them?"

I looked around confused, trying like the rest of the girls around me to figure out whom she was speaking to. She quickly clarified and, to my horror, stood and pointed directly to me saying, "YOU, why are you sitting with them? You should be over here sitting with US."

I was mortified and slightly ashamed as I realized that I was the only Black face sitting at my table and that the table right in front of me was a table full of Black faces. At that point it didn't matter either way because I was hurriedly concentrating on the tiles on the cafeteria floor as the faces at both tables stared at me while I wished the floor would swallow me to safety.

After the long, mortal, and successful fight against legal segregation, voluntary lines of racial self-segregation are being drawn, Black and White in the twenty-first century. In public schools and elsewhere, this self-segregation is a breeding ground for group stereotypes and animosity. We begin to learn to adapt to social situations as children. We carry those social adaptation strategies with us to new situations. No wonder that a White female student could tell this story about the first week at North Carolina State University. She wrote:

When I was a freshman, I attended an event on Tucker Beach where a bunch of students got together to play volleyball, socialize, and eat some hot dogs and burgers. The majority of students playing on the beach were White kids, and when I looked over by the tables in front of the tri-towers I noticed that there must have been at least 40 Black kids all sitting together social-izing with themselves with an integration of maybe 1 or 2 White kids. That is NO exaggeration, and I am SURE it was no coincidence, either.

I looked at my roommate, who is from New York, and said, "Do you see that? I've never seen such a clear-cut segregation of races in my life."

I couldn't stop thinking about it nor could I believe that this behavior was still so prominent. I've heard stories, but this was a personal experience that I saw with my own eyes. I even stopped telling my new NCSU friends about my history with a Black ex-boyfriend because of the change in judg-ment I receive from them. By reading *Blood*, I've really started to understand just how bad racism was not too long ago. Now I'm not as surprised as I was that day on Tucker Beach. It really makes me wonder what it's going to take for us to ever overcome the struggle.

On a university campus in the current century, it turns out that racial self-segregation is rampant. I worry that universities are supporting this self-segregation. Fraternities and sororities loom large in my concerns about how universities might be inadvertently authorizing self-segregation and bigotry. A White female wrote:

> It was a normal Friday night for a college student. It was my freshman year, and I was with my best friend "Emily." Emily and I were friends all through high school, so the fact that she is Black and I am White doesn't even occur to me as we are getting ready to go to a fraternity party.
>
> We didn't think we would have any problems getting into the party since we were girls, but as soon as we got there I immediately realized that we were not going to be welcomed into the party. The interaction was between Emily, the fraternity brother at the door, and me.
>
> We begin to walk through the door when the boy put his arm across to block the door so we could not pass. I asked him what was the problem, and he said they were full. I knew for a fact this was not the case, so I push further to see what the issue really was. He told us that we should go to another fraternity's party. I asked who else was having a party, and he mentions a Black fraternity's name. We then left because we knew we were not welcomed at that fraternity house.

An African male wrote:

> It was a Saturday night, freshman year, my roommate is a member of a fraternity, so he invited a group of us to come to one of the parties they are hosting. I've been to this same fraternity at least five times before, and I've never had any trouble or confrontation.
>
> On this particular night I was walking with my friends to the party, but I fell behind and they were a couple of steps in front of me. My friends, who were all White, went to the door without me, and the guy didn't ask any questions, nothing. He just let them in. I was just right behind my friends, and they were all waiting for me, waving me on to get inside, but to my

surprise, as I was walking in, this same guy walked up to me and asked me, "What are you doing here?"

I was gonna answer him and tell him that my friends are waiting for me and to check with them, but before I could even get it out, he said, "You are not welcomed here, go away."

I was really angry and got into a confrontation with the guy that resulted in a brawl between my friends and his friends.

A White male wrote:

I have an officership in a predominately White fraternity at NC State, and I experience constant pressures to conform to issues regarding race. At chapter meetings, some of the members find it "appropriate" to openly discriminate against Black people and sometimes even plot to keep "thuggish-looking Black people" from coming into our parties.

A White female wrote:

There is a website that North Carolina State and tons of other universities are on called CollegeACB. This website is composed of anonymous postings from people about their school. For some reason, the only thing on our school's campus to talk about is apparently Greek life.

One of my new friends who has also just joined the same sorority as me told me to look at that website because there was a posting about our sorority. When I went to the website and clicked on our thread, I immediately noticed people bashing the sorority for having two African American women.

Someone made a comment about my sorority saying that they have two Black girls. One person responded to this by disagreeing with the negative statement and standing up to the girls. The comments that followed shocked me.

In response to the person who stood up for the two African American girls in my sorority, someone wrote (and please, Dr. Nacoste, excuse the language, but I feel it is necessary to not edit this comment to show the stupidity of this person) . . . someone wrote . . . "Shut the fuck up you stupid coon. Fraternities and sororities were started by White people for White people. The niggers thought they deserved it too cause we 'owe' yall something. That's bullshit and because we didn't let yall join our organizations you went and formed your own, so stay with your own, and stay away from ours."

WAS THIS SERIOUS?! I truly cannot believe that someone would write this.

It honestly makes me want to punch them in the face.

Are universities subsidizing bigotry? Fraternities and sororities are not free agents. The fraternities and sororities are linked to academic institutions. Who pays for the land on which sorority and fraternity houses so often sit on a campus? On these sorority/fraternity courts with their rows of houses, who gives these sororities and fraternities access to infrastructure that allows them to have water, electricity, garbage and sewer service? Who gives these sororities and fraternities access to an infrastructure of meeting rooms on campus?

What was the word from South Africa's Johannesburg? Divest! Nations that had stocks and bonds invested in South African business were pushed to withdraw—divest—their money because that money was supporting the economics of apartheid.

Where institutions of higher learning provide the infrastructure, those colleges and universities must continually monitor the neo-diversity group dynamics. And where necessary college and university administrations must intervene and make it clear to fraternities and sororities what the penalties will be if investigations show prejudice and bigotry (discrimination) are at work. If a college or university is providing infrastructure to student organizations in which bigotry is evident, the institution must divest itself of any relationship and leave these organizations to fend for themselves. Otherwise, rather than fulfilling the aims of education—to prepare students to be well rounded and productive citizens and leaders—universities are supporting and authorizing bigotry. Such institutional support and authorization of racial bigotry reinstates racism.

Yes, based on their home experiences, students bring all sorts of tendencies with them to a campus. But the purpose of education is to give these young travelers on the road of life a perspective that allows them to look at these tendencies with a critical eye. When we as faculty and administrators don't do that job, we fail at our mandate and we fail our students. Our failure lives in students' experiences at the university. A White female wrote:

I am from an extremely small southern town where, unfortunately, prejudice still dwells deep within people. Some of these people are even my friends and family. I have always had a heart for people who are discriminated against. I went to a private Christian school from kindergarten to 12th grade. To give a mental picture of the diversity, my graduating class contained one Black male out of 40 students.

So needless to say, NC State was a bit of a culture shock. I was in amazement with the diversity on my campus and began making friends with people who were very different than myself, in terms of ethnicity.

My freshman year I became very good friends with a large, tall Black male with an afro. His name is Bobby. Bobby is from Raleigh, so he would, and still does, take me to the best local restaurants and attractions. We grew to become great friends and decided to take US History together our sophomore year. Little did I know it, but this was going to lead to my most intense intergroup dyadic interaction.

Here is what happened:

On the first class of the semester Bobby and I met in front of a classroom building on campus to walk into class together. We hugged and said hello and began moving towards our classroom. We walked in side by side and found two seats together in the front of the lecture room. I scanned the room as we were taking our seats, and I saw the familiar face whose name was Alex. Alex and I both attended the same private Christian school, but he had graduated a year after me. He had an odd look on his face, but I just smiled and waved at him.

When the class was over I looked for Alex to catch up with him, but I couldn't find him anywhere. So Bobby and I hugged good-bye and I went on my way. The next evening my roommates told me that they wanted to go hang out on one of our neighbor's porches. I agreed, and the four of us walked a few doors over. To my surprise I saw a few people who I attended high school with at my neighbors.

Before I could say hello and tell them how good it was to see them, Alex looked at me and said, "Where is your nigger boyfriend?" I responded, "Excuse me!?" Alex and three other boys began taunting me with slanders such as "We heard you've got jungle fever" and "Nigger lover."

I felt my blood boiling and became nauseous. All I could do was scream at them, "You are all full of hate!" I tried to continue, but my voice began to quiver and a lump grew in my throat. I slapped Alex across the face and burst into tears as I ran back to my apartment and cried for hours.

Every time I read or remember this young woman's story, I hurt. I would hurt for any of my students who had this experience. Yet my hurt for this young woman feels deep and personal. Like parents, professors are not supposed to have favorites. But this young woman was one of my favorites. A number of times after class she stayed to ask me questions. From those interactions with her I learned how genuine she is in social interaction. I know how filled with hope she is about life. So I hurt for her. I hurt for her having to face such monstrous, primal, bullying, bigotry.

CHAPTER 13

WHAT DID YOU JUST SAY TO ME?

There is no denying that sometimes students come to the university bringing with them people who want them to keep their old patterns of interpersonal behavior. On any campus, students do arrive with old relationships that push for keeping to the old back-at-home ways. That is why one of the goals of my classes is to help these young travelers develop a critical eye about "how we have always done things." Otherwise, again, we leave them to their own uneducated devices.

In one of our open-class discussions, my students talked about the sadness they feel about their self-segregation. My Latino, White, male, Black, Arab, female, Hindu, mixed-race students talked about the fact that here at college they have a racial mix of acquaintances, but they seldom go to each other's parties. There are Brown parties, White parties, and Black parties, all manner of segregated social activities.

Hearing lament in their voices, I ask, "Why so much self-segregation?" And they reply:

"We don't know how to talk to each other."

"We don't know what to expect."

"We don't have any helpful experiences being with each other before we come to college."

Those concerns reflect what the research shows. Tendencies to self-segregate because of being anxious about interacting with racial others is highly correlated with lack of diversity experiences. Coming from middle and high school environments that lack diversity, or that lack meaningful interactions between young people from different groups, our students come to us unprepared for the neo-diversity of a college campus. Young people come to college with group stereotypes as the only tools they have for trying to survive in a new social situation.

Keep in mind that these are not old people. For that matter, being old would be no excuse. But again we are not talking about old people, set in their ways. These are college-aged, college-going young people who are sometimes downright resistant to interaction and learning.

Sad as this is, sadder still is the fact that all too often when they get to college their stereotypes are allowed to live on, if not grow stronger. We seem to have lost faith in the power of higher education. That is why there is so much flat-out resistance among these young people to interacting across group lines. A Southeast Asian Brown student wrote:

As I finished eating dinner at Fountain Dining Hall on campus at NCSU, I sat back in my chair and started to relax and enjoy the conversations a couple of the other Resident Advisors were discussing. My friend Drew asked what I was up to this weekend. I replied by saying, "I'm hanging out with my South Asian Club (EKTAA) friends on Friday night. We are throwing a party for the President."

Drew then said, "Cool, that sounds like fun. I am on duty with this guy over here."

I look over, and across the table is Resident Advisor, Ben. Ben then looks at me and says, "I'd come and crash the party and be the odd ball out since I'm White, but I'm on duty too."

I looked over and said, "How would you be the odd ball out?"

Ben then said, "It's a "Brown" party, right?! I'm sure I'd be the only White person."

I proceeded by looking over to Drew and saying, "Our friend Ryan comes to these "Brown" parties all the time; he's White and he enjoys them. He actually loves them. He thinks they are quite fun."

Ben looks at me and goes, "I got invited to one once by my suitemate Kunal."

I said, "Kunal who? I might know him."

Ben then states, "Kunal ghisdigkhslgkhsg or something, I don't know how to say it. It's a 'Brown' name. All I know is that he hangs out with only Indians and they all smell like curry."

I then looked over to Ben, shocked, leaned over the table away from the back rest of my chair and said, "I don't smell like curry and I'm Indian. I actually am not a big fan of curry anyways. I do know Kunal though, that's his party I am going to on Friday. He's vice president of EKTAA, and I am secretary. Look what I am doing now, I'm hanging out with you and Drew and all the other RA's, of which none are 'Brown.'"

Ben then laughs and says, "Yeah, I guess you're right, you're eating dinner with us."

By this point, I get up, walk away to get some water, and get back to the table. My really good RA friend Murphy starts to talk about how he wants ice cream, and the subject changes.

If we do not give young people new and more appropriate tools to use to evaluate their tendencies to self-segregate, this is what we get. By saying no more than "You have to be more accepting" at their graduation we send them away from the university on the Wrong-Line train, and they become the "educated ones," the "leaders," who still have trouble interacting with, and showing respect to, whoever "they" are. As a social psychologist and a former university administrator I worry about the consequences of self-segregation.

For two years I served as NCSU's first vice provost for Diversity and African American Affairs (Wolcott). While in that administrative role I was sensitized to the fact that our university was not doing much to help students deal with the neo-diversity that was coming to our campus. I had taken the job to be a change agent within an institution that was fearful of change in the diversity climate. It was a turbulent two years, which I chronicle in my memoir *Making Gumbo in the University* (Nacoste).

During the time I was vice provost I learned some things. I don't know about other universities, but North Carolina State University has, for a long time, held a separate day of orientation for African American first-year college students. When this practice began in the 1970s, the idea was that Black students coming to a predominantly White university were in need of a little extra help adjusting to a hostile social climate. African American students might also need some hints to help them adjust to the academic pace of a major research university. Later, around 2001, that approach was extended to American Indian and Hispanic students, each group given a separate day of orientation.

This special arrangement for orientation of selected groups made some sense very early on as the university was opening to a more broad-based, desegregated student body. But much of this approach was based on the assumption that ALL Black, ALL African American students would have trouble adjusting to the racial college environment of NCSU. That was no longer true when I became vice provost, and it certainly is not true now. Today, African American students who enter NCSU are themselves neo-diverse. Admitted Black students are a mix on all kinds of dimensions.

I was aware of the problem before I became an administrator in 2000. From 1988 to 2000, I carried out my faculty role with no major administrative duties. As most faculty members do, I advise students in our psychology major. During that time I advised a Black male student who was already a high academic achiever, as was evidenced by the academic scholarship he received when he came to our campus.

An academic go-getter, this young Black man from Fayetteville was a founding editor for an online magazine at our university, and he went on to win other major academic fellowships. In one of our early advising meetings he asked me to explain the point of the separate orientation. He asked because he was frustrated by having someone (a Black person) assume he did not know how to manage his time. Over and over, for years and for various reasons, African American students have expressed to me their frustration with that approach to getting them oriented to the campus, including the presumption (made by some in charge of the orientation) that Black students come to the university afraid of White people.

Another student, a Brown-skinned, mixed-race female who identified as Black, expressed more than frustration. This young woman was angry because during the African American Symposium (orientation) she felt that she was being told not to trust White people on campus. Looking into my eyes she said, "I was insulted . . . my Daddy is White and I love my Daddy."

As the vice provost for Diversity and African American Affairs, I raised serious questions about the segregated orientation for Black students. In no uncertain terms, I was told not to cause trouble. It was just easier since this was the way it had always been done. In my view, both then and now, too many in the administration seem to have lost faith in the power of higher education.

Yet I was not saying that ALL Black students come to us prepared for the environment of our campus. My argument was that isolating those students by race does not help, and may hinder, their development as students. I feel even more strongly about this given what my students have written about since I began teaching my "Race" course. The student response to my class assignment "one new thought" always finds me learning a bit more about my students' lives on campus. The assignment is straightforward:

> New information is only worth something if it gives you a new way to look at the world. The new information in this course should be helping you to develop a "social psychological eye"; a way of looking at the world that is first and foremost social psychological. In particular, this course should be helping you develop a social psychological eye for looking at race, gender, ethnicity, religion, and sexual orientation at the *interpersonal-intergroup level*; in interpersonal interactions and relationships. The point of this paper assignment is for you to describe what you consider to be the most important *one-new-thought* you have about interpersonal-intergroup interactions and relationships as result of this course.
>
> In one page, explain the most important one new thought about *interpersonal interactions and relationships* that you have had that is based on a concept related to neo-diversity discussed in this class. Your assignment is to write about that one new thought describing how it will help you function better in your *interpersonal-intergroup* (race, gender, ethnic, sexual orientation, or religious) interactions and relationships.

About how the separate orientation day influenced her, an African American female student wrote:

> When I began to think about past experiences in my life that could be related to this class I began to think about when I first came to North Carolina State University. When I came to NCSU, for orientation the African American students were asked to attend a day earlier to be able to connect with other African Americans, which in this story will be considered the in-group. It is here where we bonded and formed friendships that would blossom throughout the years to come with people we met here. Towards the end of that day the upperclassmen began to tell us to be aware of tomorrow because

the fact that there are so many people here and everyone looks like you will not be the case tomorrow. A few of the people that I connected with that night got together and promised to hang out the next night after all of the festivities of orientation died down.

The next day, when I woke up to get ready for the day at eight a.m., there was a flood of the Caucasian race. As some of my acquaintances from the day before walked in and saw each other we looked at each other as if to say do not go too far and call me so we can make sure we get together. In the beginning of the day we were all separated up into different groups where for the most part there were about thirty different orientation counselors with one to two African Americans in each group. Yet, every time we got the chance to get together throughout the day we would get together and talk about how we were all going to get together later that day and how supposedly the Caucasians did not try to talk to us, and we felt as though they didn't try to include us in any of the events or activities.

But when looking back at this event I am discovering that there was a high *intergroup anxiety*, or anxiety stemming from contact with out-group members. Looking back, I cannot help but wonder if it was White students not accepting us or us Black students not accepting them? Did we even give them a chance to get in our circle, or did we already come with preconceived notions from what members of our in-group had already told us the previous day. I realize that it is hard to develop relationships with people who are members of the out-group because of the close bond that we have with members of our in-group. Looking back at the situation I wonder just how many possible relationships did I completely push out during orientation that could have been meaningful, lasting relationships.

Yet, the fact is that I cannot continue to dwell in the past because it is something that I cannot change, but I can focus on the changes I can make for the future. This change is to not judge before I get the chance to know someone because I can block out a potentially meaningful relationship.

Given a set of concepts by which to analyze interpersonal-intergroup interactions, students themselves see the pitfalls of the university's segregated approach to helping Black (as well as American Indian, Latino, and Hispanic) students adjust to the campus. This writer was able to express what other African American students have expressed to me in their own way. Yet the university persists in taking this segregated approach. The university seems to have lost faith in its educational mission and skills.

In 2012, a new administrator who read my memoir about my work on diversity in the university asked me this question: "If you had a magic wand, or institutional power, what would you do that is not being done on our campus to address diversity issues?"

I had an answer ready. For a long time I have believed that the university needs to put together a group of incoming students based on their status as the first in their family to go to college. First-generation college students are smart, but they have no informal network to draw on to get answers to their questions about college or university life. They are, after all, the first in their family, and research shows that the lack of family to advise them puts these students at risk of dropping out (Chen and Carroll). So, if I had a magic wand, I would have the university create a group made up of first-generation college students. That group would not be isolated by race or gender, because it would be neo-diverse. That group would need basic information about how to navigate college, including how to manage an environment with so many different kinds of people. But as they learned about all this, these students would be learning within a racial, gender, ethnic, and religious mix of students. Taking that approach, this group would be as mixed as the rest of the campus. In order for this course to be effective, one of its features would be student interaction with each other to deal with the self-segregation tendencies.

If I had a magic wand, I would create a requirement for all first-generation college students to be in an "Adjustment to College" course. That's what I would do in an effort to improve retention and graduation rates of a neo-diversity of students.

I don't have a magic wand. But I am a day breaker.

Colleges and universities have an obligation to teach students to evaluate critically the attitudes and the dispositions they bring to campus. We do not exist to leave in place or to reinforce the stereotypes students bring into the classroom. If that is all we do, we are not educating our students. We are leaving them to live by their own, preexisting, tendencies; to live by stereotypes. If that is all we do, we are just leaving the young travelers who come to us to stumble about the dark, narrow passageways of the Wrong-Line train. Higher education was intended to do far more than that.

I do what I can through my teaching. I am a day breaker.

As I have mentioned, on day one of my "Race" class I exhort to my students that we've got some difficult days ahead. When I go over the syllabus, in addition to the emphasis I give to the safe space rule, I specify a "seating choice rule." After the first exam, I require each student to change his or her seat so that each is sitting next to someone new.

Day two of my class, I create chaos.

After students are seated, I walk in and greet them with a hearty "Good afternoon." "Here's what we're going to do," I immediately say. "On the small pieces of paper that are being given to you now, each of you will write the following information. Write your initials. Write your answers to these three questions: One, what is your favorite type of music? Two, what is your favorite genre (or type) of movie? Three, what is your favorite outdoor activity?" I repeat while they write.

"All set?" I ask. "OK, now I want a count-off, up to four. So I will start the count with the front row. Each person will call out your number when it's your turn, and remember your number."

That done I start pointing to corners in the classroom. "Group 1, go and stand here; Group 2, go and stand here. . . ." With fifty to sixty students, each of the four groups is pretty large.

I hand each group an envelope. "Put your pieces of paper in this envelope. Mix them up."

They do.

"Now watch me," I say.

I take Group 1's envelope and trade it with Group 4's. I take Group 2's envelope and trade it with Group 3's.

"Here's what we are going to do. Group 1, please pull a piece of paper from Group 4's envelope. Let everybody in your group read the piece of paper." That done, I say, "Now, Group 1, look across at Group 4 and as a group come up with your guess of which person in Group 4 that piece of paper belongs to."

A little confusion, a lot of excitement is in the classroom. Students in Group 1 are huddled together passing the paper around, looking across at Group 4 and quietly discussing their guesses."

"OK, Group 1 . . . read out loud the answers to the questions on the piece of paper you selected." The answers are "Music: hip-hop. Movies: action films. Outdoor activity: no real preference."

"Group 1, who did you decide this list belonged to?"

They point. We figure out who they are pointing at, and I call that student to the front of Group 4.

"Group 1, read the initials."

I look at the brown-skinned male who has stepped forward, and I ask, "Is that you?"

"No," he says, shaking his head.

"Well, whoever is that Group 4 member, please reveal yourself."

A White female steps forward, and the class roars with laughter.

We do this over and over, watching each group guess wrong.

One group, on one turn, makes the right guess.

Two or three rounds later I say, "OK, here's what we're going to do now. Each of you will go around the room and meet, shake hands with, and talk with three people you do not know. And remember, I'm watching. Go . . ."

Chaos . . .

Fifty to sixty neo-diverse students are moving around the room with shyness and uncertainty. After all, it is only the second day of my class. Even so, each student is walking up to a stranger, shaking hands, and talking for a little bit. The noise level rises with voices and bits of laughter. I check in when I see a student standing alone.

"Have you met three people? Well, get to it. Here's somebody right here."

I push. But I don't have to push too much. Yes, with some shyness and uncertainty my students are nonetheless doing what I have instructed them to do: meeting strangers who look like them and some who differ from them by some obvious external characteristic.

I love watching students during this exercise. I love watching them trying to manage the social chaos in the room. Bumping into each other, "Oh, excuse me," walking up to someone quick (before they lose courage) and extending a hand for a handshake, shy smiles as they talk for about a minute and have to move on. For me, it is something to watch these young travelers standing on a new terrain figuring out how to start an interaction with a stranger, a traveler who has also just come to this prairie on the frontier.

"All right . . . has everybody met three people? OK, back to your seats."

As they move to sit down, some are still smiling, looking over at a new acquaintance. Chaos begins to settle down.

"Well, that was fun," I say. "Why do you think I put you through the exercise, guessing about other people?"

"To get us to think about our stereotypes," someone calls out.

"Of course," I say. "We all have them; we all have stereotypes. You don't have a choice about that. Your cognitive economic system searches for categories to simplify the world. So is there anything wrong with having a stereotype?"

"Look," I go on, "We all have stereotypes. And no, there is nothing wrong with that in and of itself. Think about it, you're on the brickyard in front of D. H. Hill Library, and hundreds of students are standing, talking, eating a sandwich, or just walking by going to a class. You make up stories about who they are based on your stereotypes. For me it's airports. I'm sitting there bored, watching people walk through, and I'm making up stories about those people based on my stereotypes. So we all have stereotypes. Nobody is immune from that. So what was the point of the exercise?"

"To show us they don't always work."

"Now we're getting somewhere," I say. "Stereotypes don't always work; actually, most times they don't."

A hand goes up.

"Yes," I say pointing to the student.

"Our group got one right."

"Yes, you did," I admit. "But keep this in mind . . . even a broke-clock is right twice a day. Stereotypes are a broke-clock in interpersonal-intergroup interactions. Sometimes they will seem to be right, but they are right for the wrong reasons. That is also why the real problem is our tendency to rely on stereotypes in real face-to-face interaction with a specific person. The trouble starts when we get our interaction confidence from these stereotypes. One of the interaction dynamics we will explore is how an interaction can go so quick from 'Hey, how's it going' to 'What did you just say to me?'

"When we rely on them, our stereotypes get us into that kind of trouble. So here is the first but not the last time I will say it this semester: never try to interact with a person as a representative of a group."

I stop talking. I look over the class, watch my students watching me. I speak into that moment. "Heed my warning: never try to interact with a person as a representative of a group. Heed my warning because for sure when we rely on stereotypes, we limit our social experiences. I need a volunteer."

A hand goes up. I call on this student. For reasons unknown to me, the last two semesters the volunteer has been an African American female.

"Do me a favor. Stand up and tell us what you wrote as your favorite music type, movie type, outdoor activity."

The student does so. Then I say to the class, "If any of you had at least one thing in common with the list your classmate just gave us, stand up."

Always, a neo-diverse set of students stand: male, Black, White, Southeast Asian, female.

"Look at that," I say. "Here is one of the dangers of stereotypes. Stereotypes can make it so that we do not even consider interacting with someone because the stereotype tells us that we could not possibly have anything in common with one of 'them.' Again I say, never try to interact with a person as a representative of a group. When you do that, you mess up the interaction for the both of you."

In that way, some of what I teach in the class is basic social strategy.

"Why must you act like you already know something about a person you just met? Why would you walk up to me, as people have and say 'So you were a football player.' Why would you be so presumptuous and, as you know in my case, very wrong. Look, in this age of neo-diversity you are very likely to be wrong. Everything has changed, not just race, but for instance gender roles. When you presume and assume you are very likely to be wrong. That is why so many interactions today go so fast from la de da, 'Hey, how's it going' to growling, 'What did you just say to me?' That is why at social gatherings I never ask women or men

'What kind of work do you do?' I never ask that. If I want to keep an interaction going past a handshake hello, I ask, 'What keeps you busy?'"

That small lesson resonates with some of my students. A White male student wrote:

Prior to taking this class, I had a hard time comprehending the flow of events with new people. There's small talk, maybe some observations about something in their environment, and then at some point either the conversation just dies or somebody has introduced a new subject and hopes to steer the conversation. Now, I have been on the receiving end, as well as the giving end of the "what did you just say to me?" reactions where at that point you want nothing better than to just get up and run for cover.

From the levels of interdependence hypothesis, I now understand that in this moment of anxiety we have been shoved into the dispositional-identity level of interaction to make an assumption about who the other person is and what that person likes. This is incredibly dangerous, especially when it comes to intergroup interactions because we have all been exposed to and educated through stereotypes. So when we're in an intergroup interaction, and feeling anxiety from it, these safe assumptions we have about the person we're interacting with could blow right up in our face. It is with this knowledge that I now feel more prepared for interpersonal-intergroup interactions.

I'm at a social gathering; I've been introduced to a new person through a friend and am left alone with that person to talk amongst ourselves. Instead of accessing my dispositional assumptions and trying to "talk about something they would enjoy," I can instead focus on who is right in front of me. Your example of the phrase "What keeps you busy?" is something I found remarkably effective, instead of trying to use my own assumptions to "connect" with the new individual.

On the flip side of that, I have to realize what is happening when people make assumptions about me. Instead of letting my emotions get the best of me and giving them the "you have ten seconds to get to a safe distance" treatment, I can attempt to show them that their assumption about me is a harmless mistake. This person is experiencing anxiety, and they opened their mouth and made an incorrect assumption about me. The next statement that comes out of my mouth just needs to be something as simple as "What makes you think that?"

In interracial encounters this mindset is incredibly important, as I often find myself rushed to the dispositional assumptions due to the fact that I find it hard to relate to the person in front of me. It's as simple as having a different skin color, and knowing how sensitive race is to some people, that causes me to make all sorts of assumptions about the person I am interacting with. It's from this class that I can now recognize this, and realize that there are all sorts of people. It is by having this knowledge of how the anxiety is affecting me that I can change my behavior, and instead of rushing to the dispositional level I can now recognize this and instead interact with the person in front of me.

Having interpersonal interactions, having interpersonal relationships is the most fundamental, human thing we do in life. Yet we let young people stumble about, trying to figure things out on their own. We push them to major in the right subject, we push them to get jobs, and leave them to lurch about in the social world. In her one-new-thought paper, a White female student wrote about lurching about at the university:

> I view the world in a unique way, unlike anyone else I know. In reality, I believe we all have our own lenses through which we interpret life. As a social work student, I have supposedly been trained to be culturally competent. Unfortunately, being trained how to be culturally competent is not the same as knowing why you should be culturally competent. Yes, many people are taught by their parents to be accepting of others, but that does not teach you why you are different.
>
> I am from an Eastern North Carolina town where four thousand people call home. A paper mill is the main economy in the surrounding area, along with the bulk of the job market. In a town in which over sixty percent African Americans, thirty percent Caucasian, and ten percent of other ethnic groups including a growing Hispanic population call home, the only place these groups interact is at the paper mill. Growing up, I might not have ever known Whites were the minority in the town. I went to a private school with almost completely White children in a neighboring county. Almost all the events I attended in town mainly consisted of White children. In fact, the only other ethnic groups I encountered were at the softball park. I learned only one language community.

A language community is a set of people who give specific words and phrases unique meaning in order to define the group, its mutual under-standing, and its distinctive way of interacting through verbal and some-times nonverbal manners of speaking. My first day of class at North Carolina State University was everything I wanted, but I was scared. I had class with a Black student, a first for me. I had class with a student from another country, also a first. I saw people that did not look like me, talk like me, or even care about me. I learned quickly that I must work hard to understand what other people were talking about. What I learned was that people are from different language communities; I just did not know what that was called until this semester. Understanding the verbal and nonverbal ways that people are dif-ferent is extremely important.

Just giving students a concept, language community, can change how the student, the young traveler, approaches new social interactions. That always impresses me. It motivates my teaching. Another White female wrote in her one-new-thought paper:

The minimal group effect has stood out the most during the time in this course. The minimal group effect is the automatic categorization of a person as either inside or outside of our group, with a tendency to compete when we think of that person as outside our group (Nacoste, p. 104). This concept shines more than others because it's common and happens every day, espe-cially when someone new comes into the situation. The minimal group effect automatically categorizes "us" and "them" and also involves competi-tion within those considered in the out-group.

Categorizing individuals is almost like a second nature; it happens so often and it never clicks that that's what is actually happening, separating into "one of us" or "one of them." I am guilty of this, as well as many others. Our expectations get the better of us. Since taking this course, I now realize when new interactions arise I am more patient and can mentally stop myself from causing unnecessary tension that leads to competition. It used to be awkward for me to be involved in a situation where I'm interacting with someone of a different race because I was so afraid to offend him or her. I have never been familiar with different cultures and backgrounds until I moved to Raleigh for college. Slowly I have gotten more comfortable with it, but still always had that initial competition drive when the interaction started. Since taking this course, my knowledge has been expanded, and I have learned how to stop and analyze the situation without putting individuals into a category.

This new way of thinking has not only helped me in new and unfamiliar situations but it has helped me teach others and inform them of the minimal group effect (automatically putting people into us versus them social categories). I try to always give "what if" scenarios for my friends and help put themselves in other people's shoes. It has helped me have a better understanding and actually be more understanding of those who are in an interracial relationship, not just a dating relationship but also a relationship in general.

It has made a night going out into a fun experience meeting new people and expanding those relationships instead of an uncomfortable interaction with tension. Before learning about the minimal group effect I am ashamed to say that I used to be so quick to put people in "like me" "not like me" categories all the time without even realizing it. It is difficult to recognize especially being surrounded by "competition" every single day. I have learned from this and am very proud that I can avoid such tension and help others acknowledge that this doesn't help interactions; it only makes the situation worse.

Wherever these young people travel in America, these new understandings will help. It is clear that my students learn to do the work necessary to not let their stereotypes rule what they do in a social interaction. My students come to accept the truth that we all have stereotypes and the truth that the "I don't see color" or the "I interact with everyone the same" strategies don't really work.

Stereotypes pop into all our heads unbeckoned. When that happens each of us has the job of not letting our stereotypes take over. And I am not telling you to try to suppress the thought; that is a bad strategy. Acknowledge the stereotype to yourself and recognize it for what it is: a stereotype. You already know that no person is a stereotype. So interact with the person in front of you, not the stereotype of the group. That's what I teach; that's what my students learn. Even while they are still in the class, this new learning helps students use the concepts to look back at something that was positive but still just a bit of a social puzzle. A White male student wrote:

My most intense interracial interaction was quite positive. I used to work as a waiter at a restaurant in Fayetteville, North Carolina. The worker demographic was predominantly Black; I was the only White kid working there. Sometimes I felt left out of "inside" conversations among the other co-workers and out-of-work social gatherings; however, I was always very cordial to them on the job, I just didn't know my role or how to effectively interact with my Black co-workers. My anxiety often restrained me from initiating a conversation.

One Friday afternoon, one of my big, Black, dreadlock-headed co-workers came up to me and said, "Yo dog, you ain't no regular White boy. We think you are cool as hell. You should come over to the crib tomorrow night and chill with us homies." After he made his offer, my face lit up. I was ecstatic to be "accepted" by the people, my co-workers, who at work I interact with and who I would now be able to accompany in their leisure time. Although the thought of possible deception went through my mind briefly during the interaction, I could tell that he was not trying to deceive me because his two friends, who stood in the near distance, smiled and nodded at me in a genuine manner.

What caught me a little off guard in that interaction was when my co-worker said that I was "no regular White boy." In that split second before I responded to his initial statement, I realized that his invitation was sort of exclusive, assuming that "regular White boys" generally were not sought as being adequate enough to hang out in their group. To them, I was special. My personality is what he and his friends found to be positively radiant, not my skin color. The night ended very well as my co-workers and I found that we had a lot in common.

Every time I read this story I smile and start to laugh out loud. I think it's the combination of knowing the person who had this experience and these words spoken to this reserved young White man: "Yo dog, you ain't no regular White boy. We think you are cool as hell. You should come over to the crib tomorrow night and chill with us homies." I am smiling right now. I just love this story. Our writer analyzed his words this way:

At the time that the intense interracial-interpersonal interaction took place I did not have many people that I had strong interdependence with since I had just moved to Fayetteville, North Carolina, from Cary, North Carolina. As stated, the worker demographic here was predominantly Black and was highly different from my workplace in Cary, where I was around mostly White co-workers. Not only was the group composition taken into account in my assessment of the situation but the structure of the situation at the workplace (being a waiter, I had to communicate with my co-workers frequently to make sure that restaurant procedures were going smoothly) was considered as well. So, when my big, Black, dreadlock-headed co-worker began to initiate the interaction, I assumed that he was intending to communicate something work-related to me, judging by our past interactions and equal status, employee-wise, in the workplace. In addition, the type of interdependence that my co-worker and I shared was cooperative, not competitive.

So, when I realized what he said was not work-related and was actually an invitation to a friendly association with his group ("Yo dog, you ain't no regular White boy. We think you are cool as hell. You should come over to the crib tomorrow night and chill with us homies"), I fell in a state of interaction uncertainty (not sure of my role, rules for the interaction) for what seemed to be a split second. This vague interdependence fueled my social uncertainty because I was not sure how to respond at first and was a little skeptical because my co-worker had never expressed an interest in me before. As I began to assess the possible actions/outcomes for myself in this interaction, I sorted out my options of responses that I would make to hopefully decrease my anxiety at that moment: If I said yes to his invitation, I could possibly be subjecting myself to be negatively evaluated by the in-group members at his "crib"; that risk of self-embarrassment could be psychologically damaging, and I could potentially lose motivation towards future interaction with my co-workers, whom I had to come in contact with every day.

However, the social cues I was picking up from the interaction were telling me that the positive potential consequences outweighed the negative potential consequences since my co-worker said that I was "no regular White boy." This assertion that my co-worker made elicited a cognitive image in which I envisioned myself positively interacting with people of a different race than I.

I perceived their in-group bias to be positive in the sense that they perceived me, an irregular White boy, to be superior to the out-group (regular White boys). That sense of entitlement and acceptance to the in-group elicited positive emotions in me. My evaluative reaction was positive as well since my co-worker's friends were standing beside him and seemed to be genuinely confirming the invitation to the in-group as they smiled and nodded.

Any stereotypes that I had of Black people being deceiving towards White boys were fully suppressed. As a behavioral consequence, I kindly accepted my co-worker's invitation to an afternoon gathering in hopes of possibly developing a relationship. I made sure to respond to his invitation in a tactful way which did not seem out of character or socially awkward. This positive interaction precipitated less avoidance of my co-workers on a daily basis since my social uncertainty had subsided.

According to Nacoste's Interdependence-Integrative relationship development model, my position as a waiter at the restaurant in Fayetteville entailed much surface contact with not only customers but with co-workers as well. Smiling, restaurant information exchange, and the occasional "how are you doing?" were the extent of my interactions with my co-workers for the first couple of weeks of moving to Fayetteville. I did not self-disclose any personal information to my co-workers either because I did not see an opportunity to do so, feared that they would not care to know anything about my history or personal preference, or because no one asked. This failure to provide any self-disclosure stopped my interactions with my co-workers from moving beyond surface contact into a deeper level of relationship.

Conflict is the only way that relationships can evolve, and I did not want to create conflict with one of my co-workers for fear of external factors that affect the interaction, such as an employer firing me because I said something that created conflict with a fellow employee. So, when this intense (for me) interracial interaction commenced, my self-awareness increased because I did not want to respond inappropriately. Fortunately, after the interaction with my co-worker happened, I accompanied him to his "crib" where I became more social and self-disclosed some personal information. Because of the simple social avenue that my co-worker provided, our relationship seemed to have elevated into the deeper (minor-mutuality) relationship stage, since self-disclosure had begun.

Although I liked his analysis of the situation, in a way it seemed our writer was downplaying *his* role in what happened. He seemed to think that because he came into work and was "only" polite and cordial that he might have been perceived as standoffish and not cool.

Thinking about that part of his analysis, in writing my reaction, I pointed out that he should give himself some credit. He followed the rules for the (surface contact) stage of the relationship. He didn't push. He did not try to be cool. Around his Black co-workers, even around his big, Black, dreadlocked co-worker, he was himself doing his job. He greeted his co-workers without trying to talk the way he heard one or all of his Black co-workers talk. So, in his Black co-workers' eyes, and in their experience it seems, he wasn't "no regular White boy."

This is important stuff. Learning how to interact in a neo-diverse world is a modern life skill. Segregation breeds group stereotypes and hampers an individual's development of those social skills, and so hampers important social interactions. If that is true about stereotypes regarding racial groups who are sometimes easy to see, how do stereotypes get in the way of social interactions with members of groups we know are here but who are not easy to identify and may even be invisible? What do you do when you are interacting with someone who, in the moment of the interaction, goes from group invisible to group visible? One of my Jewish students wrote:

This is what happens when people find out that I am Jewish.

"Oh, you're JEWISH. You don't look Jewish."

—How does someone *look* Jewish? I don't look at you and say, "Wow, you look Christian/Hindu/Muslim/Buddhist."

"Oh, you're a JEW. But you have blonde hair and blue eyes?"

—Yes, I know, I have looked in a mirror before.

—Moreover, why are you referring to me as a "JEW"? Judaism is my faith, being Jewish is part of my identity. It may be considered a label (by some)—You may *not* LABEL me.

When I ask people, "What does 'Jewish' look like?" They usually spew out the typical stereotypical response: large hook-noses, dark curly hair, dark skin, and dark-colored beady eyes.

Usually this awkward conversation ceases at this point, the topic is changed, or the other member of the dyad begins to talk about him or herself. However, other times, and all too frequently, the conversation will quickly take a sharp downhill turn with this announcement:

"You know you would have survived the Holocaust."

I do not know what prompts people to express this view to me. Maybe they think they are providing comfort, or they are, in some way, trying to give me their condolences. I wish that they had stopped after their first mistake. You are already in over your head, why dig the hole deeper? Whatever they are attempting, it is unnecessary and offensive.

By that statement, you belittle my past and my people's past. You demean the innocent lives lost and dishonor those who fought for their liberation.

Suddenly the person in front of you is not who you assumed they were. Your stereotype didn't work. And it seems that people can be so surprised or so suddenly filled with intergroup anxiety that they have no grace in receiving the information. It is sad that interaction anxiety can cause all kinds of awful things to be said. I am so surprised that far too many people focus the whole interaction on that person's group membership as if that makes up the whole person. This leads to the interaction shifting from "Hey, how's it going?" to "What did you just say to me?"

That is why I so often warn: Never try to interact with a person as a representative of a group.

What should a person do? Slow down, breathe, admit.

We adults have got to stop acting as if we never have and never will make interaction mistakes that have to do with neo-diversity. We have got to stop justifying our behavior saying, "I didn't mean it like that." We have to stop acting as if we are innocent. There are no innocent. So, slow down, breathe, admit.

Once we have admitted to our humanity, we can look back and learn from our mistakes. We can even catch ourselves in the middle of a social interaction and stop ourselves or admit to our interaction partner: "That was offensive."

Look, having come this far with me you know more about the dynamics of neo-diversity than ever before. Now you know how neo-diversity can influence you during a social interaction. Use what you know about the five stages of social interaction:

Stage I. Each person assesses the situation: Where, Why, When, Who? Where am I going? Why or for what purpose am I going there? When am I supposed to be there? Who else will be there?

Stage II. Each person assesses possible outcomes for self: How will I be treated? Will I have a good time?

Stage III. Each person tries to find a cognitive, shortcut way of understanding what might be going to happen (it's a party versus it's a funeral) or what is happening in the moment. We do this to avoid or to solve an actual or potential interaction problem.

Stage IV. Each person experiences large or small identity concerns that can heighten emotion: Am I being myself? How am I coming across? What am I saying?

Stage V. Each person engages in interpersonal behavior: What is said or done. We attempt to interact safely, in a way that is appropriate to the situation or interaction moment.

Use your new knowledge of those stages to think through when in an interaction you are most vulnerable to neo-diversity anxiety. Maybe you too often don't think about the situation beforehand (Stage I) and so find yourself surprised and feeling awkward in the situation. Maybe you head into the situation too worried about doing something wrong (Stage II). Maybe you start to worry too much about what other people are thinking about you as you interact (Stage IV). Be honest with yourself about your vulnerabilities in social interaction especially in a neo-diverse situation.

How? Play an interaction out in your imagination. Do it the way we all do when we are people watching. Create the story and see potential mistakes and then decide how you will behave in a way that is more appropriate to the stage of the relationship you are in with the person. Do that cognitive exercise, and that work will help you build a reservoir of strategies for social interactions of many different types.

As one of my students put it, neo-diversity is not going anywhere. So, slow down, breathe, admit; that is part of what I give my students to prepare them, and it is a strategy we all can use to prepare ourselves to live and interact well in our neo-diverse America and world.

We can't know everything about everyone we meet for the first time, or even everyone we have interacted with a few times before. To know a lot about a person takes not just time but also an understanding that people are always working on developing their authentic self. That is why it is dangerous to become complacent about knowing your new acquaintance or a friend. The minute you take them for granted is just the minute you will find something out that shakes you up. I mean, what will happen when you are in a face-to-face interaction and the other person—a recent acquaintance or a new friend—shatters your assumptions by revealing that he or she is gay, lesbian, or transgendered?

What do you do then?

PART 7

THE FARE IS CHEAP AND ALL CAN GO, THE RICH AND POOR ARE THERE

CHAPTER 14

A BEAST BENT ON GRACE

Jack Gilbert is a poet I discovered in June 2013. In the summers, I let my reading become a bit haphazard. Mystery novels, literary novels, young-adult fiction, science fiction, memoirs, and a magazine or two are part of the mix. When I picked up the *Sun* magazine in June, I just wanted to see what kinds of writing the magazine was highlighting nowadays. I discovered good articles, and then I hit a section of poetry in memory of Jack Gilbert, whose name I didn't know. I read. Then I went out and bought his *Collected Poems*.

There are no innocent, I say and know. Jack Gilbert knew it too and said we are all monsters. Yet, he said, each of us is

> . . . a beast bent on grace.
> A monster going down hoping to prove
> a monster by emphasis and for a time—
> knowing how many are feeding and crying
> they are saintly dragons on their way to God,
> looking for the breakthrough to heaven.
> But the monster goes down as required. O pray
> for this foolish, maybe chosen beast.
> (Gilbert, "Myself Considered . . . ," p. 10)

If you like, you can find and read various commentaries on Gilbert's poetry online. Having really read some of his poetry now, I say that Jack Gilbert's poetry is visceral. His poetry comes from his humane masculinity. Joy in all the hardship and hurt life and love brings to us all, expressed with strength, verve, conviction, and no surrender.

> If the locomotive of the Lord runs us down
> We should give thanks that the end had magnitude.
> (Gilbert, "A Brief for the Defense," p. 213)

Live life. Hard as that living can be sometimes, live it still. How else to live? That is the exhortation that is Jack Gilbert's poetry.

Yes, there are difficult days ahead. But that is always true. So live, learn, hope, seek, find, and accept challenge and joy. Live with integrity; live up to the standards of behavior you claim.

Sad that when it comes to neo-diversity matters, too many individuals' lives are unsure and far too quiet. We show too much tolerance for intolerance. We feed only the monster in us and the monster in those around us rather than seeking redemption as chosen beasts. Maybe that's because no one has taught us the truth. Maybe we've been so poorly taught that we believe it's all just a big joke anyway. Maybe, in our move toward a false redemption the only thing we've heard is that we just have to be more accepting.

It should be no surprise, then, that when we hear the sound of the Neo-Diversity train coming we become monsters in hiding. We cower in the corner, worried only about being run down by that locomotive. Ironic, isn't it, that if we were to come out of the corner, rather than run us down the train would slow to a stop, the doors would open with invitation for us—yes, we beasts—to get onboard, no ticket necessary. We will have been called. We will have been chosen.

Neo-diversity tests our hibernating beastliness. We have come to this era in America when no one wants to be melted, and fewer and fewer of us are hiding in closets. More and more, the closet doors are open, and when we look in we find the closet empty. We turn to walk away from the empty closet only to see that some of the people who had been in there are the people standing right next to us. A White male student wrote:

> I was in the library in between classes, playing one of the game consoles in there. This was my first year of college and very early in the semester, so

I didn't really know anyone and just kind of hung out and played games and associated with the other people playing games, one of which was a friend from high school, David. We would play pretty frequently, and about halfway through the semester I had a pretty solid acquaintanceship/ friendship with a couple of the guys in there. One of these was Charlie, who I thought I knew pretty well. We hung out outside of the library, ate dinner with friends together and such. We were pretty good friends for just knowing each other recently.

But back to the moment. I was leaving the library with David as we were walking towards the bus. I can't remember what we were talking about specifically, but some random topic came up where David was laughing at another guy for thinking Charlie was straight. "Wait, what? Is Charlie gay?" I thought. I didn't say this because just then my bus came up and I parted ways with David, just laughing off his last comment and saying I'd see him later.

A couple days later I was at dinner with friends, Charlie included, and Charlie starts telling some story about him dating some guy and some craziness ensues because neither party was completely sane but they were both trying to be good for one another. I was caught off guard again and asked, "You're gay?"

Charlie looked at me like I was crazy and responded "Uh, yeah?" like it wasn't important and continued on with his story.

I didn't bring it up again that night, but finding out that a person I thought I knew was completely different from how I pictured him threw me off balance.

Charlie was not hiding in a closet. Charlie was not trying to be invisible. Yet it took a while for our writer to see Charlie. Our writer had not been paying attention, and when doing so was unavoidable, simply, he said to himself, "That couldn't be true." In fact, in his analysis he admits that for a while he continued to not know that his friend Charlie was gay. Analytically he wrote:

> One of the new people I am introduced to while playing video games is Charlie. Charlie is a very sociable and intelligent person, so I liked him fairly easily. Over the course of a few months, Charlie and I went from just surface contact ("Please pass the controller to me; it is my turn to play") to more of a minor-mutuality standpoint. We would do things outside the library

(granted, playing video games was still principle at the beginning) and even eat dinner together. This was frequently in the presence of shared friends, but not exclusively. I was glad at my progress of making new friends, confident I had gotten to know them pretty well, Charlie in particular in this case.

So one day, I'm walking towards the bus with David when he drops a huge bomb on me—Charlie is gay, not the person I thought he was. I grew up in a pretty small town and haven't had any interactions with people who were not straight at this point in my life, so much to the point that I initially do not believe David when he tells me that Charlie is gay. Indeed, in the story I mention that I pretty much just shrug it off (ignore it) and continue on with my day. I didn't plan to ask Charlie about it, didn't plan to dwell on it at all because it was uncomfortable for me. This is textbook neo-diversity anxiety. I have never dealt with this situation before, dealing with someone who is clearly different from me in a way I've never even encountered. I did not even know how to respond to David's comment, but I was luckily saved from that due to the arrival of the bus.

Powerful and important is the admission by the writer of the neo-diversity anxiety he was experiencing and what that anxiety did to him. He searched for a way to avoid the information. The bus saved him. Yet his now minor-mutuality relationship with Charlie meant that he would again interact with Charlie. And neo-diversity anxiety being what it is, operating on us the way it can, something awkward was bound to happen in our writer's upcoming interactions with Charlie. And something did happen. Going on with his analysis, he wrote:

Let's examine my side of this interaction using the Nacoste-Nofziger model:

I. In the Stage One assessment of the situation stage, we have basically two individuals here. Myself, who is trying to be social with friends. Second, we have Charlie, who I have considered a friend, is telling me/the group conclusively that he is gay.

II. Stage Two, assessment of possible outcomes. I am feeling intergroup anxiety. Even though we are all one group of friends, I am finding out for the first time that there are splintered factions and that one member (Charlie) is not in the groups I assigned him to.

III. In Stage Three, cognitive shortcuts, I'm searching for a way to make the interaction easier for me. So I ask Charlie, "You're gay?" to make sure that this isn't just a very elaborate joke. It makes it much easier for me if I can just put him in the box he was in previously instead of creating a new one.

You see, Charlie didn't exhibit any of the traits I'd stereotypically associated with "gay guys." He wasn't effeminate at all in body language or speech, which was the chief thing I had associated back then with gay men. So it was pretty natural for me to assume that he was straight, since he didn't fit what I knew gay men to be.

At that point of the interaction, I just sort of shut down with this new information. I stop listening to Charlie's story. I only half pay attention to what is going on, and I remember being just sort of conflicted in general. My traditional father had always preached that gay is essentially an affliction of the devil and completely wrong. So, confronted with the new information that my friend is this now nefarious individual when I still thought he was a pretty cool guy was a bit jarring.

Thankfully, I let the topic drop and didn't really say much on it. At the time, I was experiencing pretty heavy interpersonal anxiety due to my background conflicting with my then-current beliefs. If I had instead acted upon that anxiety, I likely would have done so on a dispositional-emotional level rather than a behavioral one, and likely alienated myself from Charlie and/ or the group because of it.

In the end, this interaction was not a complete disaster. It did throw me for a loop, but I eventually (next day or so) worked out the internal issues I was experiencing and just ended up accepting Charlie for who he was and to revise my previous inherited thesis of "all homosexuals are the product of the devil" for when I had more evidence.

One of the relationship principles of interdependence theory and my course is: A relationship cannot evolve without encountering and managing person-to-person incompatibility of preferences, and such interpersonal conflicts come with honest self-disclosures. It turns out that the social interaction experiences that help a relationship to evolve must include experiences in which the parties discover conflicts in preferences (e.g., Why would you want to go there? You eat that stuff?) and the management of those conflicts. Our writer was clearly in the midst of such a relationship-defining moment of conflict. Now he knows for sure that Charlie is gay because when he asked that all-important question, "Charlie looked at me like I was crazy and responded, 'Uh, yeah?' like it wasn't important. . . ."

That conflict moment now requires adaptation—our writer is struggling. He now knows that Charlie is gay, but he still thinks Charlie is a cool guy. That combination butts up against the writer's father teaching him that "all homosexuals are the product of the devil." Our writer shuts down in that cognitive conflict moment. To his credit, though, he did not let his neo-diversity anxiety control him. He took time to evaluate and reevaluate what he had been taught as it related to what he knew and felt about Charlie the person, not Charlie the representative of a group. None of that internal process was easy. But more and more in America, individuals have to deal with these interpersonal situations. And interpersonal life comes at us fast.

If you think that *that* particular moment of interpersonal conflict was jarring, check this out. A White male student wrote:

> We were at one of our very first winter guard competitions of the year. In case you don't know, Dr. Nacoste, winter guard is a performance group using some of the styles of military color guards, with the performances done indoors.
>
> It was probably around mid-February. We had already performed in the early morning, and so we were sitting in the bleachers to watch the rest of the guards, as well as the drum lines. We were just minding our own business, chatting, and having a good time, when two girls walked up from lower in the bleachers and came straight to me. As I said, they walked straight up to me and said, "Hey!" I stammered a polite hello, but I was caught off guard. They then continued, seemingly not seeing my surprise. "We're actually here because of our friend Jamie," they continued. "He thinks you're cute and was wondering if he could have your phone number, but he kinda wanted us to get it for him."
>
> Bam. Punch in the gut.
>
> Not a bad punch, exactly, but one I had never expected in a million years. I was so taken aback, I am pretty sure my jaw dropped open. I was sitting in the back of our guard (we were on multiple rows of bleachers), and I saw everyone from our school group turn to look at me. And of course, I panicked. I did the first thing I thought of (of course, one could hardly call it thinking), and to this very day I have no explanation as to why. I vaguely

gestured at one of my female friends in guard and said something to the effect of "Shouldn't he be asking for her number instead?"

I don't remember the exact wording, but that was approximately what was said, albeit in a more stammered and probably more insulting way. So stunned was I that I didn't even properly realize what I had said until after the girls gave me a strange look and went back to their own group, after which I never interacted with them again.

Neo-diversity situations can come at us fast. What a moment for this young male. Someone was attracted to him, and in the high school way of doing things that person sent friends over to make the first move. Just turns out that the person attracted to our writer is also male. Taking up the task of analyzing this social interaction, our writer begins:

This is actually an event that I have pondered many times and still feel guilty about. It was only after taking this class (along with Psych 311 before it), that I understand the reasons behind my unfortunately foolish reaction and the statement that followed.

So this interaction was one that he had thought over more than once since it happened. It had hit him so hard that he really wanted to—needed to—find a way to understand what happened, in particular to better understand his own reaction. Going on, he wrote:

Before I was asked for my number, I had not thought enough about the young man (let's call him "Sam") to form any sort of conclusions—at least consciously. I was simply minding my own business, hanging out with my friends, not really having to think about what I was doing. Then, the situation was thrust upon me: I was asked for my number, because Sam thought I was cute.

Immediately, my brain jumped to assessing the situation—"What happened? I got asked for my number. Why? Because that young man over there thought I was cute. What?? He thinks I'm gay." After the rapid and unconscious assessment of the situation, we come to the transition to Stage II (assessment of outcome for self). I was immediately nervous. I had never encountered such a situation before in my life, nor had I prepared myself to react accordingly if I ever DID find myself in that situation.

Of course, this confusion and nervousness also led to vague interdependence. Vague interdependence occurs when one experiences a situation that is (1) outside the normal flow of our interdependent interactions and (2) without clear roles, norms, and relationship history. The experience Sam and I had fit that description quite well, at least on my end. I had never had a guy ask for my phone number before, nor did I consciously think to expect it. The situation, in my eyes, at least, did not have any clear norms or relationship history. I didn't really know what role I was supposed to be filling, either. Thus, I was experiencing vague interdependence that was causing me to feel anxious.

Neo-diversity anxiety was now playing a role. This was an interpersonal-intergroup interaction, and one that I had never been in. A gay guy, asking for my phone number? It was unheard of! How in the world do I handle this? I thought to myself, "What the heck do I say?" I was interacting with Sam as a representative of a group, one that I hadn't interacted with consciously before, at that. As in any other situation, making that decision would have bad consequences.

Also, another facet of my anxiety was the perception of male color guard members. I was well aware that the vast majority of color guard males are perceived to be gay, and the perception of gay males in my hometown (or at least my high school) was not a positive one. Therefore, I had that worry weighing down on me every time I went to a guard practice or event.

Now I am fully in Stage II, Assessment of Possible Actions/Outcomes for Self. Here the subject analyzes the situation for the (mostly negative) possibilities for how this interaction will end for them. In this case, I wondered about whether I would be embarrassed, whether or not people in my guard would negatively judge me, and whether or not the people in the other guard (or . . . how THEY) would negatively judge me. I didn't even realize most of this was happening, but my brain was working in overdrive, trying to process this new scenario.

The speed of processing, added to the stress of the situation, led to Stage III: cognitive shortcuts. I used schemas to interact in the situation, again, treating Sam as a representative of a group. I had increased self-awareness and an in-group bias. My motivational biases—wanting to avoid embarrassment, wanting to not be negatively evaluated, etc.—took over, and I jumped to the dispositional level on interaction.

The levels of interdependence theory perfectly describes this. It states,

"Whenever the situational conditions surrounding a social encounter between two people creates or intensifies interpersonal uncertainty, the dyadic interaction is more likely to shift from a behavioral level of interdependence to a dispositional level of interaction, making the encounter more volatile" (Nacoste, p. 180). That is indeed what happened.

The situational conditions (interacting with a member of a group I hadn't encountered before) intensified the uncertainty between the two of us, and it shifted to a dispositional level. This propelled me into Stage IV: the dispositional level. In this stage, I, as all people entering this stage do, reacted with my emotions rather than logic. "What in the world?" my brain might have thought. "That guy's not supposed to ask you for your number! He should be asking for a girl's number! You know, like a 'normal' person would do!" I was inaccurately evaluating Sam, as well as the situation. At the same time, I was aware of the stereotypes associated with the LGBT community and was doing my best to not think about them; which was about as effective as trying to NOT think of a giant pink elephant.

Moving through Stage IV, I went to Stage V: interpersonal behavior. This is the culmination and expression of the previous four stages—my external behavioral response to the situation. "Shouldn't he be asking for her number instead?" I asked.

To me, analyzing the situation, and having BEEN in the situation, this means that being gay is wrong and abnormal—that Sam should have done what was "normal" and "right," and asked a girl for her number instead. The language I used, the way I spoke, and the actual content of my statement all negatively influenced the situation and reduced the chance of the dyad developing any further.

Honestly, if I encountered the situation today, I would have no problem at all saying, "I'm flattered, but I'm actually not gay." There would be no hesitation, no panic, no nervousness. I've interacted with many people since high school and at NC State that are different than I am, in many ways, so I am more comfortable with interacting with members of out-groups. I wish that I had been then. Instead, I said THAT. The damage was done, regardless of how I felt or how much I regretted it. Any interactions that Sam and I had (mainly just seeing each other at a distance, nothing more) were negatively influenced as a result. I quickly resorted to avoidance, of both Sam and the situation itself.

I honestly think that I felt so bad about how I reacted that I made sure to consciously make a large effort to become more comfortable in intergroup situations—with members of other sexual orientations, mainly—and this actually helped, as I did encounter similar situations with different people later in that same year, which went much better. So as awkward as this situation was, it helped me learn for the future.

Dr. Nacoste, as you said in what I believe was the first Psych 311 lecture, the world is primarily social. People, too, do not just exist for us to interact with them. If you go through life as if that were the case, you will always be in trouble. That is something I have learned over the last two years, and it makes many of my experiences more clear. I plan to take this knowledge, as well as the reflection on this particular situation, to my future encounters, so I can better interact with people of different groups not as representatives of a group but as individuals—as human beings.

The story and follow-up analysis speak for themselves. Our writer was in a new experience in his life that hit him in an unexpected way, and it made him want to understand what had happened. Here then is the power of the relationship experience. It captures why we as human beings cannot mature without real interpersonal relationships. Real interpersonal relationships always involve moments of interpersonal conflict, and it is through experiencing and examining these conflicts that we find out who we really are as individuals. Through social interactions we discover what we believe. Real social interaction can help us to stop just mimicking what we have been told. If we take our relationships seriously, we discover new aspects of ourselves and we commit to what we value and cherish. As we experience new relationships, we are constantly working on the authentic identity we are always building. Another White male wrote:

This is the story of my most challenging, and yet rewarding, interpersonal-intergroup interaction. The first semester of my junior year I had a car on campus, and I got to see my best friend Jesse, who attends the University of North Carolina more and more often. One weekend I brought him over to State, and I could tell that he wanted to discuss something. We did our usual sort of hanging out, which was playing board games on my floor, and playing a TV show in the background, this occasion being "Rosemary and Thyme," I remember.

Out of nowhere he told me that he had made a friend from Poland, a guy named K. B. Now I was a bit oblivious at first to what he meant by the next line he said, which was something along the lines of "We've been getting pretty close over the past few months. I mean . . . really close."

The next bit of dialogue was like a scene from a movie with me trying to rationalize that he meant they were a couple, and we went back and forth with these short, funny, choppy sentences. Our conversation was along the lines of:

"Ohh, so wait. You mean . . . like . . . umm so . . . good friends?"

"Yeah I guess . . . I mean, I dunno. Maybe more . . ."

"So, not just friends. Together? Like you're . . . umm . . . I mean . . ."

"Yeah, I guess I mean . . ." and he took a big breath and concluded with "I just realized I might be gay. No, wait, am so."

At this point, with it out in the open, I could feel myself just freaking out, my heart rate rising, my eyes kind of racing along my character card from the board game we were playing, not reading anything on it, just focusing my attention. It was a response from left field, nothing I had thought to be hearing on that day. I had all kinds of thoughts racing through my head. I wanted to just say, "So you're attracted to men?! Are you sure? You think this is just a stage?! Did you have sex?!"

I interrupt this student's story here because anxiety, as I point out to my students, is one of the worse things that can happen to you in a moment of social interaction. When I reached this point in the story, I was holding my head, trying to control my laughter. The story is written with a vivid honesty that let me feel the writer's dismay, confusion, and anxiety. You can almost hear the voice in his head getting louder with each thought:

"So you're attracted to men?! Are you sure? You think this is just a stage?! Did you have sex?!"

Oh no . . . oh dear . . . but thankfully all that was in his head. His story goes on.

In the end I collected my thoughts, looked up at him, and said the one thing I think he wanted to hear. I just asked him point-blank, "Does he make you happy?"

I mean, I wanted to cry inside; I was shocked, a bit rattled and shaking.

He told me that he'd never felt more sure about it before, and that he was going to see where it was going. I can't tell you how difficult this was for me to find the right thoughts and express them, but I had the realization that the first thought to come up could just be thrown out the window, and it helped me keep it together.

I was actually, instead of shocked and disgusted, really happy that he had found someone. I gave more attention to him, didn't stare at the card in my hand, and we started to just chat about his love like it was, dare I say, normal. My thoughts didn't go to the idea of him being sexual with a man, and the only disgust I felt that night was with myself for thinking that in the first place. Without analyzing the changes in our friendship here, I'll just conclude by saying that I told him, "Thank you for trusting me with that," and I gave him a good hand-patting hug, and we went back to playing "Arkham Horror" on my floor as we were. We didn't even talk about it any further, but it was fine since there was nothing left to say.

I am still smiling. I am smiling because this is such a vulnerable moment of social interaction for both men. Welcome to neo-diverse America, where these kinds of social interactions can, do, and will happen. Writing from his analytic position, the young man said:

In our modern social world, we are more and more interacting with groups of people that we never have interacted with before, which has the ability to cause problems that can affect our overall interaction outcomes. Thibaut and Kelley's research supports this claim as they reported that "any failure to communicate adequately and fully in the initial phases of a relationship [or interaction] will affect the representativeness of the outcomes sampled" (Nacoste, p. 23). In our day-to-day exposure to new interaction partners of varying groups, anxieties begin to develop that can cause this failure to communicate adequately.

When it comes to my interaction with Jesse, given that we were having a normal evening of enjoying time hanging out on the weekend, self-disclosing the information about realizing that he identified as a homosexual was a huge conflict juncture for us. At this point, our choppy banter was an attempt at grounding the words we both were thinking and were expressing, but it was a bit awkward due to responding to this intense incompatibility of the moment. Grounding is defined as "the attempt to establish that what has been said actually has been understood" (Nacoste, p. 227).

In that moment, I was reeling trying to find the response I thought would be best to be supportive for my friend, since I really did value our friendship and wanted to let him know I stood beside him in this new realization. Considering how I was able to gather my thoughts and actually ask him what I found truly important, about whether he was happy, shows that we resolved the conflict of Jesse wanting me to know and accept his homosexuality, and me looking into myself and finding out whether or not I could. I honestly can say that this shift really helped to push us back into a moderate level of mutuality, since we had lost a lot of our relational intensity due to the lack of frequency of impact, strength of impact, diversity of impact, and the duration of impact that came with going to separate universities and not being in such close proximity.

To look at this interaction in even closer detail, the Nacoste-Nofziger Model of Interracial-Interdependence can be used to explain the forces at work in the interaction moment. In Stage I we assess the situation of the interaction. Basically, for this stage I was assessing what kind of interaction we were about to have based on Jesse saying he had something to tell me, and noticing that he seemed a bit nervous and reserved. I came up with the assessment that we would be having a serious talk about something, which we do often anyway, but was trying to figure out why he would feel nervous talking with me about anything. The situation was structured; I knew Jesse was going to talk about something important, and I was going to need to be attentive to find something worthy to say back. I was not prepared for what came next, and the interaction moment sent me reeling through the next few stages.

To provide a little background on my friendship with Jesse, I will say that we did not talk about women much growing up, as neither of us dated. Perhaps a consequence is that I did use the minimal group effect on him, which is when we "automatically classify someone as inside or outside our group, with a tendency to compete" (Nacoste, p. 104). I classified Jesse as being heterosexual, but I did not give thought to the idea that he might not be. The moment that Jesse said he was sure about his homosexuality, vague interdependence hit me really hard.

I started to have this battle of figuring out my actual concerns here versus the ones I expressed in my head. I spent my time worrying about myself and not considering his side of the interaction. I was on one level trying to rationalize that he was attracted to men and what that would mean about his romantic interests, but the important factor here is that I was not worried about that per se, but that I was worried about myself and being embarrassed about what could happen to me. In that moment I was focusing on the negative evaluations that might come on me from my in-group, being heterosexual people. I was thinking about more than just sexual relations he'd engage in; I was thinking about how people would be likely to assume I was gay, that he might be attracted to me, how my parents would feel if they found out about it. Basically, I was extremely worried about my outcomes here from my main close peer group, which I assumed to be comprised solely of heterosexual people, with many of them having extreme negative feelings about the entire GLBT community. I did not even admit to having these biases and thought I had worked past them, but in the interaction moment, I was actually expressing them.

Here we see hibernating bigotry raising its head again. It was asleep, but now the temperature in the sleeper car has gotten too warm. The monster of hibernating bigotry awakens. In this case, fortunately, it does not devour. Our writer was able to grab and wrestle down that slobbering beast. He writes:

In Stage 3, we try to control our experience of our own outcomes as we are working through our cognitive shortcut ways of thinking. Using thoughts such as "Did he have sex with a guy?" or "Is he attracted to me?" were simply cognitive shortcuts that I was resorting to without giving a second thought. I was using my cognitive-economic system, which is "a set of cognitive processes that serve to reduce and simplify the vast amount of information we have to process, making our processing efficient and avoiding an overwhelming overload" (Nacoste, p. 179).

I was extremely self-aware at this moment, trying to figure out what to say, but also realizing I did not want to offend him. I wanted so badly to make this easy and just say whatever thought could fly out of my mouth, but we were entering a dispositional level, and I felt that even without understanding the concept of the dispositional level, interactions at this level are more sensitive and psychological than at the behavioral level. I was experiencing escalating emotions as the intensity of the interaction was increasing.

In Stage 4, I really did experience the dispositional-level emotional reactions. I felt my heart rate start to rise, my body sweat, and a sense of fear that we were going to not be able to work past this. I kept repeating those thoughts about how he must have had sex with a guy, and it actually bothered me enough to make me feel this distressed. Neo-diversity anxieties, when experienced like this, are extremely hard to overcome, and it caused me to come up with all of these horrible thoughts. I was making a lot of bad evaluative reactions about his homosexuality, but at the same time looking for the right thing to say so I did not offend him, knowing that I could not just spout out any one thought. I was, as the Nacoste text says, searching for the "appropriate identity to display" (p. 110). I did not want to let any kind of bias get in the way of this friendship, and I could see that my nonverbal behaviors were making it obvious that I did not immediately accept what he said. I could tell that we had entered the dispositional level, because here you realize that anything you say is going to hit the other person strongly, but also your own experience is going to resonate this way as well. I was luckily able to keep my wits and not spout out anything that would harm our friendship.

Relationships are powerful motivators. Motivations can sometimes go awry, but the desire to maintain a relationship, to be the right kind of person to have this friend, can make us take a close look at our behavior and pull us out of our anxiety in order to treat another human being with respect. Going on with his analysis, the young man says:

> Entering Stage 5, my behavior based on this new information was originally expressed through slight trembling and sweating. Here I decided to not fall victim to the effects of vague interdependence and have this interaction go sour. I decided to ask him if K. B. made him happy, which is usually how we approach the topic.
>
> For this interaction, I realized that I needed to gather my thoughts to glean exactly what I felt, instead of letting the neo-diversity anxiety take over the interaction. It would have been easy to say, "Did you two have sex?" considering that I seem to hold a stereotype that homosexual couples must be intimate. Instead, I realized that that actually did not matter, and that I cared much more about whether he was happy with this new identity that

he had accepted. We have not had perfect interactions based around sexuality since then, but the neo-diversity that we live with is not always readily adapted to, and we just have to be patient.

Jesse knows that I do not feel like his homosexuality is a negative thing, and getting past that was a huge step in bringing us closer as friends, but also for helping me to become even more accepting and understanding of the GLBT community. Neo-diversity presents its challenges, but the potential payoff for both in-group and out-group members can be extremely rewarding, as long as we are able to understand the emotional intensity that it brings with it and control our behaviors to be able to make it an enriching experience.

This is why I teach what I teach the way I teach. Wow, what a clear example of what I mean when I say we have to interact with the person in front of us, and not the group stereotype. We have to slow down, breathe, admit. In his analysis, we see this young man understand how he used the slow-down, breathe, admit strategy to full use so that he could interact with his friend as another, vulnerable, human being. So, we have got to stop worrying about damaging young people's faith in America. Young people want to learn; they want to live in a more humane society. How could it be otherwise?

A White female had this to say in her one-new-thought paper:

A little background information first: My whole life I have always been an outspoken (perhaps a little too outspoken) individual. With that said, I am careful to not say anything that may offend anyone, but I still let my opinion be known. When I started attending my family friend's church when I was eighteen, I began to add people from that church on my Facebook in order to keep up with church events. At nineteen, I emerged as a leader within the church, as I played the piano during the services with the praise band. Around this time, our church welcomed a new youth pastor, his wife, and two young children. I got to know the family, and they worked with me during my process of becoming baptized a second time.

Now, here's the story. In May when Amendment One was up for vote in North Carolina, I made it clear on my Facebook that I did not want it to pass and would be voting against it. Several people in my church spoke out against me and said that "I must not believe in the Bible if I believe it's okay for gay people to get married." Another person said, "By accepting Jesus as my savior, I must accept ALL that the Bible says and because it states that homosexuality is a sin, gay people shouldn't get married."

It gets better.

The youth pastor I mentioned earlier took me aside after church one day and basically said that women should be silent and shouldn't speak out about anything. After already feeling attacked for seeing nothing wrong about two consenting adults getting married, I'm now being told that because I'm a woman I shouldn't speak my opinion. I very calmly replied (although inside I was seething) that I would take his opinion into consideration and walked away.

Needless to say, after that conversation I did not attend my church again.

Once again, maternal, paternal, pastoral bigotry backfires. Neo-diversity in communication technologies means that we no longer live in an age where information can be controlled. All of us are exposed to alternative ways of thinking about living socially. We all know that no American citizen has to be married in a church. No one has to be a member of a church to be married. I guess that somewhere in the world there are societies in which marriage is *only* a church-given right and rite. But America is not such a society. There is no Church of America.

Does our Declaration of Independence read this way?

When in the course of Church events, it becomes necessary for one people to dissolve the Church bands which have connected them with another, and to assume among the powers of the earth, the separate and equal station to which the Laws of Nature and of Nature's God entitle them, a decent respect to the opinions of other Religions requires that they should declare the causes which impel them to the separation.

We "The One True Church" hold these truths to be self-evident, that all of the churched are created equal, that they are endowed by their Creator with certain unalienable Rights, that among these are Life, Liberty and the pursuit of Happiness.—That to secure these rights, "The One True Church" is instituted, deriving its just powers from the consent of the churched.

No, it does not read that way, because that was one of the main obstacles to liberty that our Founding Fathers were working against. That is why the First Amendment of our Constitution includes the separation of church and state.

No American has to be wed in a church, synagogue, temple, or mosque to be legally married. For some of us, having the ceremony in a religious place performed by a cleric of a particular denomination is the only way we would consider ourselves to be married. But that is not a legal requirement. Surely we all know that no one has to even belong to a religion to get married. Atheists have the right to, and do, get married. In America, marriage is a legal right and rite so long as the couple is of legal age and obtains a marriage license properly signed by a legally recognized officiant and witnessed. It is also true that no one, not even the government, can tell a religion which persons it can marry. No one can decide which couples a religious group must marry. That is up to the particular religion and its specific rules and views of who has the right to be married by that religion. No church or denomination can even be forced to recognize a marriage the religion does not condone.

Married twice, I was never wed in the eyes of the Roman Catholic Church in which I was baptized and confirmed. With no regrets, neither ceremony was performed in any church. Still, not at the same time, mind you, I have been twice married. And in my and my then wives' view, and in the legal view of the United States, I was married. So in America, when it comes to marriage we live with a tension between legal rights and religious rights. That is as it should be in our democracy given our founding principles. We get in trouble when we try to make one dominate the other. We lose sight of our history and our nation's historical purpose and legacy.

Living in a society with such freedoms, people young and old have alternative ways of understanding the world and the options for how to live in that world. Knowing this I take my teaching responsibilities very seriously. I stand on the wall and teach. I do not worry that young people can't handle the truth.

I have faith that young people can not only understand and appreciate real teaching, but that from that teaching they can and do learn how to live better in our continually evolving neo-diverse nation. We ain't going back, so we better prepare our children. And I know it can be done.

A White male used his one-new-thought paper to offer these observations:

Before taking psychology courses I gave psychologists a bad rap. I felt that all the information they shared was just observations of everyday life, but I was wrong. Psychologists analyze everyday life and break it into pieces, making it easier to handle. The push hypothesis that you presented in lecture, Dr. Nacoste, states that the presence of race can push the interaction to a dispositional-identity level before the dyad is ready to be there. What that means is that an intergroup difference between two people can cause people to say or do things they would not normally do due to different races being involved in the interaction.

After learning about the push hypothesis in that lecture I began to feel this tension in my own interactions. It's not that I had not felt this tension before; I just was not aware of its specifics. It is almost pathetic how this tension is present even though I was raised in an area fairly diverse in race.

The push hypothesis is a relevant topic in today's interactions, and I feel as if it will be for a long time. The number of different races and even just different colors of people are so great in the United States, and our history is segregated. When confronting race, these factors lead to premature dispositional-identity ways of trying to interact. As I go into the world I will use my knowledge of the push hypothesis to avoid the early dispositional-identity level. I will be more aware of my actions and of the actions of those around me, allowing me to recognize and adjust to the dyad.

The information I have learned from this course will be crucial to the rest of my life. Two semesters with Dr. Nacoste has changed me to be more open-minded and understanding. When I first took these courses I would say I was slightly prejudiced and homophobic, but now I can honestly say that there is no hate in me for any particular group. I'm not saying that I'm perfect now, but only that my mind has been fully opened to different cultures, races, and beliefs. Every person I meet I recommend your courses to. I hope you continue to open minds as you have mine because I gravely needed it and greatly appreciate it.

Faith in humanity is the key to my teaching, and my students bolster my faith every semester. A White female wrote:

My "one new thought" about interpersonal relationships and race is the discussion of gay, lesbian, bisexual, and transgender people's rights. Being a

GLBT college student I have grown to understand that there are more and more people of my generation that are willing and able to discuss this topic of diversity in educational settings. However, I have seen an intergenerational gap on the topic.

Although some of the strongest allies that the GLBT youth have are of older generations, there is a gap in experience and viewpoint that lies between generations today. Baby boomers have lived through a different time than we Millennials have, creating perspectives that sometimes distance themselves from one another. Equal rights, specifically those of GLBT people, are a new topic in our American society today. People of my generation have come to see it as our own "civil rights movement." This has been clearly shown through the reelection of President Obama and the many changes made in our government officials this year. It is obvious that this "issue" is one of great importance to many young Americans, and the fight has just begun.

I see a direct correlation between the theory of neo-diversity and the equal rights movement. Neo-diversity is defined as "a new social uncertainty brought about by the ongoing, rapid and substantive social changes." (Nacoste, p. 185). It is truly a "rough beast" that Americans and the rest of the world will be facing over the years to come. This will most definitely become an age of interpersonal anxiety, due to those different experiences and viewpoints brought by different generations. Although I see plenty of hardship and fights ahead, I have faith in America as a great nation.

We have been through so many "rough beasts" in our nation's history from women's rights to African American rights to immigrant rights that it is obvious we know how to stay strong. We know how to come together as one nation and stand up for our diversity. My faith in this nation and in my fellow GLBT people grows stronger every day. As I see myself and my Millennials take charge, make decisions, learn from one another, and create the world they want to live in, I feel hope.

This is our time, our nation.

There you have it; America just won't sit still. New people, new social forces are always calling on us to more fully embrace our credo "We hold these truths to be self-evident that all men are created equal." The poet Langston Hughes once wrote, "I too sing America. I am the darker brother. . . ." (Hughes).

Yes, the darker brother, the lesbian sister, the Muslim sister and brother, the atheist brother and sister, the Christian brother and sister, the Latino brother and sister, the gay brother, the Brown sister and brother, the Buddhist brother and sister, the Little-Person brother and sister. I too sing America; I am America.

But that neo-diversity can create anxiety about who are the "we" and who are among the "they." So all of us have to pay attention and not let ourselves be misled. That's true in whatever contexts Americans live and work. We have to get past the superficial and deal with each other as equals.

Must everyone in America, in a particular work environment or in a neighborhood like each other? No. But to live up to the advanced citizenship that America requires means that we must understand that it is inappropriate to make fun of, to belittle our differences of group origin. To live up to the advanced citizenship that can make America truly the land of the free and the home of the brave means that no matter our groups of origin, we have to interact with each other with respect.

CHAPTER 15

PEACE THROWN LAVISHLY AWAY

No one should want to be me. As I mentioned earlier, I was born and reared in the Louisiana bayous, in a family of Black people, when Jim Crow was the law of the land in the South. In 1972 I left there to join the navy, where racial tensions existed in the midst of the new desegregation. Tensions that ran so high I lived through a three-day race riot onboard a US aircraft carrier loaded with weapons of mass destruction. Also while in the navy, when I was just twenty-three years old, as the military escort I took my friend Benson home in a coffin. When at the University of Michigan, by way of a cooking accident I set my left hand on fire and spent thirty days in a hospital burn unit. When I was an assistant professor at Auburn University I had knee surgery and developed a blood clot that turned into a pulmonary embolism (blood clot in my lung) that almost killed me.

No one should want to be me.

I am making a fuss about this because, lately, it feels like people have been hunting me down. I try to get a moment to myself, and out of nowhere, I hear a voice calling, "Dr. Nacoste . . ." People want to talk to me. Given my faculty position, that's not too unusual. A lot of those same people say they want to learn from me, which is both flattering and encouraging, as it relates to the courses I teach. But lately, too many say they want to *be* me.

Truth is, when a student says to me, "I just want to be you, Dr. Nacoste," I kind of understand. Young people want role models, and some of my students see me as a model of how, at least, to be a professor. Even so, the desire is out of order. But here's where I go from feeling chased to feeling tracked.

I don't teach classes in the summers, but it's more than not teaching. I hide in the summer. I avoid the campus and, except for a few close friends, I avoid people. You see, I know too many people. Actually, to be honest, there are too many people who think they know me when in fact the truth is they only know *about* me. We do not have the moderate-mutuality relationship some people seem to assume. Even so, that doesn't mean people won't run up to me and start talking as if they know me.

So, I hide in the summer. I use my summers to give myself time alone to read, to work on writing projects that are not academic, and to travel. In the summer of 2012 I did all these things.

One morning that summer, I was heading into a grocery store all relaxed. In North Carolina the heat of that particular summer was outrageous. There was a week when every day the temperature reached 105 degrees. That is why I was headed into the store in the morning before the temperature made being outside unbearable. I thought I was safe. But just as I got to the door, there came a voice from an SUV that was sitting nearby. "Dr. Nacoste . . ."

It was a young, relatively new NCSU faculty member. This faculty member said, "I know when you heard my voice you had to be thinking, who is this person stalking me?" Then this faculty member just started talking.

"I have people in my life, mentors that I look up to, and look to learn from. You are one of my most important mentors . . . I want to learn from you . . . I know its summer, but could you meet with me? You have to understand . . . this is so important . . . I just . . . I just want to be you."

Now, as a psychologist, I am worried, maybe even a little frightened. What the hell is going on? We all have a history that brings us to where and who we are. It's not all up to the individual. To be me would mean having the same experiences I have had. No one should want to be me. No one should want to live through some of the things I have lived through. I don't think people who say "I want to be you" really mean that. It took me a while to figure out what was really going on.

Part of that figuring-out process was a conversation I had with my good friend Craig Brookins, who is also a faculty member in the Psychology Department. Over a good craft beer I told him about my grocery store encounter. Sitting in Raleigh's Flying Saucer, I told him how much I was puzzled by the sentiment "I just want to be you." As Craig sipped his IPA (India Pale Ale), I could see he was thinking about my query. After a little while, he told me that I have to understand that when people on campus observe me, they observe someone at ease with who he is, someone who does what he thinks is the right thing to do.

Sipping my own IPA, I listened and I got it. Craig was saying that people look at my behavior and see someone who lives their authentic self. OK, I thought, that makes sense. Who doesn't want to live in an authentic way?

But I think too many people want a shortcut to get there. That's not how it works. To be me would mean having the same experiences I have had and finding a way to integrate those experiences into a coherent self—a gumbo self. Each of us has to develop our own authentic self. There is no shortcut through that process.

I am the son of August (pronounced O-geese) and Ella Nacoste. I loved my parents, and my parents loved me. I learned from my parents. When Mr. Ogeese (1918–1998) and Miss Ella (1922–2002) died, I felt a hurt like no other. But even so, I never wanted to *be* my parents.

John W. Thibaut was one of the great minds in the history of the field of social psychology. A short White man of slight build, he was my mentor, a man who played a major part in my education and intellectual development. I learned a great deal from Dr. Thibaut. I admired him. I came to love John as a friend. And he loved me. Upon his death in 1986, at the request of his family, I was one of the three speakers at his memorial service. While John's impact on my personal and professional life was enormous, it was never my goal to *be* John.

I admire many of the poems written by Sterling Brown, a poet of the Harlem Renaissance. His poem "Nous n'irons plus au bois . . ." is all about what can happen to a person who tries to take an easy way to developing their authentic self. In the poem we hear a person looking at the life they have lived up to now, looking hard at past choices made by giving their life over to someone else's goals. The speaker says: I met your friends, listened to their silly chatter, and contributed to the trivial conversations. I fawned over your friends, the nothings that they said, and I even responded with less, without concern for my own thoughts and beliefs. I gave up my integrity, and you gave me what I deserved. You rewarded me for my cowardice with your ridicule. It is in that moment now that I am thinking back to my own dreams for a life of honor, and I realize the peace I have thrown lavishly away for you, for this.

Don't put yourself in that position. Don't give up on yourself. That's what that poem is about. It is the lament of someone who gave up on themselves to follow someone else. The person followed someone else's goals, followed someone else's values, and followed a path chosen by that someone else. In the end the writer felt empty and cheated, but it was their own doing. The person had behaved in a cowardly fashion and now, too late, realizes what that cowardice had cost. None of us should put ourselves in that position. Through formal schooling or life experiences, each of us should be confronting and exploring questions about our own values.

The point of getting an education is to develop your authentic self, not just get a degree or a job. Each of us should be asking ourselves: What are *my* values? Not what are my parents' values or my friend's values, but what are *my* values? To put it simply, values are *standards*. Each of us should have *standards* for our own behavior. These *standards* help guide our decisions about who our friends are. You should have values, *standards* for how you let people interact with you.

I find that too many people are afraid to follow the values, the standards, they claim to have. After the November 2012 presidential election, I had too many students ask me what to do about their friends who use ugly racial language about our president.

A friend calls President Obama—the president of the United States—an ape or a nigger, and *you don't know what to do?* Numerous students say that person is using language that goes against *their* values, but *they also don't do anything about it.* They don't speak up to object. Or they speak to their friend about it, and that person says they can say whatever they want about citizens of different neo-diversity groups, about President Obama. And the student who has asked me about this is trying to find a way to stay friends with that particular person.

If you have respect for the president, there really is only one thing to do. Speak your objection in the moment of the interaction when it presents itself. If the person continues, walk the hell away from that person.

Too many people behave as cowards, afraid to follow the personal values they say they have. Weakened by a vague interpersonal desire, they let another person drag them down into the pit of racial, gender, ethnic, religious, bodily condition, sexual-orientation bigotry.

We do indeed have some difficult days ahead. Right now the challenge facing Americans is how to talk to, with, and about each other. Intolerant intergroup language is the greatest threat to productive exchange between individuals in our nation. Some think all the beastly language is just a big joke, that it has no real meaning or personal/social impact. But if we do not address the rampant intolerant language in our everyday social interactions, our great nation is degraded in our own eyes and in the eyes of others.

Here is a connection we need to make. Much of the intolerant language that threatens America today is a threat because it is the language of bullying. One expert on bullying, Barbara Coloroso writes:

> There are three kinds of bullying: verbal, physical, and relational. . . . Verbal abuse is the most common form of bullying. . . . Verbal bullying can take the form of name-calling, cruel criticism, personal defamation, racist slurs and sexually suggestive or sexually abusive remarks. (p. 14)

Bullying is everywhere in America today. Yes, we see it in the hate-filled comments people make online. But bullying is also happening in many face-to-face interactions that occur in middle and high schools, in colleges and universities, in the workplace, and in professional sports of all places. Two other examples are:

MUSLIM-AMERICAN MAN WINS NEARLY $1.2 MILLION IN JOB DISCRIMINATION CASE
His co-workers may have not seen past his beard, but the jury did.
A Muslim American man from Ypsilanti has won a nearly $1.2-million jury award after successfully arguing he was harassed, taunted and discriminated against at work because of his religion, race and appearance—most notably, his long beard. (Baldas)

N-WORD USE AMONG BLACKS PUT ON TRIAL IN NYC WORKPLACE CASE
Jurors awarded compensatory damages to a black employment agency worker who was the target of an N-word laced rant by her black boss

A federal jury in New York has rejected the argument that use of
the N-word among blacks can be a culturally acceptable term of love and
endearment, deciding its use in the workplace is hostile and discriminatory
no matter what. (Neumeister)

Much of the bullying we are seeing across America is the outgrowth of
neo-diversity anxiety. The bully is not just asking himself how he is supposed
to interact in the given situation but also how he is supposed to keep the
upper hand among all of "them."

Much of today's bullying behavior is expressed in the form of casual anti-
group slurs or name-calling, which is motivated by neo-diversity anxiety. Too
many Americans feel anxious when they have to interact with people from different groups. This is not just my opinion; it is the conclusion of a report from
an *Esquire*-NBC News survey. It begins by saying, "'Diversity' is on the rise in
America and people are 'very anxious' about it" (Dokoupil). A major statement
in the report indicates that many "are worried about how 'increasing diversity'
in America will affect the country's future, with almost one in five saying diversity makes them 'very anxious'—and a super-majority (65 percent) reporting
that diversity inspires in them no sense of hope in the future, or at least no sense
stronger than the anxiety they reported here" (Dokoupil).

The results of that survey show us that most Americans are surprised at
what seems to be the sudden appearance of so much, and so many different
forms of, diversity. We have been startled by the roar of the Neo-Diversity
train. We have been so startled that we have not prepared our children. We
have left to their own devices young people who are still developing the social
skills that will give them the self-confidence to interact in a lot of different
social situations. Without adequate social skills, any situation that is vague
will activate neo-diversity anxiety, an interpersonal frustration or confusion
about how to interact with a new person. Feeling anxious, struggling to find
a way to feel safe in a social interaction can make people lash out at the source
of their anxiety—the "other." Our evidence is in all the stories of too many
Americans lashing out at Muslim Americans, males lashing out at females,
Blacks lashing out at Whites ("What are you doing here?"), Whites lashing
out at Blacks ("Who brought the nigger?"). But all of this amounts to bul-

lying; trying to put oneself in a high-status position by putting another person in an inferior position.

When I teach my students about neo-diversity some have to admit that in the past they have confronted someone in a way that amounts to bullying. Yes, some have to admit that they have witnessed bullying and let it pass. And others have to admit that in the past they have been the target of what amounts to bullying. But when my students learn about neo-diversity anxiety, they learn that it can influence how they and others interact. These young people gain interpersonal confidence from understanding that anyone can experience this anxiety and that others are experiencing it in the same type of situation. This recognition reduces the anxiety-driven tendency to lash out.

In making her analysis, parenting educator Barbara Coloroso points out that "if verbal bullying is allowed or condoned, it becomes normalized and the target dehumanized" (p. 16). In America today we are showing too much tolerance for intolerance in our everyday social interactions. We let people who interact with us make comments about others that amount to *name-calling*, *cruel criticism*, *personal defamation*, *racist slurs*, and *sexually suggestive or sexually abusive remarks*. In doing so we condone our interaction partners' bigotry, and we make it possible for these individuals to move from one situation to another, spreading their bully language far and wide.

Parents, teachers, counselors, coaches, and others who interact with groups need to be taught about neo-diversity. Too many of these shapers of children's behavior are unaware that their own behavior can teach children how to bully or set the bad example of excusing such action. These shapers of behavior need to be made aware that once-acceptable ways of talking to control a child's behavior now amount to bullying. For example, telling girls that nobody likes a girl who is bossy amounts to gender bullying. Shapers of behavior also need to be made aware that you can bully people who are not in your presence. Telling boys that to be weak is to be "a pussy" is almost guaranteed to make those boys speak to girls and women in demeaning ways.

Understanding how the interpersonal dynamic works means that with training about neo-diversity, behavior-shapers of all types can begin to address the underlying cause of modern bullying—neo-diversity anxiety. Concrete lessons about the true nature of America and its struggles with neo-diversity will, I believe, lead to a reduction in the amount of intolerance and unacceptable intergroup behavior we witness far too often in this country. Part of this task must be to teach young people to speak up when they witness instances of intolerance. Not all of us want to condone bigotry. Many would do something to combat the problem if only they knew what strategy to employ. That is why I have worked so hard to offer in my social psychology classes a research-confirmed strategy for addressing intolerance in our interpersonal interactions.

Neo-diversity bullying is growing for two reasons: First, the sheer number and combination of groups is growing. Second, as I have said before, in the midst of all the neo-diversity changes, too many of us show too much tolerance for intolerance. The interpersonal strategy I teach my students is one that reduces tolerance for the intolerance of bullying. With more people speaking up to object to intolerant language (stereotypes and slurs), the less confident will be any potential bully.

It's strangely sad how much we seem to relish calling someone a "racist" from distance. If a politician, celebrity, or some simpleton makes a racially intolerant remark that goes viral, we sit back comfortably and say, "What a racist." But when at dinner, at a party someone uses a racial slur, makes a negative gender remark, spews an ethnic insult, degrades a religion or religious belief, or starts to talk about retards and crips, we say nothing; we go quiet. Yet it is important to recognize what the poet W. H. Auden pointed out:

> Evil is unspectacular and always human.
> And shares our bed, and eats at our own table.

We seem to relish pointing out the spectacular but do nothing about the unspectacular and ordinary examples of bigotry and prejudice that swirl around us every day. No wonder young people tell me about so much intolerant language in their daily lives. A female student of mine wrote in one of her papers: "I have heard 'nigger, bitch, Whitey,' and multitudes of others." These are not the types of neo-diverse expressions that any young woman should be recounting these days. It's not just one or two students who report this, and it's not just students. I work with a lot of different age groups from middle-school students to folks in their eighties. In every one of these groups, someone brings up the problem. Someone will eventually volunteer that "when we get in our own demographic group, when it's just us, the language changes and somebody there starts using anti-group slurs." Muslim Americans become sand-niggers and ragheads. Women become sluts and whores. President Obama becomes . . . you get the idea. The person who brings this up usually says, "I am very uncomfortable when this happens, but I don't say anything; I don't want to be the odd one out."

And so the sales pitch about an ever tolerant America lives on.

People freeze in the moment, often because the author of the slur claims, "I have free speech; I can say what I want." Relevant here is a scene from the 1995 movie *The American President*, when the film becomes much more than a romantic comedy. It's just a moment, but what an important moment, when the president makes this declaration at a press conference:

> America isn't easy. America is advanced citizenship. You gotta want it bad, 'cause it's gonna put up a fight. It's gonna say . . . "You want free speech? Let's see you acknowledge a man whose words make your blood boil, who's standing center stage and advocating at the top of his lungs that which you would spend a lifetime opposing at the top of yours. You want to claim this land as the land of the free? Then the symbol of your country can't just be a flag; the symbol also has to be one of its citizens exercising his right to burn that flag in protest."
>
> Show me that, defend that . . . celebrate that . . . in your classrooms. Then, you can stand up and sing about the "land of the free." (Sorkin)

Far too many Americans misunderstand our US Constitution's statement of the right to freedom of speech. It says:

> Congress shall make no law respecting an establishment of religion, or pro-hibiting the free exercise thereof; or abridging the freedom of speech, or of the press; or the right of the people peaceably to assemble, and to petition the Government for a redress of grievances.

Free expression and freedom of speech are not the same thing. In America, no individual has a right to total free expression of opinion; any of us can land in court for slander or libel. What the Constitution says is that "Congress shall make no law . . . abridging the freedom of speech." The First Amendment protects citizens from their *government* trying to silence their expression of ideas and claims. Freedom of speech, however, protects no citizen from rebuttal by other citizens. That's advanced citizenship. And it takes an understanding of the advanced nature of American citizenship to know that we can make our claims in public, but that others can stand right next to us and object and rebut our claims with their own arguments and views. If you believe that you can say what you want and everybody just has to accept what you say, when you say it, without making objections or counterclaims, you misunderstand the meaning of the Constitution in this case. Your understanding of American citizenship is unsophisticated and primitive.

Lately, the mistake that so many Americans have been making is exactly this misunderstanding. For some reason we have it in our heads that since Americans have freedom of expression, there is nothing to be done when bigotry and prejudice raise their heads. At least, that is what some people claim. That's why we sometimes end up with the odd situation that when someone makes ugly racial, anti-gay and lesbian, anti-some-group statements, people claim embarrassment, admit being outraged, and inwardly condemn such language, but they act as if there is nothing to be done.

Lately, we have been acting as if we think that freedom means that we have to shut up in the face of someone else's ugly use of that same freedom. But we don't have to remain silent, and we shouldn't. People often freeze in such moments because they don't know how to confront the bigotry of intolerant language. They do not have a strategy to act upon. But there are strategies.

There's a group of Americans who turn out to yell and scream at the funerals of soldiers. Members of the Westboro Baptist Church say that the death of a soldier is God's punishment for the sins of America. So they come out to a funeral to make that point in front of a family burying a loved one who served our country. And they have the free speech right to do so. Indeed, based on the First Amendment, the US Supreme Court ruled that they cannot be stopped from doing so by any agents of government. This was the appropriate application of our Constitution. But this does not mean other Americans cannot use their freedom of speech to confront this mean-spirited, intolerant behavior at the funerals of American soldiers.

That's what happened when the Westboro Baptist Church members showed up at the funeral of Elizabeth Edwards (former wife of presidential candidate John Edwards). Since Ms. Edwards had been in support of marriage rights for gays and lesbians, members of the church came to her funeral to shout out that she was damned. But that group found themselves peacefully blocked by a "line of love" (Knickerbocker).

At the funeral of Ms. Edwards, when that church group assembled in the permitted area, other Americans were there to block their position. This kind of response is also happening at the funerals of soldiers: people line up early to stand in front of the assigned position of the Westboro Baptist Church members, to block their signs from the sight of those attending the funeral. This is also a legitimate way to exercise freedom of speech.

So, too, was what people did in New York City on the first day that gays and lesbians could be legally married in that state. Knowing anti-gay and lesbian protesters would be present, people, many of whom were strangers to each other and some heterosexual, showed up with colorful umbrellas. With those umbrellas open they took positions that blocked the view of the protesters from those couples who, in love, had showed up and lined up to get married (New York *Daily News* Writers, 2011, July 25).

That, too, was legitimate expression of freedom of speech.

Here's some relevant "breaking news":

MEXICAN-AMERICAN BOY, SEBASTIEN DE LA CRUZ, SINGS ENCORE PERFORMANCE OF NATIONAL ANTHEM AT NBA FINALS IN RESPONSE TO BIGOTED COMMENTS.
    The fifth-grader demonstrated maturity beyond his years when he dismissed the hatred. "With the racist remarks, it was just people—how they were raised," de la Cruz said. (Knowles)

I watched the video of Sebastien's second performance of the national anthem. The mayor of San Antonio and his wife introduced him. Sebastien sang and acted out the song; the kid is amazing. As his performance ended, the fans in the auditorium went crazy: screaming and giving him a standing ovation. Then as Sebastien took his bow, the two coaches came out and shook his hand.

All that happened in response to tweets from bigots after Sebastien's first performance. Apparently some of the bigoted tweets had to do with Sebastien's dressing mariachi-style in the tradition of his American ethnic group. These were tweets filled with primal bigotry against our Mexican American sisters, brothers, their children, and their style.

The community action taken to bring Sebastien back was to show that San Antonio would stand against bigotry and that the two team leaders would stand against it as well. That is part of the challenge of our new American social frontier. In the past, the enemy of America was its own racism that was embedded in the law. It took marches, protests, and far too many deaths to show the nation that the laws had to be rewritten to be consistent with the values expressed in our Constitution.

We have succeeded in doing that for the most part, but now the work is different. In a nation with equal protection under the law for all, we have to show that the majority of us will not give bigotry a pass. Our work now is to speak out against bigotry when it happens around us, in any sphere of social interaction. What happened in San Antonio was a community using its legitimate freedom of speech on a very big stage. But strategies at such a spectacular level are not the only way we should stand against bigotry.

Understand that it is the ordinary and unspectacular interpersonal moments that can have tremendous impact on our lives and the social fabric of our nation. When a person in conversation utters some intolerant, racial, gender, ethnic, religious, bodily or mental condition bigotry what should we do? When our neighbor uses bigoted language toward a group, how should we react? When our classmate or a co-worker spews a prejudiced remark, how should we respond? We need an interpersonal strategy for these interpersonal moments.

Too often we let our neo-diversity anxiety and uncertainties freeze us in a moment when we should be speaking up to call intolerant language offensive. We show too much tolerance for intolerance. In these moments we should speak up and call out the offense; we should take action. One citizen's freedom of speech does not negate another's. Let's not forget that. We cannot afford to forget that, because when we do we allow ugly speech to rule the day and no positive change takes place.

When I started working on race relations issues in the US Navy in 1974, diversity was all about Black-White relations. But today, in twenty-first-century America, diversity being only about Blacks and Whites is a dead reality. Neo-diversity is what we live with today, a time and circumstance when all of us encounter and interact with many more people from different bodily conditioned, racial, religious, ethnic, sexually oriented groups, and that contact is unavoidable. Too many Americans are having trouble adjusting to our neo-diverse country.

Today my work is about that neo-diversity with groups on and off campus. From college students, middle and high school students, and people over fifty, I have learned that one of the biggest neo-diversity problems we face is that moment when someone in a group utters words of intolerance and bigotry, and people in the room are at a loss for something to say. But there is hope because social psychologists have been studying the effects of different ways of confronting that moment, of confronting intolerance in interpersonal interactions and relationships.

Alexander M. Czopp, Margo J. Monteith, and Aimee Y. Mark have been conducting experiments to discover ways for any person to effectively confront group bias that pops up during a social interaction. In their 2006 report of three experiments these researchers make this important point: "Some people would rather remain silent and not want to create a stir, but perhaps creating a stir can have an impact and induce change in others. By speaking up and addressing the person who made prejudiced comments and voicing displeasure, people have the opportunity to confront prejudice directly and perhaps help reduce the likelihood of [intolerant language from this person] in the future" (p. 784).

Turns out, there is no point to reacting with hurtful and demeaning responses to another person's bigoted language. There is no need for name-calling. Such an equal and opposite reaction to bigotry and prejudice is just another form of "us versus them," and it merely perpetuates the problem. Although they note that a harsh confrontation may be effective, the researchers rightly point out that most people will only be comfortable taking action if the confrontation can be conducted politely. Yet even a polite confrontation can be effective because these encounters hit the perpetrator in the place we all live; these encounters hit the person's concern not just with their self-image but with the person's concern with how other people will think of them. In that context, Czopp, Monteith, and Mark are pointing out that a polite confrontation is powerful in two ways. One, people are more likely to get the courage up to make a polite confrontation. Two, everyone wants to be liked, so a polite confrontation has the interpersonal power to influence a person using stereotypes and slurs to stop in that moment, given their self-concerns.

So when someone you are interacting with uses anti-group language, when that someone speaks about a person as a stereotype, stop the interaction. Put your hand up and then quietly say, "Oh, I'm sorry. I am very uncomfortable with that kind of language. I find it offensive. It hurts me." That's it, that's all you have to do. By the way, saying, "Oh, I'm sorry" is not apologizing and giving up your power. It's just being polite. One could also say, "Oh, excuse me but . . ." That's taking action. That's interpersonal action appropriate to the interpersonal moment. And it will work. I know this not because it's my opinion but because the data from social psychological experiments demonstrate it.

The research conducted and reported by Czopp, Monteith, and Mark shows there is power in speaking up to say, "I would prefer not to hear that kind of racial/gender/ethnic slur. I find it offensive. It hurts me." Or "I really don't like to hear people referred to as stereotypes. I find it offensive. It hurts me."

In the experiments, a person who was confronted in this polite way about using a racial stereotype was really influenced by the polite objection. Results of the experiments show that when confronted, the perpetrator experienced a powerful mix of self-relevant emotions. As measured in the experiments, those confronted reported feeling a mix of feelings, such as "anger at myself," "annoyed at myself," "regretful," and "disgusted with myself."

Why does the quiet, polite confrontation have such a strong influence on people's self-evaluations in the moment? Looking at the results of their three experiments, among a number of conclusions Czopp, Monteith, and Mark say that "confrontations from others are likely to be more effective (immediately and perhaps in the long term) to the extent that . . . feelings such as guilt and self-criticism are elicited. Individuals may attempt to customize their confrontations so as to induce the most [negative self-evaluations] (e.g., by increasing empathic concerns)" (p. 799). That is why when I teach the confrontation strategy, I emphasize that a person say, "It hurts me." If the person being confronted cares anything at all about you or continuing their interaction with you, the statement will have power.

As soon as I read the work of Czopp, Monteith, and Mark, I incorporated what they discovered into my presentations on neo-diversity. One place I made sure I did that was in my TEDx talk at our university. "TEDx" stands for "Technology, Education, and Design" talks that emphasize "Ideas Worth Spreading." These presentations are made to a local audience and are videotaped. After watching and listening to my TEDxNCSU talk, my niece Tresha e-mailed me.

> Dear Uncle, The sales pitch does live on, doesn't it? Yet . . . to call upon all peoples to consider or perhaps reconsider the idea of America the beautiful is long overdue. "Who are the 'we'? Who are among the 'they'?" Timely. Important. Necessary.
>
> I have been in the very situation you described in your talk numerous times. That moment . . . that moment when you feel the warmth of uncomfortableness slowly creep upward and over your face because someone has said something . . . some nasty, derogatory thing about a group of people or person . . . and you find yourself paralyzed by discomfort, but never really knowing what to say or how to address it. Been there . . . far too many times to admit. Thanks for giving us the words. "It hurts me." I love that. It personalizes it. It encourages the receiver to hear the message in a different way. "It hurts me."

That is an eloquent and moving description of the moment I am trying to help all Americans navigate with dignity while at the same time being true to their own values. In all of the groups I talk to about neo-diversity someone in the group brings up that moment when "someone has said something . . . some nasty, derogatory thing about a group of people or person." Brought into the discussion, every audience I have talked with has acknowledged experiencing such a moment as being uncomfortable. And, like Tresha, the people who say they experience this awful discomfort also say that "you find yourself paralyzed by discomfort, but never really knowing what to say or how to address it."

But now we know there is a strategy. There is action each of us can take.

Even though I don't teach courses in the summers, if I think it important enough sometimes I do come out of hiding to do one or two one-shot presentations at the university. And I am a bit of a sucker when it comes to speaking to students just coming into our university. Summer 2013, as part of one of my presentations on neo-diversity, I asked a set of new students, "Why do you think that this polite confrontation has such a big effect on the person confronted?" New to the campus as part of an early-start program, this neo-diverse set of first-year college students did not hesitate. A red-haired White male said, "It lets the person know how you are feeling." With what I later learned was a Haitian accent, a young, dark-skinned male said, "It lets the other person know how you have been affected by their words." An obvious but important response.

But in that moment of interaction, there was something more going on than the obvious. From both students I was picking up emotion in their voices, in their eyes. I was looking into the eyes of a young person who had not only listened attentive to my presentation on neo-diversity but who now was experiencing a revelation. Looking into their eyes, I had no doubt that each had lived through that awful interaction moment when someone voices a stereotype or slur about some group. Now I was moved to know that what I was teaching mattered to these young people because it let them know they had power. I was moved to know that this empowerment made them feel true emotion. What hit them was the same thing that hit my niece Tresha. They were given words to help personalize the moment and to encourage them to speak out with a response like "It hurts me."

Keep in mind too that in the moment of polite confrontation, the person confronted also experiences emotion. Anger at being confronted comes first. So understand that. You need to be ready to see anger in the eyes of the person you confront. But also know that the person confronted experiences other emotions, too. As explained by Czopp, Monteith, and Mark the person confronted also reports feeling negative self-evaluations (e.g., "anger at myself"), which I mentioned before.

Such negative self-evaluations are activated by the polite yet firm confrontation. Not only that, but those negative self-evaluations predicted that the confronted person was less likely to use a stereotype or slur again in the immediate situation. And those negative feelings about self also predicted that the person was less likely to respond with approval to use of a racial or gender stereotype in a different context. As one of their major conclusions, Czopp, Monteith, and Mark say that "confrontation situations involving individuals who frequently interact with each other may be especially effective in changing behavior. A confronted person may change his or her behavior to avoid the discomfort of similar interactions with the confronter in the future. In addition, because of the repeated contact between the individuals involved in the confrontation, the confronter may become an especially strong cue for control for the confronted individual and facilitate self-regulation of future responding" (p. 801).

The logic of their findings and thinking leads me to this speculation: The more people have the experience of another person standing against their use of a stereotype, the more people will experience tension and reluctance when in their informal (being a dinner guest) or formal (being a teacher; being a police officer) social interactions they are about to rely on a stereotype.

By our own behavior we have the interpersonal power to influence another person's experience of the moment of interaction with us. Such interpersonal power can be used to create a quiet revolution against the stereotypes that we all still carry with us.

That is why I teach the interpersonal strategy every chance I get. And people have very powerful responses to learning that there is a strategy that works and that it is one they can understand and employ. I offered this approach in a guest column for NCSU's student newspaper, the *Technician*. It was titled "Wake Up to Your Own Power":

> Each of you has the power to influence your social interactions. When the
> person you are interacting with uses negative racial, gender or ethnic lan-

guage, do not tolerate it. But, don't call that person names, like racist, sexist, homophobe. Instead of name-calling, speak for yourself. Don't try to tell that person they are wrong. Don't try to tell that person it's just not a good idea to talk that way.

Let that person know your standards for continuing to interact with you. Just quietly, but firmly, express your personal standard for the interaction. Speak into that moment and speak for yourself. Simply say, "I am very uncomfortable with that kind of language. I find it offensive. It hurts me." If the person persists, walk away from the interaction. It's time for all of us to wake up and take personal responsibility for what goes on in our interactions with other people.

CHAPTER 16

A QUIET REVOLUTION

*H*owl of the Wolf: NCSU Students Call Out for Social Change is a small book I wrote on the topic of neo-diversity for the NCSU campus. Not just because we are the Wolfpack did I call my book *Howl of the Wolf*. Sure, I wanted a hook, an attention-getter, relevant to our students' sense of identity at the university. But when I settled on the title I was also thinking about the change I hear in my students' new thoughts about neo-diversity issues on campus and in America. In their writing I hear a loud howl of new motivation that calls out to others. In chapter 5, "Children of Light," I state:

> If we really want change, silence is no longer an option. When we are silent we give power to the idea that speaking in stereotypes and slurs is ok. That is why history repeats itself. But now is our opportunity to begin to change that. You see, it is in the small interaction moments where the next big change will occur. Now is your opportunity to create change in the small moments. (p. 93)

After teaching this, I have seen the light go on in my students' eyes. Now they have a way, a path to take, to stand up to intolerance in their everyday, social lives. That gives students power.

One White female student of mine clearly understood her role in perpetuating the problem and in becoming part of the solution when she wrote:

> Throughout my life I have been surrounded by terribly negative words like "bitch," "nigger," and "faggot" from the likes of the media, rap music, my schooling, and even my Grandfather. I always knew these words were wrong and hurtful to others, but they were used so frequently and in a playful manner that their true meanings were gradually downplayed.

While I wish I could say differently, because I did know better, I confess I often took part in using these words. Reflecting now on my past, I can see that I made a choice to use those vile words in order to seem "normal." In fact, the use of these words was and is normal, but I have grown to find that the use of these words can be very dangerous.

I, being a huge supporter of the GLBT community, am ashamed to know that I ever allowed myself to utter the words "fag," "homo," or "that's so gay." Now when I hear such hateful speech, I do not join in, in fact I make a point to let a person know they are offending me when they use such words or phrases. One thing I like to point out to people is how odd it is that "that's straight" is used to describe something as being cool or good whereas "that's gay" is always a completely negative phrase.

I believe many times it is these silent decisions to use such language and that keep this language so prevalent. Many people, I am sure, are now numbed to these words and thus use them in their daily vocabulary. The danger of these words was displayed just months ago when many teens took their lives after being publicly ridiculed and harassed for being openly gay. Stories like these tear at my soul, and I hope others have learned from these suicides that words are powerful.

I have come to understand the power of words, especially negative words such as "bitch," "slut," "nigger," and "faggot." Though I too once participated in throwing these words around, I now know why. I made a silent choice. In the future I hope to turn others away from making that same choice. Informing another person that their words are offensive to us gives them a negative stimulus to attach to those words, and hopefully they will reassess their use of such hateful terms. I will not put up with these horrific words. Though I have begun to speak out against their use because they are offensive to me, I cannot do it on my own. These words are nothing but terribly, tragically, unfortunately hateful terms and I will not be silent.

Hear that? I call that the Howl of the Wolf. A lone wolf howls, but in howling it calls to other wolves that eventually join in the howl as well. She is calling to all on our campus (and elsewhere). It is a call to redeem us all, because we are all monsters.

I distributed *Howl of the Wolf* to students on our campus to try to help them recognize the dynamics of neo-diversity and to confront it in their own lives. That approach went along well with the efforts of the student group I was advising, called Wake Up! It's Serious: A Campaign for Change.

Wake Up was a student advocacy group that grew out of my "Interpersonal Relationships and Race" class. In the fall of 2010, we had an incident of hateful, racial graffiti in our so-called Free Expression Tunnel. That time many students across campus were outraged enough to organize a protest rally. At the same time, I led a discussion in my class and asked the students if they wanted to keep this energy going. Students said yes, and over the following six months Wake Up! It's Serious: A Campaign for Change was born. As a social action advocacy group, these students' mission was

> to design campaigns to help North Carolina State University students learn how to speak up in the presence of intolerance by refusing to be silent when another person uses derogatory group terms. We have committed ourselves to speaking up when a fellow student utters words of intolerance toward a group of our fellow student-citizens. We have also committed ourselves to creating and participating in concrete educational activities toward positive change in the campus diversity climate with the aim of strengthening the social bonds of our community.

Two years later, the group put on a magnificent event to introduce *Howl of the Wolf* to the campus. To get the word out they used e-mails, social media, and flyers. This was a coffeehouse-style evening event, with a spoken-word artist, skits about neo-diversity interactions, piano interludes by a student musician, and me as the main speaker at the end.

That November night, along with about two hundred students, to my surprise, a few staff and faculty members from the College of Humanities and Social Sciences showed up. Each spoke to me after the event, and each was very complimentary about the organization, the content of the event, and the turnout. I assured them that all the credit was due to the students in Wake Up. It was quite a night. We gave away about two hundred books.

Later in the semester I learned that at least one student who came to the event was there to get credit for a course. My friend Dr. Craig Brookins requires that his students attend a number of events that are relevant to neo-diversity. To get credit for attendance, though, his students must write about their experience of the event. That student who attended the *Howl of the Wolf* event wrote the following:

> I attended Dr. Nacoste's event, which featured student skits and performances and his discussion about the content of his newest book *Howl of the Wolf*. The skits featured scenarios in which students interacted with someone of a different culture or sexual orientation but did not handle the situation correctly. We then had an open discussion about the proper way to handle these types of situations and why we think they occur. We also watched a spoken-word performance in which the poet described his mother's life as a maid. Finally, Dr. Nacoste tied in the importance of all of these things amongst students on the campus.
>
> In the first skit, two girls were discussing their holiday breaks and one student was of Middle Eastern descent. The friend made an ignorant comment in relation to the Middle Eastern student's culture. The second scenario involved two guys who were becoming good friends, but one was homosexual and the other was heterosexual. The heterosexual friend was often too aware of his friend's sexuality and made conversations awkward. Both these scenarios relate to the importance of socialization. As Americans who live in a diverse nation, it is important that children are socialized to deal with people of different backgrounds in a way that won't offend them, and it is also important for the child on the other end of the incident to know how to deal with an awkward situation and not allow negative incidents to alter how they identify themselves.
>
> The book *Howl of the Wolf* is a compilation of stories written in Dr. Nacoste's class in which students described their awkward experiences with people from different backgrounds. Dr. Nacoste said that we live in a neo-diverse age in which it is important for people from all walks of life to know how to interact with one another. This is especially important on such a diverse campus where despite our differences, we all howl the same. We are the neo-diverse Wolfpack.

Starting with that event and the Wake Up! group's energy, passion, and work in creating and putting on events, we gave away over a thousand copies of the book that semester. Why all the effort? Why all the passion from this group of young people? After taking my course, students come to believe it is time for a real conversation about neo-diversity. Together we were starting with our community, to heal our own—to truly nurture our pack.

The message of *Howl of the Wolf* began to be heard off campus, too. I gave copies to a Sanford, North Carolina, community group. One-by-One is community-action group started by a set of mostly elderly White women. Their goal is to improve race relationships in the Southern, Tobacco Road hamlet of Sanford. Even there, the Neo-Diversity train had come to town and brought with it a number of intergroup anxieties. I have worked with this group since the spring of 2008, so when I published *Howl* I gave members of the group copies, and then a month later I went back to facilitate their discussion of the book. This group of Sanford citizens, which later included a few men, Black and White, and a few Black women, read *Howl* and were eager to discuss it.

During the group discussion there were a number of important moments. One came when one of the younger African American women said, "I had to put your book down for a little while, Dr. Nacoste. There were things your students learned that made me look at myself. Now, that's the gospel."

Another such moment came when a White woman threw up her hand to speak. She began by telling us the struggle she had been having with her own mother using racial slurs. How she was hurt every time it happened but felt helpless. Then she said, "When I read the strategy about speaking up, I felt good. I felt empowered. I said to myself, 'I can do that . . . I can do that.'" A comment made by a woman in her late sixties echoed the emotion of many of the new students I spoke to during the summer of 2013 as well as that of my niece who said: "Thanks for giving us the words. 'It hurts me.' I love that. It personalizes it. It encourages the receiver to hear the message in a different way. 'It hurts me.'"

Later, at my request, the One-by-One group sent me a list of insights they gained from reading *Howl*. Here are a few:

> Learned about neo-diversity and the anxiety it can cause during a social interaction.

Learned how to deal with that neo-diversity anxiety during a social interaction.

Learned that we limit ourselves if we don't figure out how to get along with people who are "different" from us.

Learned how to speak up in the face of intolerance.

Whenever and wherever I can, I teach the "It hurts me" interpersonal strategy. "Speak into the moment of bigoted language," I tell every audience. The power of this style of confrontation rests on one fundamental interpersonal principle: *A relationship cannot evolve without encountering and managing person-to-person incompatibility of preferences that come with honest self-disclosures.* Honest self-disclosures require that we speak for ourselves. We must speak in the "I" not the "You." Trying to object to someone's behavior from the mountaintop, from the burning bush, is ineffective because the other person also has a mountaintop stance. What matters at the interpersonal level, in the interpersonal moment, is how you reveal to the other person how *you* are doing in that moment. Being honest with and vulnerable to your interaction partner is what makes the interaction authentic. It is potent, then, to speak for yourself, to say to the person with whom you are interacting, "I am very uncomfortable with that kind of language about people. I find it offensive. It hurts me."

When my students badgered me into giving a TEDx talk, I worked it into my presentation on the American sales pitch, "Speaking Up for Neo-Diverse America." Students in my classes began to send the YouTube link around to other students, to friends, and to members of their families. I received an e-mail from a father. J, a White man in his sixties, wrote:

Let me begin by saying I have watched your TED lecture twice and have sent it on to several friends. The problem is I received it about 48 hours too late!

I have a group of about 30 guys who play golf every weekend, so we all know each other pretty well. After golf, we go to the bar, talk and joke, and wait until everyone finishes. This past Saturday I was sitting at the table with 5 of the guys, discussing sports in general, and college basketball in particular. Suddenly, one of the guys, "Benedict Arnold," blurts out a racial slur as the reason basketball has gone downhill.

At this point, I could have used your advice on how to deal with ignorant comments; instead, my reaction was quick, loud, and firm. I turned to Benedict, who was seated next to me, and said, "Shut up, Benedict, that's F-ing Stupid!"

He was so shocked, he couldn't respond.

The group then returned to our conversation as if Benedict wasn't there. Once Benedict left, I was concerned with how the other guys (all pretty conservative) would react, *if* at all. To my surprise, one of the guys looked at me and said, "That needed to be said!" The others all nodded in agreement, which, given their political views, was quite unexpected. I left the bar sometime later very proud of my golfing buddies. The following morning when I arrived at the practice tee, the incident was being discussed by some of the guys. Apparently I am not alone in my disdain for bigoted racial slurs!

I wish I had seen your video prior to the incident so I could have responded in a more intelligent and less threatening manner! But, my choice of words also seemed to be effective! Change is slow, but it is coming; keep up the powerful work you do!

I quickly responded to this important e-mail:

Sir: You spoke into the moment! That's the major point I am trying to give to people. Speak up; say something. Given the group you were in, your style was dead-on. In other situations, the softer approach might be better. But now, you will have a couple of strategies to draw on as you judge the situation.

The other important part of your story is how other people in your group evaluated your action. I am of the belief, and your story supports my belief, that many, many Americans will support someone speaking up. Many are silent because they are "caught off guard" and worry too much about how their objection will be received by other members of the group. But once someone speaks into the moment, as you did, the speaker finds strong support for shutting down the ugly use of slurs or stereotypes.

Thank you so much for sharing your story.

It was no exaggeration when I said that other people will support someone speaking up. About that one of my tattooed and pierced students wrote:

So, I decided to join (rush) the Christian sorority on campus my sophomore year. I had to go through a week of different activities to learn more about the sorority and the girls. I had noticed that one girl in particular had been staring at me the whole time.

My appearance may be misleading to some people who know that I am a Christian. I have several tattoos, several piercings, and I wear different clothes. So some people assume that because of the way that I look I am a terrible person.

Well, it was the last night, and they do something called "Sister speed date" where you go around and talk to each sister and they ask you questions about yourself. Most questions are "Why do you want to join the sorority?" and several "What is your major?" This was not the case for one girl—let's call her Emily for privacy purposes.

I sat down at her chair, and she just stared at me for a good minute. So finally, I said, "Hi, I'm Katie. What's your name?"

She glared at me then said, "Name's Emily."

I was smiling awkwardly because I had no idea what to do. Then it started. I knew when I sat down in her chair something was about to happen. Very bluntly she said, "Do you think this is funny? We take this serious and your mocking isn't appreciated."

I was just sitting there like, "What is going on?" and by then everyone in the room stopped talking and stared at me. In a second I had over 100 pairs of eyes staring at me for something I did not even know what it was about.

Emily continued . . .

"You come in here pretending you believe in God, which we can all see that is not true. In the Bible it does not say anything about body modification, and since it's not in the Bible it's a sin and sinners go to hell, therefore you're going to hell."

I was stunned.

Yes, because of the way I have chosen my outward appearance to be I get the usual stereotypes, but they are never usually voiced. Before I could say anything, she said, "No, let me finish. We do not allow devil worshippers or drug users in this sorority. Unlike you, we don't worship Satan, we pray to an almighty God. So before I have to get the whole sorority involved, will you and your devil-worshipping ways please leave? Actually just leave . . . NOW."

Every girl in the room's eyes were giant, all looking at me for what I was about to say. I looked at her and said very calmly, "I'm sorry you have such a narrow view on the world. I hate to inform you not everyone who has tattoos and piercings worships the devil or is a drug user; I don't do either. I've been a Christian my whole life, never have I ever worshipped the devil. I am sorry my appearance makes you feel that way, but the Bible preaches that we should accept all of God's children, not ostracize them because they don't look like you."

She looked at me and then replied, "Wow, I didn't know you knew such big words."

That pushed me over the edge. I got up and started walking out of the room because I did not deserve to be treated that way, especially when I had not done anything. As I was leaving she said, "She's gone girls, now the room is pure again."

I turned around and thanked them for inviting me, and then for once I kind of stood up for myself. I said, "Emily, if I follow your logic you're not in the Bible, therefore it's a sin, and sinners go to hell, therefore you're going to hell."

And then something weird happened: all the other girls clapped when I said that and asked me to stay. They all hugged me, and the president sent Emily home. Later, I found out she got kicked out for what she said, which I am glad because I had never been attacked like that before for no reason, in an environment that is supposed to be safe and accepting. They later also told me that they were hoping I was going to punch Emily.

Primal bigotry is nasty, ugly, and anything but chaste; it is monstrous. Punching, however, will not change that or make the interpersonal moment positive. But speaking up calmly and politely but firmly during such social interactions in order to object to the bigotry that has been voiced definitely has power. Often the power rests on giving courage to others who see what is going on.

A Black female wrote:

From Pre-K until high school I attended private school, which, with the exception of Pre-K and Kindergarten, were predominantly White schools; therefore, I have had a lot of interaction with White people. When I started to attend my last private school I was in the fourth grade.

From fourth to eighth grade there was this one particular boy in my class whose name was Steve Turberville (not his real name). Through all these years Steve would make comments about me being Black and always talked about White being the smarter and most dominant group, continuously talking about the Confederacy. Going to the administrators several times about the different comments he would make, and the administrations' lack of response, led me to this intense interaction. The only consequence he would receive was getting talked to and told "don't do it again."

On Valentine's Day of 2003 I had decided that I could no longer take anymore of Steve. In eighth grade, we would sit in alphabetical order, so "Turberville" happened to be right behind me. On this day, the teacher had left the room while we were all sitting in our chairs doing some work.

He came out of nowhere and said, "That's why all Black people are ugly because they look like monkeys." When I heard him say this I became so infuriated that I got up from my seat, turned around, and loudly said, "This is the last time I am going to listen to you talk down against Black people, just because you have a hatred for us, and the next time you try to say something degrading like that again it will only get worse."

It was at this moment that all of the other kids, all White kids, got up and started cheering. They came up to me and said, good job, he really deserved it because he had no right saying any of that stuff.

Her classmates knew Steve's behavior was out of order and just plain wrong. Yet, at least the way the story is told, none had ever even offered private support to the writer. What a shame. Yes, she had to stand up for herself. But she did so not even knowing that her classmates would support her attempt to retain her dignity against a racial bully.

We are at a critical train stop on our nation's journey to its full humanity. Intolerant language is all around us as we struggle with the new tensions and anxieties being activated by neo-diversity. I am proud to be an American, but the only America I can be proud of is one that corrects its mistakes. To redeem America, to stop our inner monsters from devouring our own flesh from the inside out, we need to take up strategies to confront intolerant language as a primary national superordinate goal.

I have made it well known to you that I served in the US Navy during a very tough racial transition, with race riots occurring aboard warships. Under Admiral Elmo Zumwalt, that major national security problem was addressed through mandatory, organized racial sensitivity discussions (Sherwood).

The genius the navy showed through those "Understanding Personal Worth and Racial Dignity" (UPWARD) racial sensitivity sessions, the groups I and others facilitated, was to get navy personnel to focus on carrying out their mission. That is what unified us: the mission, to protect this nation. It was not whether we liked each other, but that we had to respect that each of us had a job to do to complete the shared mission.

It was an ingenious move because it tapped into what we social psychologists call a superordinate goal, a task that cannot be accomplished without cooperation between people from different groups. To accomplish the superordinate goal, all in the navy had to put aside their stereotypes and intolerant language to interact in a productive way with the real people in their work group, and in the navy writ large.

For his one-new-thought paper, a White male student wrote:

No person is an island. The phrase has stuck with me through not only Psychology 311 but also into Psychology 491, albeit with a different meaning for the current course. It struck home especially when the topic of a superordinate goal was introduced. Superordinate goals are tasks that require cooperation between two antagonistic groups, which can directly relate to the correspondence of outcomes between the two groups. This teamwork between two different groups of people, whether they be White or Black, gay or straight, Christian or Muslim, is for me, perhaps the biggest piece of the puzzle when dealing with the rough beast that is neo-diversity. A single person being an island to himself prevents the cooperation necessary to achieve superordinate goals, in our case preventing the slaying of the beast that is neo-diversity.

Before this class, I had thought of race especially as being something that each of us must overcome through our own means. To overcome prejudice, one must simply spend time around those unlike themselves and have their minds changed to squash previous stereotypes. What I have now realized, however, is how everyone must be involved together to achieve a superordinate goal such as dealing with neo-diversity. Today through classes, sports teams, the workforce, or simple dyadic interactions we are all working towards the superordinate goal of dealing with and finding the answers to our age of neo-diversity.

Moving on from this class with a changed mind and perspective on many issues, this new thought and knowledge of superordinate goals that we all face together will help immensely just in everyday life and encounters. Having an interpersonal-intergroup interaction now represents so much more. Knowing that we all are different, knowing the dangers of stereotypes, knowing that we all suffer anxieties in interactions, and knowing that we are all part of something bigger than ourselves will help me work towards superordinate goals for the betterment of the whole, not just myself.

As we move through the twenty-first century, I believe we Americans must take on confronting intolerant language as a superordinate goal. Why? Because language is not just words; it can reflect our behavioral tendencies. Words we choose to use can reflect how we are likely to behave toward the people and groups we use language to describe. For example, a White male wrote:

> The days normally blend together working at a national sporting goods store. I stock shelves, I sell rifles, and I help customers find what they need to hunt and fish. However, the normal quickly went away when an older Hispanic man came in to purchase a rifle to get ready for hunting season.
>
> He did not speak English very well and he could not read or write. I spent a good amount of time speaking with him in broken Spanish and finding out exactly what he was looking for and what he was hunting. He explained the exact type of rifle he needed, and we picked one off the shelves for him to purchase. After I explained how the paperwork process went we began filling it out. I asked him the questions, his friend filled out his answers, and I signed that I was a witness along with his friend. This is exactly how the paperwork instructs filling out the form if reading and writing is a difficulty for the purchaser of the rifle. Once that was completed I called the FBI to do an instant background check, which he passed, and all that was left was a manager signing off of the weapon.

Manager-A came to the counter, looked at the customer, and politely denied the sale. "What?" I said. "Why?"

He replied with a simple response of "I can't sell the rifle if he did not fill out the paperwork."

I explained that the FBI gives specific instructions on what to do if this is the case.

He then began to get defensive and said that I was putting him in a tough position and pressuring him into selling the rifle. I then began to get annoyed and pulled him away from the customer to ask him in private why he would not sell the rifle. Then . . . the truth came out. "I'm not selling this gun to some Mexican that can't even speak English!" he snapped at me.

Knowing that this was a deep issue with Manager-A, I quickly said, that's no problem, I will ask the Hispanic man to leave. I then walked back to the customer and called Manager-B over to sign off on the rifle against the wishes of Manager-A. Manager-B signed off on the rifle, and I walked it out to the Hispanic man's car with him, wishing him the best and good luck hunting.

When I returned to the store Manager-A was there to greet me with a stern "You disobeyed my direct command to not sell the rifle. You are going to be let go today because we will not have that here."

I replied, "Do what you have to do. I was comfortable with the sale, and he was a respectable man."

When I got back to the counter Manager-B, who had signed off on the rifle, informed me that there was a phone call for me in the back office. I went into the back office with both managers. Once we were all in the office I spoke into the speaker, "This is Scott."

The response was, "Scott, this is the CEO. Can you tell me about what happened today?"

I explained the story, which was incredibly awkward because both managers were in the office with me. After I finished the story there was a pause, and then the CEO spoke.

"Scott, I appreciate you standing up for a comfortable sale and not allowing discrimination to come into the workplace." The CEO then proceeded to tell Manager-A that because of the way he showed severe discrimination that the company was going to let him go and that he needed to pack his things. I was shocked.

After Manager-A left, the CEO continued, "Scott, that was a very bold but correct move you made today. I especially appreciate it because I am of Puerto Rican descent. We could use more people like you within the company."

"Thank you sir" was all I said, and we said our good-bye.

After that moment my desire to stand for what I believe in has become even stronger, and I am well respected by our customers no matter what the race.

America is now a neo-diverse nation, and we ain't going back. To help that along, we need to commit ourselves to a new superordinate goal, which should be to stop showing so much tolerance for intolerance. We have to speak up in the face of intolerance. We have to speak up and defend our neo-diverse nation wherever we are and with whomever we interact. We have to stop showing so much tolerance for intolerance.

A quiet revolution against intolerant language should be our shared goal in America. To reach that goal, we have a clear, quiet interpersonal strategy. All over America people experience the moment my niece Tresha describes as "that moment when you feel the warmth of uncomfortableness slowly creep upward and over your face because someone has said something . . . some nasty, derogatory thing about a group of people or person . . . and you find yourself paralyzed by discomfort, but never really knowing what to say or how to address it." In that moment, no longer should we be paralyzed because now we know of an appropriate interpersonal strategy. Each of us can speak up. We can say, "I am very uncomfortable with that kind of language. I find it offensive. It hurts me." This statement, while simple and (seemingly) benign is not only powerful and disarming toward the offender but encouraging to those around us who need help in their effort to stand up to bigotry.

In his one-new-thought paper, a White male student wrote:

> Living in a fraternity house this year has been quite the experience. I live in a room with two of my pledge brothers (brothers that went through pledging with me, called "Spring 12s") and in a house with about 40 brothers all together. Within each pledge class, pledge brothers are always very close; it is a bond created through the pledging process. When someone has an issue with another pledge brother, he will address the brother directly, which is why I decided to initiate my "end to silence" within this group.

After your last few lectures focused around the "N-word," as I know you expected, I cannot hear the word without it mentally teleporting me back into my seat in Riddick, where I hear you speak the lecture. I think about every word. Most especially, the words you quoted from Dr. Martin Luther King Jr.: "The greatest tragedy of this age will not be the vitriolic words and deeds of the children of darkness, but the appalling silence of the children of light." One task of mine day-to-day is to be as humble as possible, although I like to consider myself of the children of light. To hold this mentality though, one must act, because as you said, silence is agreement.

Although many rather stereotype my fraternity, each brother, like anyone else, is a unique human being with rich backgrounds. Even with this being so, as it is a large part of popular culture, rap music is ubiquitous to most brothers' music libraries. One of my roommates is from Greenville, and along with electronic/party music, rap is his predominant music choice. Living in the same room as him, when he plays music, my other roommate and I both hear it and likewise for him.

Since your "N-word" lectures, I am literally baffled by how much I hear the word in the house through music, alone. Brothers sing along, and I hear it when they say it. And, I mean, I did not just sprout ears, but now I hear it. Even though it should, hearing it in music does not bother me (past that unfortunate, uncomfortable feeling for its commonness) because the musician is not a part of my group. However, the other day after the first part of the "N-word" lecture, I walked back from class to the house and up to my room. My frat roommate A. J. was already there, and I was greeted with an ever-so-happy and cheerful "What up, my nigga?" Without realizing it, I just stood there, staring down at my bass guitar in front of me. A. J. looked at me and asked if I was all right. I said I was fine. But I was truly disappointed in not knowing how to address how I did not want that word used in my presence, or preferably at all.

This past Sunday, while studying for a nutrition test the next day, I took a break and decided to watch your TEDx talk on YouTube. When I finished with the video, I chuckled at how simple your recommended response was. It made perfect sense. You are not attacking the other person. You are simply explaining how you feel. Yet, I thought about how I could execute it, and it scared me. I wanted to address someone when they used the "N-word" or any other slur of any sort, but I feared the consequences. I feared being socially exiled, especially from my fraternity brothers who I consider good friends.

When I got back to the house and my room, once again A. J. was in there as well as my other roommate Con. Once again, A. J. saw me and said, "What up, my nigga?" I stopped once again, finding myself staring at that very same spot on the bass guitar. I returned to the moment with the mentally rehearsed response, "A. J., I'm sorry, but I am very uncomfortable with that kind of language. I find it offensive; it hurts me." Con turned at me somewhat wide-eyed. A. J. responded with an honest yet simple "My bad, man." And the weight of my mental tension fell with those words. The next step and challenge . . . is to repeat. . . .

Reading this account, I know that my teaching matters. There are no innocent. We are all monsters, but we are monsters who hope to prove our full humanity. I am called to get people ready for the journey by train. It is a long journey to our humanity. But the Neo-Diversity train is coming down the line, ready to take us on that journey.

At the end of the course in the fall of 2012, at the end of his one-new-thought paper, a White male student wrote:

People, please be ready, there is a train coming, we don't necessarily need a ticket, but we must fasten the seat belt for the ride. I am determined to stop accepting the status quo with intergroup relationships. Don't get me wrong, there are obvious differences between people, and I will never say that I do not see color or that there are no differences; that would be silly. What we should do is admire our differences and use them as strength.

How can this happen, you might ask? It seems clear to me that we need to end this sense of competition between people. In theory this might seem easy to do on paper, but it will actually be difficult. The first big step will be to educate people, especially when they make mistakes.

I have friends all the time that say, "Well, at least I'm not gay," or "Well, at least I'm not Black" when things don't go well for them. However, there are no innocent. Before coming to college, all the time I would say statements such as "That's so gay"; heck, I have even used negative statements toward other races in high school.

We are splitting ourselves into groups with those statements of "us" versus "them," but we are all playing for the same team, humans. From now on I will be observing the world and when negative statements toward another group occur I will speak out and let them know that I am not okay with that type of language. I have been trained and forever changed in a good way, and I would never like to go back to where I was before. Letting others know that I disapprove of language that they use towards other groups will help them change like it changed me. Now I am standing at the train station, my bag is in my hand, I am ready to get onboard the train, and I just hope America will be ready to go with me!

PART 8

NO SECOND CLASS ABOARD THIS TRAIN,
NO DIFFERENCE IN THE FARE

CHAPTER 17

WE'RE ALL TRAVELERS

I have had a very successful career as a professor. One of the things I am known for is my teaching style. That is why some on campus consult with me about classroom dynamics and teaching techniques. That is why that young man I mentioned earlier was in my office asking about teaching techniques. My advice to him was "humanize the material." A bit later that semester, I received a letter from him.

> I wanted to thank you for the time you spent talking with me before break. I truly appreciate your openness and engagement with students.
>
> Many of the topics we discussed that Friday have stuck with me, but one has probably impacted my life. I told you I was teaching an introductory problem-solving section for Meteorology. Over break one of the other teachers had a family emergency requiring him to return home for the remainder of the semester. I volunteered to take over his section, which placed me in the uniquely awkward position of becoming a new teacher, a new set of rules, a new environment for thirty students.
>
> Tuesday of this week was my first time with that class. As I was preparing my PowerPoint, I decided it was important for me to start by leveling the playing field; setting my expectations of the students, letting them know what to expect of me. The first set of slides were all rules and policies. I imagined myself as a student during this portion of the lecture and felt I would view my instructor as a dictator or a robot.
>
> I immediately thought of our conversation of humanizing the material. I threw in a slide about something in my personal life, about my girlfriend being in Guatemala. During my lecture, the whole room was tense for the first few slides. I could see in the students' eyes a distant, impersonal look. As soon as the slide with my girlfriend popped up and I started my short

story, the room exhaled. Everyone was smiling. They realized I was human, just like them.

It's amazing what a little honest self-disclosure can do.

Sincerely, C. W.

On the campus of NCSU I am asked to give teaching workshops. "Neo-Diversity in the Classroom: Creating a Safe Space" is a workshop I conducted in February of 2013. I showed how any professor can create a safe space in the classroom. I told the story of the "who pays?" discussion (see chap. 5), the student reaction, and my firm reminder to my students of the safe space rule. Given my confrontational teaching style, some of my colleagues wonder how I can be so challenging and yet have students feel safe to ask questions and give opinions during class discussions. I should not have been surprised by the question.

Throughout my workshop presentation I take questions about the specific point I am making, and then at the end I take general questions from the faculty and staff who attend. An African American faculty colleague put her hand up and said, "You really challenge your students on diversity issues, but yet you have a large following of White students. How do you pull that off?" I was surprised but not put off by the racial bluntness of the question. I took a moment, and then I took time to give an extended answer to that question. But there is really only one thing going on. I am a day breaker.

Just the week before that workshop I was allowed to inform people that I had won the University of North Carolina System Board of Governors Award for Excellence in Teaching. In the fall of 2013, my department and the College of Humanities and Social Sciences had nominated me. It is indeed quite an honor to be nominated for that award, but quite a lot of work, too. As classes for the semester were ending, in addition to dealing with grading final exams and final papers, I was also putting together the extensive teaching portfolio that the evaluation process required. I had help; no one is an island. Faculty colleagues and students helped me put together the various parts of the portfolio. I was exhausted but happy with every component and thankful that fall semester was over.

A month later, just after our spring semester started, I walked into my office on the morning of January 11, 2013. My phone message light was blinking. That always irritates me. So early in the semester, it could only be one of two irritating things: a student confused about something with an obvious, on-the-syllabus answer, or a student wanting to force-register into one of my classes, which at that point was impossible.

Rather than let it blink for hours, as I have done in the past, I decided to just listen to the irritating message. I hit the button. A voice said, "Good afternoon, Dr. Nacoste. This is Chancellor Woodson. It is my pleasure to inform you that I am forwarding your teaching portfolio to the Board of Governors as our campus winner of the Board of Governors Excellence in Teaching Award. . . ." I sat at my desk holding my head.

Chancellor Randy Woodson went on to inform me that for reasons of protocol I could not yet tell anyone that I had won. He also let me know that, having left me his message, the formal letter would be brought to me. It would give me the details of all that had been set in motion because I had won the highest teaching award given by the university and by the UNC system.

Much was about to happen. I was to attend and be the speaker for the luncheon at the Office of Faculty Development Teaching and Learning Symposium. I was invited to attend the Chancellor's Celebration of Faculty Excellence Dinner. In front of twenty thousand people I would be formally presented the award at the Spring Commencement, during which I would join the chancellor on the platform along with "other" dignitaries. Then there was this that caught me off guard: *The awarding of the BOG Award for Excellence in Teaching is also celebrated by the lighting of the Belltower.*

What? Really?

What an extraordinary honor! On the North Carolina State University campus the Memorial Belltower is an icon. It is lit red only under very special circumstances: winning a basketball game, a football game, winning a national championship. When it is lit red, students, alumni, and fans of the university drive by and blow their car horns, over and over.

Now I learned it would be lit red for me. That made me giddy.

About a month after receiving the chancellor's call and the subsequent letter, I received official notice from the UNC System Board of Governors. Now I could tell my colleagues, students, and the whole campus. Starting in the just-past fall semester, I had been working very closely with the 2012–2013 editors of the *Technician*. In fact, already in that spring semester, these editors had published one of my guest columns, "A Wake Up Call to Neo-Diversity Gumbo":

I am a Louisiana Black-Creole from the bayous. Just think swamps, alligators, crawfish and gumbo and you get the right picture, and if your imagination is really good, the right smells.

Delta Upsilon Fraternity had a gumbo gathering on Jan. 16. One of their member's families is from Slidell, La. and he made gumbo. With his gumbo, he represented my "who dat" nation very well.

So no, I didn't cook. I was there to lead a discussion of neo-diversity. You see, we no longer live in a society where our racial contacts are controlled and restricted by law. Not only that, but nowadays, every day, on the NC State campus each of us has some occasion to interact with a person from another racial, gender, ethnic, religious or sexually oriented group. That's true all over the United States.

Using some words of Dr. Martin Luther King, Jr., I introduced the idea of neo-diversity and got the fifty-five or so students talking. To help our fellow Wolfpackers understand how much and how fast things have changed I let them know that I, a dark-skinned Black man, grew up in the Jim Crow South—that time of legal segregation and legally supported bigotry. We have gone from that to neo-diversity where our racial contact and interactions are not controlled by law or anything else. We have gone from that to the second inauguration of a Black, racially mixed man: President Barack Hussein Obama.

This neo-diversity has come to America quickly. That is causing some people to panic and try to avoid everyday social interactions on our campus. So, I challenged the students to learn to interact across the superficial group lines. Learn now because when you leave this campus, employers are looking for people who can do that. But learn it now, I said, because everybody here at NCSU is Wolfpack.

WOLF! PACK!

Though it's fun, that cheer is empty if you don't mean everybody on our campus. Wherever we are in America, we have to learn to interact with each other as individuals, not as representatives of a group. If you try to interact with someone as a representative of a group, that interaction will go bad because your strategy will require that you rely on stereotypes. And no person is going to respond kindly when they feel you aim a stereotype at them. In this age of neo-diversity we all have to learn to interact with the person standing in front of us and not with our ideas about the group.

That night at Delta Upsilon I felt good because everybody seemed to be willing to engage in dialogue and take on new thoughts. For an hour we had a good time, but I had to bring things to a close because my old knees were telling me to go home.

Many students came up to me to thank me for coming, talking, and making it fun. One young White woman was struggling to find the words to thank me. "Thanks," she said, "that was . . . that was . . ." Someone else standing there said, "Compelling." The young woman who was struggling shook her head and said, "No . . . yes, it was that . . . but it was . . . a wake-up call."

That's why I give talks and presentations about neo-diversity. I do what I can to get every audience to wake up and see our neo-diverse America. I want everyone to wake up to the fact that America just ain't what it used to be. I want all of us to wake up, acknowledge, and appreciate our wonderful, American neo-diverse gumbo.

Given my strong relationship with the *Technician* editors for that academic year, I sent them a copy of the Board of Governors' official letter. I was blown away by the editorial they published on February 26, 2013. "An Award Well-Deserved" was the title of the editorial, which read, in part:

In addition to his academic achievements, Nacoste is a strong supporter of civil rights and social justice. His research on interpersonal relationships and modern racial tensions has led him to publish multiple essays on what he calls "neo-diversity." His classes, often called tough or intense, include his thoughts on the false claim that we live in a post-racist United States, and he challenges his students to confront prejudice on campus and within their personal lives. He seeks to genuinely educate students about these tough topics.

"Wherever we are in America, we have to learn to interact with each other as individuals, not as representatives of a group," Nacoste recently wrote in a guest column in *Technician*. "If you try to interact with someone as a representative of a group, that interaction will go bad because your strategy will require that you rely on stereotypes."

We greatly respect Nacoste and completely support the Board of Governors in their decision to recognize him with this award. He is a model of both academic excellence—through the respect he garners from students—and civil rights activism—through his willingness to promote diversity and thoughtfully discuss hard topics.

So Nacoste, this goes out to you.

Who Dat?

When the university set the date of the Belltower lighting, it was close to the end of the semester. I only had a few days of notice. I wanted my former and current students to know. I hoped a few might come out that night. So with the subject being "Dr. Nacoste honored," I sent this e-mail to students from the past three years of my classes:

> *From the Chancellor's office, here's the announcement:*
> "To celebrate Dr. Rupert Nacoste for being the Campus-Winner of the UNC Board of Governors' Award for Excellence in Teaching, the Secretary of the Faculty has requested that the Belltower be lit red on this Tuesday, April 30th. Dr. Nacoste is the only Psychology-faculty-member to win the award in the entire UNC system this year. Also, he is the first Psychologist to win on any system campus since 2009.
> To honor Dr. Nacoste the NCSU Memorial Belltower will be illuminated just at dark, around 8pm or a little later. Dr. Nacoste will be at the Belltower at 8pm."
> *From me:* So I would be honored to have some of my former students come out for this lighting of the Belltower. I will be at the Belltower by 7:45 or so. If you have the time, come out and celebrate with me; come howl with me.
> I hope to see some of you out there.

And that's when the howling started.

I wasn't really thinking. I had the idea that maybe a few students might show up, and we would shake hands, chat, and when it got dark enough and the Belltower turned red, we'd say, "Wow, look at that," and then go home. After sending the "Dr. Nacoste Honored" e-mails, almost immediately e-mail responses began to come in. I realized that my idea was way off.

There were e-mails of congratulations:

> Congratulations on this well-deserved honor. I had the pleasure of being in your class for both introductory psychology and social psychology, and you are one of the greatest teachers I've ever had. I graduated from NC State in 2011 and am heading to medical school at UNC this fall, but I will never forget some of the lessons I learned from you about "life in the social world." I hope you'll be "comin' in hot" for many years to come!

There were e-mails of regret:

> This is great news! I'm not even surprised you won because honestly, I always tell everyone that "He is the best professor at State!" Anyone who didn't take your class is missing out for sure! If I could, I would come take another one of your classes. Haha! Any-who, congrats on your award and I wish I could celebrate with you if I wasn't all the way in Philly . . .

Or St. Thomas
Or George Washington University
Or Indianapolis
Or San Diego
My current and former students were excited. I mean, really excited. One student was so excited that he wrote:

> I was so ready to go to this I forgot to look at the date. I got out there right on time, *about 24 hours early*. I would gladly go again tomorrow, but my band is playing at the Pour House and we'll be heading over to unload around that time. Congratulations, though!

Regrets from near and far made me begin to see that my students were really excited for me. But what made me realize I was in trouble were the many e-mails that read:

Thanks for the invite, and I will most definitely be attending! Again, congratulations.

So many e-mails declaring, "I will be there" was the alert I needed. Now I knew I had to prepare a few words for those who would be at the Belltower that night.

The night of the Belltower lighting I decided to get an early bite to eat to hold me for a while, and then get on over to the event. As I pulled into one of the spaces at the Belltower, I saw that some of my students were already there, and it was only 7:30 p.m. As I had said in the e-mail announcements, nothing was going to happen until 8 p.m. So I was surprised to see about ten students already there and waiting. When I walked up the steps I said, "What are you guys doing here so early? We won't start until 8 o'clock."

An answer came from an Arab American male student who had just finished my "Introduction to Social Psychology" class on interpersonal relationships. Despite the two-hundred-person auditorium class and the fact that he sat almost at the very top of the auditorium, I recognized him. I remembered him by his dark eyes, well-kept haircut, neatly trimmed black beard, his always mischievous smile, and because he always asked good questions in a bold way. Also memorable was the poem he wrote for the one-new-thought paper for that class. Apparently my lectures on the mistake of being too friendly on a first date really hit him. The interdependence theory concept of autistic friendliness (Thibaut and Kelley), a rigid predisposition to be friendly, is what he wrote his poem about. He wrote:

> The day you brought up this term: autistic friend-li-ness
> I realized what it was, and why it was such a mess
> You see, I had thought about that sort of thing before
> I decided I would pay attention! I wanted to hear more
> It's not that I wasn't listening to you at the start
> I came into class with an open mind and an open heart
> People said take Nacoste! Hear what he has to say
> His class is very interesting, and taught in his own way

> I figured how could it be different? I thought I'd seen it all
> And then this Cajun Black Creole walked into the hall
> He said my name is Rupert, don't let me hear a pen
> Don't write something down. Unless I say it again.
> I said okay, I'm listening. . . . And then . . .

And then, he said, he learned to sit back in my class, listen, learn, and take notes when I gave the signal by repetition. It was this young man who answered me when I walked up the steps of the Belltower. Smiling, he looked me in the eyes and said, "Oh, well, we know you don't like it when we are late for your class."

I fell out laughing.

"But," I said, "this is not a class period."

He just smiled wider.

I found it funny that I kept getting that same answer as I asked the same question of others who were already there and those who started showing up right after me. The refrain was always—"We know how you are about people being late."

The demand for punctuality is part of my reputation among students. I just didn't think it would apply so broadly. As I shook hands and hugged students as they showed up, they just kept coming. Suddenly the steps of the Belltower were full, and I could still see students coming.

It was turning into quite a celebration. A current student, Lydia Bravo-Taylor was walking around taking pictures. Then my colleague, my friend, a man I consider a brother, Dr. Craig Brookins showed up with cameras. He started taking pictures and video. Around 8:15 he got us organized for group pictures.

Nacoste and his neo-diverse students in front of the NCSU Belltower. Image courtesy of Lydia Bravo-Taylor

What a turnout. I was almost speechless. Almost, but I had prepared something to say to these young travelers. And they were ready to hear from me. When I said, "OK, now I have something to say," they just stood there waiting. I said, "Well, I would feel better if everyone sat down first." So they did, and I felt their presence as if they were in class with me, attentive, ready. And so I spoke:

I am a day breaker.

In my teaching in the college classroom, I am a day breaker.

You see, in my opinion teaching is getting people to understand, embrace and use the knowledge your discipline has to offer. To make a lecture or speech zing, I always try to make a provocative statement of my theme in the first sentence.

I am a day breaker.

Intriguing and capturing the audience right from the start is an idea that I take seriously when I am preparing a lecture. But I am trying to do more than that. I am also trying to create a struggle.

Human beings, you see, are designed to live in a social world.

If adults can survive while the young cannot, the latter are obliged to ask their elders for knowledge from the start.

Turns out that to acquire the skills to survive, humans must be engaged in an interactive struggle; we are built to wrestle knowledge from our elders and from each other.

That is why, as most of you know, I start one of my courses with a poem, and then I say, "You're not going to like this class."

I do so because I am trying to create a struggle; an intellectual struggle. From the first day of any of my classes, I am trying to wake up my students to the realities of the social world. I am a day breaker.

The poetic motivation behind what I do comes from the Arna Bontemps poem "The Day-Breakers." In that poem Bontemps says that in the fight for human rights some of us must be willing to die if that's what it takes to beat a way for the rising sun. I take that seriously. My major teaching goal is to beat a way for the rising sun. I am a day breaker.

I want to thank all of you for standing up to that challenge. And when I say standing up to the challenge I mean putting yourself in a position to be challenged and to learn from that challenge. It takes a grownup to do that.

No man is an island. . . .

I recite poet John Donne to say that I stand here because other people in my life have encouraged and supported me.

My parents: Mr. Ogeese and Miss Ella. They taught me to have the joie de vivre; the joy of life; eh toi (oh yeah) . . . c'est, c'est bon (it's so good) . . . laissez les bontemps roulez (let the good times roll). . . .

They started the gumbo that is my life.

My colleagues; when I was first on the faculty here, Jim Kalat and Bob Pond helped me think through classroom teaching techniques. Other colleagues have always supported me; standing over there, Dr. Craig Brookins in particular.

And finally, I stand here because of you, my students. All of you . . .

It is you, my students, who have motivated me to keep at it and get better at it.

Who dat!? It's you.

Eh toi (oh yeah) . . . it's you, all my students are part of the gumbo of my life.

Who dat!? It's you . . . wolf . . . pack . . .

Thank you, Wolfpack, for staying in the classroom with me, for being open to the challenges my teaching presented to you; thank you for taking the opportunity to learn how to live better in the social world. Thank you.

I am a day breaker; I am always trying to beat a way for the rising sun.

But the world is primarily social. So I know that I do not do my work on my own. The world is primarily social. Never forget . . . no woman or man is an island. . . .

Thank you for coming out tonight. I am honored to have all of you here to share this moment with me.

Thank you, thank you . . .

Quite an evening, filled with smiles, hugs, laughter, and picture taking. When the Belltower went red, everyone cheered, and from the street, car horns started to blow.

Logan Collins, one of my former students from ten years back and now one of my dearest friends, was there. Logan, a White female, told me she was blown away by the neo-diversity of students who came out to be with me. That made me think of the comment made and question asked of me at the teaching workshop I held on neo-diversity in the college classroom. During the question-and-answer period, a faculty member, an African American, marveled at what she had heard about me on campus and from whom she had heard the comments. She asked how I could pull it off.

"You really challenge your students on diversity issues, but yet you have a large following of White students. How do you pull that off?"

I "pull it off" by addressing my students as twenty-first-century citizens, and with respect. My classroom is one of mutual respect. I demand respect and I give respect. I don't tell my students what to think. I do not try to indoctrinate them. I teach social psychological concepts and how to use those concepts to analyze what is going on. Yes, I have a real agenda based on my experiences and personal values. But I believe in and trust the framework of my discipline. My personal experiences and values fuel the passion that comes through in my teaching of the concepts of social psychology. I teach concepts and analysis with passion in order to beat a way for the rising sun, to get my students ready.

Yet I must also say that my faculty colleague was wrong to say that I have a large following of White students. That is not true. As the turnout for my Belltower night showed, I have a large following of a neo-diversity of students. Why?

No matter their skin color, bodily condition, sexual orientation, ethnicity, mental condition, gender, or religion, without meaning to, I become a father figure to many of my students. I become Chingachgook.

In the 1992 movie *Last of the Mohicans*, we meet the Mohican Chingachgook and his two sons, Mohican Uncas and "adopted" White Nathaniel Hawkeye. Chingachgook had spent much energy in rearing these two into men of integrity who have respect for nature, nature's creatures, and respect for people of all kinds. That integrity is what gets Hawkeye in trouble with the British forces. Seeing that the British are betraying them, Hawkeye helps a number of colonials escape a fort that is under siege by the French. He himself does not escape because he is in love with Cora Munro, the daughter of the British commander. Staying behind to be with Cora and with the word having gone out that he helped the "traitors," Hawkeye is arrested.

British soldiers storm into the room where Hawkeye, Uncas, and Chingachgook are sleeping. The soldiers grab and cuff Hawkeye as his brother and his father are about to fight the soldiers. Hawkeye stops them from doing so, telling Chingachgook that this is not their fight. Watching as they take Hawkeye away, in a plaintive voice, Chingachgook calls out, "What will they do . . . with my White son?"

Every semester I get quick visits and quick e-mails early on. In the fall of 2013, a female student wrote:

> I hope you are well and that the summer months were wonderful for you. I cannot believe I begin this semester without one of your classes on my schedule. Other than that fact, this semester's classes seem to be promising. I would love to meet with you sometime soon when time permits to tell you about my summer and talk about the upcoming year. Can't wait to catch up!
>
> P.S. My parents say hello and still love telling people the story of the time they got to meet you before last semester ended :-)

Even after the semester is over students sometimes come to me for a fatherly moment. They come to me for advice on friendships and romantic relationships. Some write to me about relationship issues, troubles, and adjustments. A male student wrote:

> I feel like my love life has turned into an Otis Redding song. After over 5 years, my time with my girlfriend is coming to an end. I've been looking for someone to help me get this off my chest, and of course the first person to come to mind was the one who taught me so much about relationships. Though it's not been easy on me, I wanted to thank you for all you taught me in Social Psychology. I read through my notes from class recently, and they were extremely valuable in figuring out what's happening between us.
>
> I think the most pertinent subject was that of authentic self-knowledge. She wants, and I need (though I may not actually want it yet), a chance to see what we are like as individuals. We need this as a chance to define ourselves as people rather than as a couple. I am slowly coming to grips with the notion that I may never be with her again. I am also getting better at accepting that it can happen again if it's meant to be. That's a comforting thought, but I know better than to hold out for it since that will only hurt me.
>
> Luckily, we're both level-headed and nobody is angry or bitter. We're spending the last few days of summer celebrating what we have and what

we had. After that, my last year of undergrad will be my first year of single college life.

I hope the years have been kind to you. I noticed you published another book. I'll get myself a copy very soon. My band recorded and put out our own CD. If you're ever around campus, I'd love a chance to drop by and give you one.

Once again, thank you for all you taught me, and for giving me the tools and understanding I need to get through this. It's a huge change for me, and you were so helpful in preparing me for it. Your friend, D. L.

To D. L. I replied:

Oh D. L.,

Your words have touched me, deeply. I am so thankful that you took my course and that through our honors discussion I really got to know you. I found you to be a young man who was growing in all kinds of ways, including being open to learning. I am grateful that you have found in my teachings a path to adjustment and healing in this period of transition in your life.

I will be on campus again in the fall. Let's please do find a time to get together to catch up. We can do that in my office or over coffee somewhere.

Here and now you sound very balanced in what I know is a tough time. For that I am grateful. Your friend . . .

During any semester, a neo-diverse set of my students begin to respond to me as a father figure. Some come to me for advice on how to deal with a troubling neo-diversity situation. Remember "I'm at a party right now" Maggie? No, I did not answer her that night. My students know better than to expect that. But I did respond to Maggie. Here is our full exchange of e-mails:

I'm at a party right now . . .

And a 21-year-old White male just said the word "nigger." I told them that I didn't think that any use of that word was acceptable in any situation. This started a conversation with everyone explaining to me it all mattered about the "inflection" and "connotation" it was used in. I was at a loss for words. What can I say if that happens again?

Thanks Dr. Nacoste, Maggie

Hi Maggie,

OK, the mistake you made was getting into a discussion. Your statement was almost the right one. Remember, the idea is to make the point that the word is unacceptable to you; "I find it offensive; it hurts me." Then you should reinforce that by walking away . . . from anyone who wanted to argue that the word "nigger" can ever be acceptable. If that means leaving that party, then so be it. Dr. Nacoste

I'll keep that in mind if it ever happens again, Dr. Nacoste. I'm just sorry I dropped the ball last night. I hope your semester is going well, and that your speech at Talley yesterday had a big turnout! Maggie

Maggie,

You didn't drop the ball. You actually got people thinking about the issue, even if they argued with you. To argue, they had to think about the issue more than they had before. So, again, you didn't drop the ball. Remember, you are still learning how to stand up for change. I am very proud of you for working on that. Dr. Nacoste.

I don't do counseling. I tell my students, "No one wants my version of counseling." When I say that, all of my students go wide-eyed and shake their heads side to side in understanding and agreement. I don't do counseling, but I will not ignore one of my students. I will not leave them hanging, and they know that.

Neo-diversity is a tough reality to learn to manage. Even after graduating, students seek out my perspective on current events. One student e-mailed me with a query about the LA Clippers situation. He wrote:

I thoroughly enjoyed taking your "Interpersonal Relationships and Race" class last spring and have found the course's topics ever relevant since taking the class. I have this week been particularly intrigued by the events surrounding Los Angeles Clippers owner Donald Sterling. I'm sure you've heard about his racist comments and the league's response. I was wondering, what is your reaction to the news?

Mr. Sterling strikes me as a man with a slave-owner complex, hiring more Black coaches and GMs than any other owner in the league over the past 30 years as well as having a half-Black girlfriend. His history of racist behavior is additionally concerning. The more I learn about this story, the more interested I become, so I was hoping to get your perspective on the events and your take on the psychological analysis of Mr. Sterling's behaviors.

Thanks, Benjamin.

Here is my reply:

Benjamin,

Yes, there continue to be lots of neo-diversity stories in the news.

So first, Mr. Sterling's verbal behavior is bigotry. But as the owner of the Clippers (with organizational power), his behavior may indicate racism. Remember racism is institutional and organizational. If his bigotry informed his hiring practices as the owner then the organization is engaged in racism. Even though he hired Blacks his motivations were based on racial paternalism; as you put it, a slave-owner mentality; I take care of them, I feed them, I pay them. All the use of the word "them" makes his decision-making in-group–out-group.

Also, one of the neo-diversity dimensions is that his "girlfriend" is mixed race, yet he hoped she would think of race in the same way he did. So in his interactions with her he was struggling with the neo-diversity anxiety about "who are the 'we' and who are among the 'they?'" His shaky assumption of belief similarity got him into this trouble because it made him feel free to openly talk about Blacks as "things," with a person of mixed-race heritage.

The NBA also had to deal with the neo-diversity question "who are the 'we' and who are among the 'they?'" If the NBA had let this go, that would mean that the NBA is engaged in racism; organizational support for racial bigotry among the owners. That would have been immoral. But it also would have damaged the NBA brand; the NBA global corporation. The NBA could not let that happen, and they acted rightly and swiftly.

Yet this is still America. To oust Mr. Sterling will take following the rules of the NBA commission. There is still a fight ahead, and Mr. Sterling has plenty of money to fight with if he chooses that route. On that, we will all have to see.

Nice to know you are still keeping yourself aware.

I enjoyed that interchange. It forced me to be analytic about what was going on. That is what I hope my class does for my students.

Once my students grasp the meaning and far-reaching implications of neo-diversity, their new awareness puts them in situations of vague interdependence that they will struggle with. Toward the end of my class, I begin to warn them about this. I do that more than once because I know in ways they don't yet that they have gained a new awareness that will catch them off guard.

I get e-mails over the summers. An e-mail from a male student came to me with the subject "Help with N word reduction." He wrote:

> I took your relationships and race class last semester and was hoping you could help me with something. I am working in a summer counseling program that targets kids in the 7–12 age range. The vast majority of these kids are African American, and the N word is running rampant in our sessions. I am a White male and have yet to bring up the topic for fear of losing rapport with my clients. You do a very good job at getting through to us in class, and I was hoping you might have some advice or a line of thought that would get through to these kids. I appreciate any help you can offer and best of luck with your book writing this summer.

Being summer, it took a little while, but I replied:

> Truth is, you as an individual can't do anything about the language used by these children. For this to be addressed at the camp, the camp (as an institution) would have had to lay out a language policy for attendance. That would have alerted the parents who let this language go on at home, and it would give the camp (as an institution) a rule structure about language. Also, a language policy would give the camp (as an institution) a reason for making that part of the first-day orientation for the camp, and a platform for explaining why certain words are demeaning.
>
> Hang in there my friend.

He wrote back to say:

> I very much agree with your thinking, and in all honesty, I now see the preparation put into this program was subpar. I am writing a report on the

program for the company, and your thoughts have helped me to organize my thinking.

No worries on the delay; I know you are a busy man. Enjoy the remainder of your summer.

Thank you . . .

Also one summer, a young White female e-mailed me to get my advice on how to deal with family members who use intergroup slurs. She wrote:

Once again, I'd like you to know that I really enjoyed and benefited from PSY 491. I have learned so much, and my way of thinking has changed a lot. I was so happy with the positive classroom environment I got to experience all semester.

However, I am in the real world now and am struggling. In particular, I am struggling with my family. Racial slurs are being used once in a while, and stereotypes are being used a lot. I try to stop the use of these devices, but to no avail. My efforts have been crushed by my siblings and occasionally by my parents, and I get blamed for causing a fight or a controversy. The last straw happened this past week while my family and I were on vacation in Florida. My brother, a rising sophomore in college, was angered at the way a male Hispanic waiter was treating my father; he was being rude to my father, so we left the restaurant. When we got back to the car and were driving away, my brother called the man a racial slur. I immediately became frustrated and exhaled loudly. My parents responded, "What?!" and I said, "I'm tired of hearing racial slurs!" They had not heard what my brother said, and my brother said the word was not a racial slur. He repeated the word, as well as another racial slur, and my parents yelled at him for using that language.

Ever since the fight, things have been weird and awkward within the family. My sister told me I was being ridiculous by getting upset with the use of racial slurs, and was defending the negative actions that had brought about the use of those slurs. ??? How can I help my family to see that I am just against the use of stereotypes and slurs? I don't know why they are struggling so much. They do not want to listen to what I have to say and are content with living in a world that promotes hate. Please let me know if you have any advice. I could really use some help with this one, especially since they are my family.

I warn my students about this, too. Toward the end of the semester, I tell them that because they have taken the "Interpersonal Relationships and Race" course, they now have new social sensitivities. I tell them those sensitivities will be activated especially at home. "Where before you did not react to intolerant language, now you will react in some way that will be obvious to the people you are interacting with. That reaction could be verbal or nonverbal." But even having been forewarned, this young woman needs help in figuring out what to do now that, as she put it, "I am in the real world now and am struggling. In particular, I am struggling with my family. Racial slurs are being used once in a while, and stereotypes are being used a lot."

I responded to her as soon as I read the e-mail:

> No doubt this is a real struggle. So first, remember no one changes overnight. Second, let them know you are not condoning rude behavior of other people, just pointing out that the behavior has nothing to do with the person's group membership. Third, make the point that you would prefer they not use slurs . . . in your presence . . . because those words hurt you.
>
> Also point out that slurs create hostility. Racial slurs are no different than gender slurs, slurs against women. Point out that when people think slurs against women are OK, they set up an environment where women become devalued and are to be used. That's what all slurs do; they devalue individual people and make them targets.
>
> Say all that and then go to your room or out to a movie.
>
> Remember, no one changes overnight . . . so say your piece and then let it go. If someone does it in your presence again, then don't point it out and argue; leave the immediate situation. Walk the hell away. Come back later and act like nothing happened. You have said your piece. If it happens again, do the same thing: walk the hell away. Keep repeating that exit behavior when you need to. And stay true to yourself.

A day or so after I responded to her, this young woman wrote back saying,

> "Thank you so much. I needed to hear that."

Somehow, I have become a father figure. Chingachgook: that source you go to for advice when you know you are on the right track but need a little help, a strategy for staying on that right track, and some encouragement to do so. And so at the end of any semester, I get hugs, cards of thanks, and tears as these young people head off into the world. Often after such a moment I have the feeling that I believe that Chingachgook had as he watched the British soldiers take away Hawkeye, his White son. With that feeling, I say to myself:

What will they do with my Chinese daughter?

What will they do with my New Jersey son?

What will they do with my Muslim daughter?

What will they do with my Little-Person son?

What will they do with my Black daughter?

What will they do with my Long Island daughter?

What will they do with my lesbian daughter?

What will they do with my African American son?

What will they do with my Jewish daughter?

What will they do with my Christian son?

What will they do with my Nigerian daughter?

What will they do with my White Johnston County, NC, son?

What will they do with my . . .

One last time, we have gathered together.

Image courtesy of Lydia Bravo-Taylor

We are back at the platform. We stand together shaking hands, hugging, with smiles, laughter, a few tears, looking each other in the eyes, listening to the diesel humming, listening to the train that's coming.

Such gatherings are important because we are social beings.

> No man is an island,
> Entire unto itself.
> Each is a piece of the continent,
> A part of the main.
> If a clod be washed away by the sea,
> Europe is the less.
> As well as if a promontory were.
> As well as if a manor of thine own
> Or of thine friend's were.
> Each man's death diminishes me,
> For I am involved in mankind.
> Therefore, send not to know
> For whom the bell tolls.
> It tolls for thee. (Fallon)

The poet John Donne wrote these words to remind us that we are social; we are all involved in humankind.

And we are all involved in mankind. That at least is what the actor Robert Duval says as a character in the television movie *Broken Trail*. A group of cattlemen are moving their herd across the Western plain to sell them at the end of the trail. Yet, during this difficult cattle drive, these men, led by the old, wise cowboy Prentice Ritter (Duval), end up caring for five immigrant Chinese girls who had been sold in their homeland and brought to America to be sex slaves. Reluctant at first, these cattlemen, all White men, rescue, watch over, and try to keep these Chinese girls out of harm's way. With no common language, Prentice Ritter gives the girls numbers as names: Numbers One through Five.

Alas, on the Western plain, in despair of having been raped, one of the Chinese girls, Number Four, throws herself at the hooves of the fast-moving cattle. She is trampled and dies. As the group gathers to bury Number Four, Prentice Ritter makes a pronouncement: "We're all travelers in this world. From the sweet grass to the packing house. Birth 'til death. We travel between the eternities."

He says we're all travelers in this world. And we travelers do, of course, gather when the bell tolls for endings. We gather to say good-bye to fellow travelers. We do this because we are social; we do this because of what we have been to each other while we traveled together.

Now the Neo-Diversity train hisses to a stop in front of us. And the doors open. It's time for my students, these young travelers, to get onboard. Like any parent, as I watch them get on the train, I want the best life for them. I wonder, "What will the world do with them?" Yet I do not worry because I believe I have prepared them. I know they have listened. I believe they have learned from the challenges in the lessons. I have faith that in the midst of being challenged by my teaching, they have worked out new ways of thinking and motivations for themselves as they struggled to take in the knowledge of the real world of neo-diversity.

I have faith in each of my former students, and every now and then I get word that confirms my faith. "Ferguson and Neo-diversity" was the subject of this young White woman's e-mail to me:

Hi Dr. Nacoste—To say that your thoughts and teachings have been in my mind over these past few months would be an understatement! As I see the events unfolding around the nation, due to recent events in Ferguson, Missouri, my mind is drawn back to deep discussions on race relations and neo-diversity and social dynamics. Many of my peers are confused and lost, and I'm so thankful for the opportunity to have been in your classes throughout my academic career and to be able to have a frame of reference for understanding what's going on around us. It's been 6 years since my days in your class, and your class still rings strong in my mind and has shaped much of me and what I do today! Thank you!

As our nation continues to struggle with group dynamics of neo-diversity, I have faith that former students of mine are continuing to work on becoming citizens who can bring perspective to the goings-on. "It's been a hell of a time" was the subject of the most recent e-mail I received from a former student. An African American female, she wrote:

Good evening, Dr. Nacoste: I hope all is well. With everything going on in the world I wish that I could be a fly on the wall during your class next semester. After Michael Brown in Ferguson, after Eric Garner in New York City, I have heard so many conversations about race, some of them positive and some not so much, and to be honest it hurt me (this is all your fault, by the way).

I was hurt because I had to remember the biggest lesson I learned in your class: there is NO they! These young Black men could never go home to their families, never see their kids, and I couldn't say I hate "them" (the police; White people). This idea seemed to be what I saw in general on social media and even listening to some friends at home; "They don't care about us," "We will never be respected by them," "Nothing has changed." When I hear all these comments and see what seemed to be a new Black person dead every week, I was angry and I have to admit I thought maybe those comments are right. But every time I went to say something like this out loud, I couldn't fix my lips to say it. All I could do was think about the stories I heard in your class and the people I met during my time at State, and I realized it was not a "them" but it was a WE.

We need to be better as people, we need to treat people better, we need to acknowledge our flaws, and we need to figure out how we can stop history from repeating itself . . . we need to be honest with ourselves. I feel like if we honestly thought about people as other human beings just like us, a lot of the problems we face will be gone. I feel like if someone like you who has been through so much and seen some of the ugliest things and the ugliest people and still treats people as individuals, there is no reason why me and the rest of the world cannot do the same. I guess what I have been trying to say throughout this e-mail is thank you. Thank you for taking the time and the energy to ruin as many students as you can so we don't go out and ruin the world.

This is why I am confident that working through the information and challenges I offered, my students have developed their own abilities and perspectives to navigate our neo-diverse America. I am confident that they board the train and with respect treat others as individuals in the neo-diversity world they are going to travel and live in. I believe that there is hope for all of them. That is why I do not worry as they get onboard the train—no ticket necessary.

As the Neo-Diversity train starts to pull out, through the windows my former students smile and wave to me. Suddenly a surprise; I hear it soft at first, but then it comes to me fuller and stronger. My students are humming and singing Curtis Mayfield's "People Get Ready." Then singing, smiling, waving, they point to something behind me. I turn to look, and see that from the other platform a new set of young travelers has stepped off the Wrong-Line train. Through iPhones, iPads, Facebook, RateMyProfessors.com, and actual face-to-face social interaction, apparently word had spread. The word that reached some was that real lessons were being taught off the Wrong-Line; lessons that would help travelers identify, name, and analyze the something they had been sensing, experiencing, and been surprised and confused by on their travels. Now, this new set of young travelers had come off the Wrong-Line train into the station looking harried but hopeful.

Remaining on the platform but looking back into the station, I can see the newbies asking questions at the ticket counter. A brown-skinned woman who takes tickets is shaking her head. She closes her window. Her bright, multicolored hijab complements her uniform as she comes from behind the counter. Still shaking her head but smiling wide, she leads this new group to the benches. Then, as those young people start to sit, I see her turn and point to me. Smiling, she waves for me to come inside.

I am being called.

As I make my way inside, I hear the whistle of the Neo-Diversity train moving away. I know it will return, but for now the Neo-Diversity train is going on with its travel down the line to pick up passengers, coast to coast.

Now inside the station, having answered the call, I stand before this new group of young travelers sitting on the benches. As they go quiet watching me, I gather myself and say, "We've got some difficult days ahead."

AFTERWORD

The train's a coming
I hear it just at hand
I hear the wheels a rumbling
And rolling through the land
The fare is cheap and all can go
The rich and poor are there
No second class aboard this train
No difference in the fare
Get on board, little children
Get on board, little children
And Fight for human rights
We're gonna fight for human rights!
—African American spiritual (1872)

ACKNOWLEDGMENTS

Every writer needs a first reader. Questions, critique, support, and encouragement are all parts of that role, all at the same time. Ms. Logan Collins is my first reader. Logan is always the first person to read the beginnings of one of my nonfiction writing projects. And as I find my way to organizing and continuing the project, Logan reads and reads. Thank you, Logan, for your strong critique, strong support, and strong encouragement as I worked on this book. Thank you for your strong, positive influence on this book. I thank you too, Logan, for your generous friendship.

Once I had a real draft of this book, I turned to my ever-ready copyeditor, Mr. Gideon Brookins. As I have said elsewhere, I have watched Gideon grow into the fine young man he is and to the excellent technical editor he has become. Thanks, Gideon, for working me through the details of grammar and formatting that helped make this a stronger book to present to Prometheus Books.

After I submitted my book proposal to them, Steven L. Mitchell of Prometheus Books was quick to ask to see the full manuscript. Even in our first correspondence it was clear that Steven was getting it when he began to use the term "neo-diversity. It was my pleasure to work with Steven and with members of the Prometheus Books staff. Thanks to you all for such a cordial and productive experience in getting my book ready and out to market.

And now let me give praise to libraries. My brother Phillip and I are great fans of public libraries. To him and me, it just seems magical that any of us can walk into a library in pretty much any American town or city and be allowed to read. As a professor I also have the privilege to always have available to me a university research library. If you want to see and tour what I consider a twenty-third-century university library, come to North Carolina State University's James B. Hunt Library. Summer 2013, that library was where I wrote *Taking on Diversity*. With its open-air design, unique colorful furniture, generous seating areas, large windows with views, that library was a wonderful, stimulating haven and incubator for my thinking and writing. I know I am not alone at the university in thanking Vice Provost Susan Nutter for her vision in bringing together the people and resources that got the Hunt Library built and up and running. Thanks, Susan.

And now let me praise students. With twenty students in 2006, I taught my "Interpersonal Relationships and Race" course for the first time. It was at the insistence of those twenty students that I began to consider increasing the course enrollment. Those students expressed with strength their belief that more students needed the opportunity to learn about neo-diversity. That is why I started to let the enrollment begin to climb and to get as many as seventy-five students one semester. Given the demand, I also went from teaching the course once a year to teaching it in both the fall and the spring semesters.

Not just seeing the impact on students but having students tell people away from campus, I began to realize that more Americans needed to learn about neo-diversity. As I say in the book proper, Americans are sensing something, but sensing something is not enough.

So, to the first twenty students who took the challenge of my course, I say thank you. And to all the students who have now taken my course and challenged me to get the word out, I offer my heartfelt gratitude. You have my salute. You, my students, you are the reason that more Americans can now begin to understand neo-diversity and learn how to manage the neo-diversity challenges of these difficult, but quintessentially American, days.

WORKS CITED

INTRODUCTION

The Blind Boys of Alabama with Aaron Neville. "People Get Ready." YouTube video, 4:39, posted by "pannellctp," February 5, 2011, https://www.youtube.com/watch?v=2k3roW1 -Nvo. Accessed December 8, 2014.

Dickinson, Amy. "In the End, It's Still an Offensive Word." Ask Amy. *Raleigh News & Observer*, September 9, 2009.

CHAPTER 1: NOBODY TELLS US WHAT THAT MEANS

Brown, S. A. "Transfer." In *The Collected Poems of Sterling A. Brown*, edited by Michael S. Harper. New York: Harper & Row, 1980.

Tyson, T. B. *Blood Done Sign My Name*. New York: Three Rivers Press, 2004.

CHAPTER 2: A SALES PITCH?

Gilovich, T., D. Keltner, S. Chen, and R. E. Nisbett. *Social Psychology*. New York: W. W. Norton, 2013, pp. 421–22.

Nacoste, R. W. "In Racial Transition." In *Nubian Message*, December 3, 2008.

———. "Who Are We?" In *Technician*, October 17, 2011.

Simpson, G. E., and J. M. Yinger. *Racial and Cultural Minorities: An Analysis of Prejudice and Discrimination*. New York: Harper & Row, 1953, p. 721, n. 65.

Tyson, T. B. *Blood Done Sign My Name*. New York: Three Rivers Press, 2004.

Vander Zanden, J. W. *American Minority Relations*, 3rd ed. New York: Ronald Press Company, 1972, pp. 28–29.

CHAPTER 3: WE'VE GOT SOME DIFFICULT DAYS AHEAD

Kelley, H. H., and J. W. Thibaut. *Interpersonal Relations: A Theory of Interdependence*. New York: Wiley, 1978.

Stephan, W. G., and C. W. Stephan. "Intergroup Anxiety." *Journal of Social Issues* 41 (1985): 157–75.

CHAPTER 4: DJANGO UNCHAINED

Asim, J. *The N-Word: Who Can Say It, Who Shouldn't, and Why*. Boston: Houghton Mifflin, 2007, p. 4.

Bruni, F. "Paula Deen, Our Deep-Fried Boor." *Raleigh News & Observer*, June 25, 2013.

Carter, C. J., and H. Abdullah. "The Color of Valor: 24 Minority Veterans Receive Long Overdue Medal of Honor," CNN Politics, March 19, 2014. http://www.cnn.com/2014/03/18/politics/medal-of-honor-vets/index.html. Accessed December 15, 2014.

Schwartz, N. "Eagles Receiver Riley Cooper Uses Racial Slur at a Kenny Chesney Concert." *USA Today* Sports, July 31, 2013. http://ftw.usatoday.com/2013/07/eagles-receiver-riley-cooper-uses-racial-slur-at-a-kenny-chesney-concert. Accessed December 15, 2014.

Sherwood, John D. *Black Sailor, White Navy: Racial Unrest in the Fleet during the Vietnam War Era*. New York: New York University Press, 2007.

Sommers, S. R., and M. I. Norton. "Lay Theories about White Racists: What Constitutes Racism (and What Doesn't)." *Group Processes & Intergroup Relations* 9 (2006): 117–38.

Tarantino, Quentin. *Django Unchained*. Directed by Quentin Tarantino. Columbia Pictures, December 25, 2012.

Thibaut, J. W., and H. H. Kelley. *The Social Psychology of Groups*. New York: John Wiley & Sons, 1959. Note: From Thibaut and Kelley's interdependence theory, the social psychological concept is fate control: the ability of person-A to influence person-B no matter what person-B does.

CHAPTER 5: PREACHING TO THE CHOIR?

Kelley, H. H. *Personal Relationships: Their Structures and Processes*. Hillsdale, NJ: Erlbaum Associates, 1979.

Kelley, H. H., and J. W. Thibaut. *Interpersonal Relations: A Theory of Interdependence*. New York: Wiley, 1978.

Rusbult, C. E., and P. A. M. Van Lange. "Interdependence, Interaction, and Relationships." *Annual Review of Psychology* 54 (2003): 351–75.

Whitehead, B. *Why There Are No Good Men Left: The Romantic Plight of the New Single Woman*. New York: Broadway Books, 2003. Note: According to sociologist Barbara Dafoe Whitehead, American society has shifted from using a marriage-dating system to lead a couple to a marriage, to using a relationship-dating system that is designed only to put people in intimate relationships, without regard to those relationships leading to marriage.

CHAPTER 6: PISTOL SHOOTING?

Altman, D., and D. Taylor. *Social Penetration: The Development of Interpersonal Relationships*. New York: Holt, Rinehart & Winston, 1973.

Werber, B. *Empire of the Ants*. New York: Bantam, 1999, p. 84.

Williams, M. "Virgin Mobile US Takes Down Christmas Advert Suggesting Sexual Assault." *TheGuardian.com*, December 9, 2012. http://www.theguardian.com/media/2012/dec/09/virgin-mobile-us-holiday-ad. Accessed December 17, 2014.

Yeater, E. A., K. L. Lenberg, C. Avina, J. K. Rinehart, and W. O'Donohue. "When Social Situations Take a Turn for the Worse: Situational and Interpersonal Risk Factors for Sexual Aggression." *Sex Roles* 59 (2008): 151–63.

CHAPTER 7: THAT'S PRETTY GOOFY

Appadurai, A. *Fear of Small Numbers: An Essay on the Geography of Anger*. Durham, NC: Duke University Press, 2006. Note: Appadurai argues that there is a new social uncertainty spreading across the globe that is caused by the increased visibility of minority groups. He says: "This species of uncertainty is intimately connected to the reality that today's ethnic groups number in the hundreds of thousands and that their movements, mixtures, and cultural styles, and media representations create profound doubts about who exactly are among the 'we' and who are among the 'they'" (p. 5).

Duval, S., and R. A. Wicklund. *A Theory of Objective Self-Awareness*. New York: Academic Press, 1972.

Nacoste, R. W. *What Rough Beast: Interpersonal Relationships and Race*. Unpublished manuscript used for academic course.

Yeats, W. B. "The Second Coming." *Poets.org*. http://www.poets.org/poetsorg/poem/second-coming. Accessed December 15, 2014.

CHAPTER 8: WE TEACH CHILDREN

Allport, G. W. *The Nature of Prejudice*. New York: Double Day Anchor, 1958, pp. 250–68.

Altman, D., and D. Taylor. *Social Penetration: The Development of Interpersonal Relationships*. New York: Holt, Rinehart & Winston, 1973.

Kalat, J. *Introduction to Psychology*. Belmont, CA: Thomson Wadsworth, 2008, pp. 99–113.

Pettigrew, T. F. "Generalized Intergroup Contact Effects on Prejudice." *Personality and Social Psychology Bulletin* 23 (1997): 173–85.

Werber, B. *Empire of the Ants*. New York: Bantam, 1999, p. 84.

CHAPTER 9: HIBERNATING BIGOTRY

Giammona, C. "Alabama Police Chief Apologizes to Freedom Rider Congressman," NBCNews .com, March 3, 2013. http://usnews.nbcnews.com/_news/2013/03/03/17167907-alabama -police-chief-apologizes-to-freedom-rider-congressman?lite. Accessed December 17, 2014.

Pastis, S. "Pearls Before Swine." *Tie-Dye* (comic strip). *Raleigh News & Observer*, December 16, 2012.

Shipkowski, B. "Police: Boy, 16, Made Racial Comment at NJ Walmart," Associated Press, March 20, 2010. http://www.denverpost.com/ci_14720166. Accessed December 29, 2014.

Smith, G. "Medgar Evers: Lost in a Search for the American Dream," *Fayetteville Observer*, June 11, 2013.

CHAPTER 10: SURPRISE, SURPRISE

Hax, C. "Boyfriend's Bigotry: Deal Breaker or Not?," July 10, 2012. http://www.startribune .com/lifestyle/relationship/161981565.html. Accessed December 17, 2014.

Kelley, H. H. *Personal Relationships: Their Structures and Processes*. Hillsdale, NJ: Erlbaum Associates, 1979.

Kelley, H. H., and J. W. Thibaut. *Interpersonal Relations: A Theory of Interdependence*. New York: Wiley, 1978.

Oxendine, D. B., and R. W. Nacoste. "Who Would Claim to Be That Who Was Not: Evaluations of an Ethnic Evaluation Procedure." *Journal of Applied Social Psychology* 37 (2007): 1594–1629.

CHAPTER 11: THINE ALABASTER CITIES GLEAM

Altman, I., and D. A. Taylor. *Social Penetration: The Development of Interpersonal Relationships*. New York: Holt, Rinehart & Winston, 1973.

Associated Press. "White Americans no longer a majority by 2042." NBC News. Wed., Aug. 13, 2008, http://www.msnbc.msn.com/id/26186087/. Accessed December 29, 2014.

Binning, K. R., M. M. Unzueta, Y. J. Huo, and L. E. Molina. "The Interpretation of Multiracial Status and Its Relation to Social Engagement and Psychological Well-Being." *Journal of Social Issues* 65 (2009): 35–49.

CNN Staff. "Miss America Crowns 1st Winner of Indian Descent." CNN. September 17, 2013, http://www.cnn.com/2013/09/16/showbiz/miss-america-racist-reactions/. Accessed December 29, 2014.

Devos, T., and M. R. Banaji. "American = White?" *Journal of Personality and Social Psychology* 88 (2005): 447–66.

Thibaut, J. W., and H. H. Kelley. *The Social Psychology of Groups*. New York: John Wiley & Sons, 1959.

CHAPTER 12: LET'S GO TO THE RODEO

Adams, John S. "Federal Judge Admits He Sent Anti-Obama, Racist Email." March 1, 2012. USA TODAY. http://usatoday30.usatoday.com/news/nation/story/2012-02-29/Montana-judge-racist-email/53307060/1. Accessed December 29, 2014.

Associated Press. "Interracial Couple Denied Marriage License; La. Justice of the Peace Cites Concerns about Any Children Couple Might Have." MSNBC.com, October 15, 2009. http://www.msnbc.msn.com/id/33332436/ns/us_news-race_and_ethnicity/. Accessed December 21, 2014.

Associated Press. "NJ GOP Lawmaker Quits over Wife's Racist Email." MSNBC.com, August 22, 2011. http://www.msnbc.msn.com/id/44233833/ns/politics/#. Accessed December 19, 2014.

Cass, C., and J. Agiesta. "Poll: Young People See Online Slurs as Just Joking." MSNBC.com, September 20, 2011. http://www.msnbc.msn.com/id/44591677/ns/technology_and_science-tech_and_gadgets/#. Accessed December 19, 2014.

CBS New York. "ESPN Apologizes for LINsane Headline (Chink in the Armor)." February 19, 2012. http://newyork.cbslocal.com/2012/02/19/espn-apologizes-for-linsane-headline/. Accessed December 21, 2014.

Coffey, L. T. "Anchor Called Too Fat for TV Is Now International Role Model." *Today News*, December 29, 2012. http://todaynews.today.com/_news/2012/12/28/16194156-anchor-called-too-fat-for-tv-is-now-international-role-model?lite. Accessed December 21, 2014.

Hananel, Sam. "More Men Filing Sexual Harassment Claims; Percentage of Complaints Filed by Men Has Doubled over Last 20 Years." MSNBC.com, March 4, 2010. http://www .msnbc.msn.com/id/35706595/ns/business-careers/. Accessed December 19, 2014.

Hinxman, D. "Hawaii Football Coach Uses Homosexual Slur in Reference to Notre Dame." *Reno Gazette Journal*, July 30, 2009.

MSNBC.com. "US Judge Forwards Racist Email about Obama." March 1, 2012. http://usnews .msnbc.msn.com/_news/2012/03/01/10549045-us-judge-forwards-racist-email-about -obama. Accessed December 29, 2014.

NBClatino. "Penn State Sorority Apologizes for Having Offensive Mexican-Themed Party." December 4, 2012. http://nbclatino.com/2012/12/04/penn-state-sorority-apologizes-for -having-offensive-mexican-themed-party/. Accessed December 19, 2014.

"Obama Wins. . . ." *Raleigh News & Observer*, November 5, 2008. Front-page headline.

Sudekum, M. "Missouri Fair Clown Draws Criticism for Obama Mask." Yahoo! News, August 11/12, 2013. http://news.yahoo.com/missouri-fair-clown-draws-criticism-obama -mask-004950184.html. Accessed December 21, 2014.

CHAPTER 13: WHAT DID YOU JUST SAY TO ME?

Chen, X., and C. D. Carroll. *First-Generation Students in Postsecondary Education: A Look at Their College Transcripts*. Washington, DC: National Center for Education Statistics, US Department of Education, Institute of Education Sciences, NCES 2005-171, July 2005.

Nacoste, R. W. *Making Gumbo in the University*. Austin, TX: Plain View Press, 2010.

Wolcott, R. "Seeing beyond the Skin: A New Diversity Movement Takes Shape." *Alumni Magazine of NC State University*, Spring 2001: 11–15.

CHAPTER 14: A BEAST BENT ON GRACE

Gilbert, J. "A Brief for the Defense." *Jack Gilbert Collected Poems*. New York: Knopf, 2012, p. 213.

———. "Myself Considered as the Monster in the Foreground." *Jack Gilbert Collected Poems*. New York: Knopf, 2012, pp. 10–11.

Hughes, L. "Epilogue," *The Collected Works of Langston Hughes, Vol. 1*. Edited by A. Rampersad. Columbia: University of Missouri Press, 2001, p. 61.

CHAPTER 15: PEACE THROWN LAVISHLY AWAY

Auden, W. H. "Herman Melville." *W. H. Auden Collected Poems*. Edited by E. Mendelson. New York: Vintage Books, 1991, p. 251.

Baldas, T. "Muslim-American Man Wins Nearly $1.2 Million in Job Discrimination Case." *Detroit Free Press*, February 28, 2014. http://www.freep.com/article/20140228/NEWS05/302280130/Muslim-discrimination-beard. Accessed December 21, 2014.

Brown, S. A. "Nous n'irons plus au bois . . ." *The Collected Poems of Sterling Brown*. Edited by Michael S. Harper. New York: Harper & Row, 1980, p. 123.

Coloroso, B. *The Bully, the Bullied, and the Bystander*. New York: HarperCollins, 2003, pp. 14 and 16.

Czopp, A. M., M. J. Monteith, and A. Mark. "Standing Up for Change: Reducing Bias through Interpersonal Confrontation." *Journal of Personality and Social Psychology* 90 (2006): 784–803.

Dokoupil, T. "'Very Anxious': Is America Scared of Diversity?" NBCNews.com, October 15, 2013. http://nbcpolitics.nbcnews.com/_news/2013/10/15/20961149-very-anxious-is-america-scared-of-diversity?lite. Accessed December 22, 2014.

Knickerbocker, B. "Westboro Picketers Outnumbered at Elizabeth Edwards' Funeral." *Christian Science Monitor*, December 11, 2010, http://www.csmonitor.com/USA/2010/1211/Westboro-picketers-outnumbered-at-Elizabeth-Edwards-funeral. Accessed December 29, 2014.

Knowles, D. "Mexican-American Boy, Sebastien de la Cruz, Sings Encore Performance of National Anthem at NBA Finals in Response to Bigoted Comments." *New York Daily News*, June 14, 2013. http://www.nydailynews.com/news/national/mexican-american-boy-national-anthem-performance-sparks-racist-backlash-article-1.1371990. Accessed December 23, 2014.

Nacoste, R. W. "Wake Up to Your Own Power." *Technician*, March 13, 2011.

Neumeister, L. "New York Jury Punishes Use of Racial Slur by Black, Defendant Loses Lawsuit, Plaintiff Cites Degradation." *Boston Globe*, September 04, 2013. http://www.bostonglobe.com/news/nation/2013/09/03/case-puts-word-use-among-blacks-trial/CKTcxBY0aZqUADqBfv0oQJ/story.html. Accessed December 29, 2014.

Sorkin, A. *The American President*. Directed by R. Reiner. Columbia Pictures, 1995.

CHAPTER 16: A QUIET REVOLUTION

Nacoste, R. W. *Howl of the Wolf: NCSU Students Call Out for Social Change*. Raleigh, NC: Lulu.com, pp. 93–95.

Nacoste, R. W. "Speaking Up for Our Neo-Diverse America, The Beautiful." TEDxNCSU,

James B. Hunt Library, North Carolina State University, Raleigh, March 2013. YouTube link: https://www.youtube.com/watch?v=Y73bRAwJY6I. Accessed December 23, 2014.

Sherwood, John D. *Black Sailor, White Navy: Racial Unrest in the Fleet during the Vietnam War Era.* New York University Press, 2007.

CHAPTER 17: WE'RE ALL TRAVELERS

"An Award Well-Deserved." *Technician*, February 26, 2013, editorial page.

Bontemps, A. "The Day-Breakers." *A Sudden Line of Poetry*, December 11, 2012. http://asudden line.tumblr.com/post/37723248584/the-day-breakers-arna-bontemps. Accessed December 23, 2014.

Cooper, J. F., M. Mann, and C. Crowe. *The Last of the Mohicans.* Directed by M. Mann. Twentieth Century Fox, September 1992.

Donne, J. *No Man Is an Island: Selected from the Writings of John Donne.* Edited by K. Fallon. Los Angeles, CA: Stanyan Books, 1970, p. 1.

Geoffrion, A. *Broken Trail.* Directed by W. Hill. Canada: Butcher's Run Films, AMC TV miniseries, 2006.

Nacoste, R. W. "A Wake Up Call to Neo-Diversity Gumbo." *Technician*, February 1, 2013.

Thibaut, J. W., and H. H. Kelley. *The Social Psychology of Groups.* New York: John Wiley & Sons, 1959.

INDEX